Forex
DeMYSTiFieD®

DeMYSTiFieD® Series

Accounting Demystified

Advanced Statistics Demystified

Algebra Demystified

Alternative Energy Demystified

Asset Allocation Demystified

Biology Demystified

Biotechnology Demystified

Business Calculus Demystified

Business Math Demystified

Business Statistics Demystified

C++ Demystified

Calculus Demystified

Candlestick Charting Demystified

Chemistry Demystified

Commodities Demystified

Corporate Finance Demystified, 2e

Databases Demystified, 2e

Economics Demystified

Energy Investing Demystified

Environmental Science Demystified

ESL Demystified

Financial Accounting Demystified

Financial Planning Demystified

Financial Statements Demystified

Forensics Demystified

Forex DeMystified

Genetics Demystified

Grant Writing Demystified

Health Assessment Demystified

Hedge Funds Demystified

Human Resource Management Demystified

Intermediate Accounting Demystified

Investing Demystified, 2e

Lean Six Sigma Demystified

Linear Algebra Demystified

Macroeconomics Demystified

Management Accounting Demystified

Marketing Demystified

Math Proofs Demystified

Math Word Problems Demystified

Mathematica Demystified

Microbiology Demystified

Microeconomics Demystified

Multimedia Demystified

Nanotechnology Demystified

Operating Systems Demystified

Options Demystified

Organic Chemistry Demystified

Pharmacology Demystified

Physics Demystified

Physiology Demystified

Pre-Algebra Demystified

Precalculus Demystified

Probability Demystified 2e

Project Management Demystified

Public Speaking and Presentations Demystified

Quality Management Demystified

Quantum Mechanics Demystified, 2e

Real Estate Math Demystified

Robotics Demystified

Sales Management Demystified

Six Sigma Demystified, 2e

SQL Demystified

Statistical Process Control Demystified

Statistics Demystified

Supply Chain Management Demystified

Technical Analysis Demystified

Technical Math Demystified

Trigonometry Demystified

Visual Basic 2005 Demystified

Visual C# 2005 Demystified

XML Demystified

The Demystified Series publishes over 125 titles in all areas of academic study. For a complete list of titles, please visit www.mhprofessional.com.

Forex
DeMYSTiFieD®

David Borman

McGraw
Hill
Education

New York   Chicago   San Francisco   Athens   London   Madrid   Mexico City
Milan   New Delhi   Singapore   Sydney   Toronto

1 2 3 4 5 6 7 8 9 0   QFR/QFR   1 9 8 7 6 5 4 3

ISBN	978-0-07-182851-2
MHID	0-07-182851-6

e-ISBN	978-0-07-182853-6
e-MHID	0-07-182853-2

Library of Congress Cataloging-in-Publication Data

Borman, David.
   Forex demystified : a self-teaching guide / by David Borman.
      pages cm
   Includes index.
   ISBN 978-0-07-182851-2 (alk. paper) — ISBN 0-07-182851-6 (alk. paper)   1. Foreign exchange market.   2. Foreign exchange futures.   3. Investments.   I. Title.
   HG3851.B673 2014
   332.4'5—dc23   2013033972

McGraw-Hill Education books are available at special quantity discounts to use as premiums and sales promotions, or for use in corporate training programs. To contact a special sales representative, please visit the Contact Us page at www.mhprofessional.com.

This book was written for all those who like to have a sense of control over their financial destiny – they know that even though they might not "pick up every penny in front of the steamroller" their efforts go a long way in keeping their and their family's fortunes and security on track – Also a shout out to my Mom, who has kept our family's fortunes going well past the typical retirement age – Bravo, Mom!

About the Author

David Borman has been investing and trading since 1999. He has worked at Deutsche Bank, Merrill Lynch, and the Federal Home Loan Bank. He has traded mutual funds, stocks, Forex, and precious metals. He has also worked in the High-Net-Worth Accounting and Offshore Hedge Fund business. Today he spends his time reading about the economies of Europe, Asia, and the U.S. while searching for Forex trading setups. He holds a bachelor's degree in finance from Southern Illinois University, a Masters in Accounting from DePaul University, and has studied financial markets and financial modeling at Northwestern University. He lives in Chicago, IL.

Contents

Introduction

Market participants who trade in currencies, or foreign exchange (Forex) traders, trade in the largest and most liquid market in the world. The Forex market is a connection of banks, brokerages, and market makers worldwide that allows traders to buy and sell upwards of 50 currencies, 24 hours a day, 6 days a week.

While currency trading is a relatively new market, many individual traders have learned how to study the interest rates, economic information, growth rates, and trading patterns of the United States, Europe, the United Kingdom, and Asia for a profit. They know that this information, coupled with charting skills, can allow them to trade in the exact same way as large institutional traders do: They trade Forex in the spot market online.

Trading Forex in the online market comes with many advantages that go beyond those of typical equities trading. As with equities trading, Forex traders are allowed to use margin to amplify their buying power and returns in their accounts. But with Forex trading, the margins or "gearing" are much, much greater than those allowed with equities trading. This coupled with 24-hour trading and worldwide markets means that Forex traders are on an even par with hedge funds, mutual funds, and other worldwide institutional traders.

As you read this book you will learn the basics of what makes up a Forex currency trade. You will also learn the concepts behind the huge amounts of leverage that can allow even the smallest of FX accounts to produce very large profits.

It is true that it is possible for you to make 10%, 12%, or even 15% profit on a trade in one day. It is also true that it is possible to make this amount of profit by trading in the evening hours and close out the trade in the morning, allowing you to trade Forex while still having a full-time job.

It is also possible to get to those levels of overnight profit and limit your risk. You will learn these risk-management solutions in this book, as well as methods for using software to automatically close out your trades at set profit points, allowing you to "set it and forget it" and walk away from your trading desk.

In this book you will also learn how to search out and use what is known as fundamental information about a currency and make your own conclusions as to which currencies will be good to trade. This, in addition to lessons on how to use charts, adds up to a good, solid introduction to the subject of Forex trading.

The reason to read this book is simple: You're not new to the markets; you might have tried your hand at stocks or mutual funds. Now you'd like to move on to something more exciting, and possibly something more challenging. While it is often said that trading equities is the most basic form of trading, you will see that learning how to trade currencies is not hard. You will see that once the basics are learned, it can be quite doable to read the news, interpret the market, see the values in Forex pairs, and place FX trades, all while managing risk.

It should be mentioned at the beginning that Forex trading can be one of the riskiest types of trading known. With gearing levels of upwards of 50:1, a 1% gain in a currency pair would translate to a 50% gain in your Forex account! Gains of this nature often lead to traders making huge overnight, weekly, and monthly profits. This is precisely the reason so many people (including institutional and professional traders) are attracted to the FX market.

At the same time, the huge gearing levels in your FX account can lead to losses of 50% with every 1% move against you, which can lead to disastrous results to your profit and loss statements, or worse, margin calls or even the account automatically closing out all positions.

The Forex market can be learned either the easy way or the hard way. The hard way would be to open an FX account, deposit your money, ramp up the leverage ratio, and begin trading. At 10:1, 20:1, or 50:1, things happen fast. Not knowing how much capital to commit to a trade, not knowing when to get in or get out, or just simply not knowing whether to go long or short which currency can lead to a total loss in your FX account in a matter of minutes. Trust me, I've been there, done that. My first trade was going long on the Swedish kroner. I had no clue what to do, and bam! The account was at a margin call in about 5 minutes. I just sat there, scratching my head and thinking "What happened?"

It took quite a bit of study coupled with working in the institutional hedge fund business to get to the point where I was trading with consistent profits in a demo account. I developed my own system at that point, and it's the one I've shared with you here. It's based on good clean information, without bogging you down in data. It's also based on the fact that I really like to trade Forex, but I really don't like to lose money. Consequently, the system is simple and conservative. I'm one for believing that if a trading system works, then use it, and don't make it more complex just because you can.

Forex accounts are just like brokerage accounts. You should have the attitude from the get-go that you are in FX to make money, to enjoy it, and to learn. You'll find that Forex trading is actually simpler than most people make it out to be, and at the same time very fun!

You should have as your goal during your reading to start following the world's markets and economies, if you haven't already. Because FX trading is a world market, your trades and your profits will be *directly* tied to the well-being or not-so-well-being of different countries and economic zones. As you read this book you will begin to see how China's economy is related to others, how the Euro zone is related to Eastern Europe and Scandinavia, and how the United States is related to all the world's economies combined. You will begin to ask and answer the question: What would I trade in today's markets?

These questions are the core of Forex trading. With the system that you will learn in this book, you will develop a way of getting into good trades with a high degree of success. You will learn that unlike stocks, where you have over 5,000 equities to choose from to trade, you might specialize in two, three, or four currency pairs. You might find that these currency pairs are the favorites of your trading desk because they turn out the most predictable profit, trade after trade.

How to Use this Book

First and foremost, Forex trading needs to be hands on. The best way to get experience with Forex trading is to open a free practice account at one of the hundreds of available online Forex brokers. As you work through the examples shown in the book, get your hands on your computer and place trades in the practice, or "demo" account. This is where the real learning takes place. Take your time working through this book to get the gist of what is being said. There is a bit of common thread to how to trade. Most professional traders go with a combination of gut feeling and science. You will learn to use both as you spend more and more time trading Forex.

Trade after dinner in front of the TV. Trade in the mornings. If you are at work, check your trades on you cell phone or iPad at lunch. Read this book and get into trading by looking for setups and working some trades. Practice makes perfect, and before you know it you'll be ready for trading with real cash. Earnings from FX trading can be very exciting, or even thrilling! They are best when you know why you entered into the trade, and why it worked out for you. This way, the trade can be repeated again and again, winning again and again.

This book serves as the start of your journey into the fun, fast, and rewarding world of Forex trading. Study, read, trade. These are the secrets to success in Forex trading.

David Borman

Forex
DeMYSTiFieD®

Chapter **1**

Introduction to Forex

CHAPTER OBJECTIVES

In this chapter you will learn the following:

- What it means when people say they trade Forex
- The basics of Forex Leverage
- The basics of the Forex Pair
- The best times to trade Forex
- The history of Forex Trading

1

When people say they trade Forex, which means buying and selling money in the worldwide Foreign Exchange market, what they are saying is that they trade money. It is as simple as that: Forex traders buy and sell different types of money. After all of the strategizing, technical analytics, and fundamental analysis, the basic Forex trade is betting that one country's currency will be worth more than another country's currency at some point in the future. You as a Forex trader might use a mathematically based diversification theory to minimize the risk of your Forex trading account. You might wait until a technical indicator such as a 200 day/50 day moving average cross signals you to "go long" the Euro and short the U.S. dollar. You might study the Bank of England's website http://www.bankofengland.co.uk/ and discover that the UK's economy is shaky, leading you to "short" the Great British pound against the Swiss franc.

Either way, you are placing an educated bet that one currency will be worth more of another currency at the end of the holding period. How is this done? Currencies are traded in pairs. In the case of the Euro/U.S. dollar pair, a Forex trader has the choice to bet that the U.S. dollar will get stronger in relation to the Euro, or that the Euro will get stronger in relationship to the U.S. dollar. If you were the Forex trader and you thought that the Euro was going to get stronger against the U.S. dollar, you would "go long" or "buy" the Euro/U.S. dollar pair. What this means is that you are simultaneously betting that the Euro will go up, at the same time betting that the U.S. dollar will go down. Extending this out further, a long Euro/U.S. dollar trade is in reality a long Euro/short U.S. dollar trade.

How Is Money Made on a Forex Trade?

In order to see how money is made on a currency trade you first have to understand what is going on behind the scenes in a trade. If you thought the Euro was going to get stronger against the U.S. dollar, we have seen that you would go long the Euro and short the U.S. dollar. In reality, what happens is that by shorting the U.S. dollar, you are in effect "borrowing" U.S. dollars and using the money to "buy" Euros. When this is done, you then have an IOU to your Forex broker for the amount you shorted. This IOU is denominated in U.S. dollars. When the Euro gets stronger than the U.S. dollar, you would then close out the trade, take the Euros, and use the money to settle out the IOU from when you "borrowed" U.S. dollars. Since the Euro got stronger, you would be able to use less Euros to satisfy the U.S. dollar IOU and pocket the difference as a profit. This works due to the exchange rates of the two currencies having changed (see Figure 1-1).

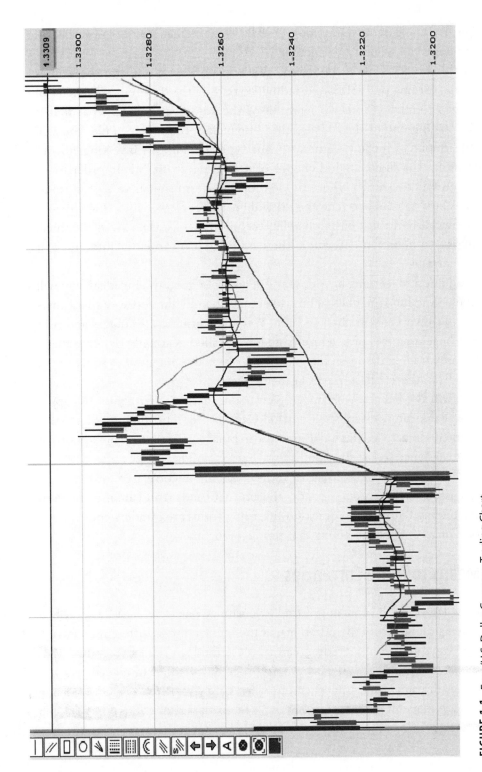

FIGURE 1-1 • Euro/U.S. Dollar Currency Trading Chart

At the beginning of the trade, you would have one exchange rate, and at the end of the trade you would have another.

In this book, *Forex Demystified*, you will be lead along the sometimes twisting, turning path of Forex trading, or trading the different currencies of different countries. You will learn all of the key ideas behind what makes Forex trading one of the most exciting financial products to trade. You will also learn one of the key elements in any type of trading or investing: how to spot trades that have a good chance of becoming profitable. In order to do this, you will be shown where to look for long-term signals to a good trade, such as how to read between the lines of central bank websites. You will also be shown how to use basic charting techniques—also known as technical analysis—to help you determine the best price level to enter into and exit out of a trade.

In addition to learning how to seek out and spot good trading ideas, you will be shown the fundamentals of how to actually handle the software that comes with your own Forex trading account. You will learn the advantages and risks of the huge amounts of leverage (sometimes called gearing by Forex traders) that Forex trading is known for, and what creates the potential to squeeze out profits from the smallest moves in the market.

You will also learn how to match your trading activities with your risk appetite, available time, established portfolio, and lastly, your long- or short-term investment objectives. You will learn how to build a grouping of Forex positions that are designed to last six months to two years, and have Forex effectively act as an alternative asset class that has returns that are uncorrelated to your traditional assets such as stocks, bonds, and mutual funds. You can also use your Forex trading skills to earn quick profits; using your Forex trading endeavors as a form of second job—a hobby that produces income.

What It Means to Trade Currencies

Trading Forex, or the concept of trading currency pairs, can best be described as making money from the difference of the money of two different countries. Other ways that Forex trading can be described are: (1) using very high amounts of leverage to benefit from the price differentials of one currency as it moves in value against another, or (2) a method of placing bets where the trades are made in currency pairs in a 24-hour market of overlapping trading time zones.

Trading currencies is like trading stocks, ETFs (Exchange Traded Funds) or mutual funds. A trade is made on a trading software platform with the hopes that it will create a capital gain. Forex traders make capital gains when they can accurately predict the direction of the movement of one currency against another. Forex trading is simple: one currency gets strong, the other gets weak.

When trading equities, stocks move either up or down, with most market participants taking a bullish stance (meaning they set their trades to make money when the stock gains in value). When you are trading currencies, you not only have to decide what currency will go up, but you will have to decide what currency that currency will get stronger against. In other words, not only will one currency go either up or down in price, it will do so at different rates against different currencies (called the counter currencies). While this may seem to make the process of deciding which Forex trades to place a difficult one, any complexity is greatly outweighed by the simplicity of the relatively small number of currency pairs to trade: Equity traders have thousands of stocks to trade, Forex traders only have somewhere between 20 and 50 currency combinations to worry about. This makes the process of trading Forex easier than picking stocks, as it is quite possible to become an expert in and trade only three, four, or five currency pairs day in and day out.

The most heavily traded currency pair is the Euro/U.S. dollar pair. With this pair, traders will bet if the Euro will get stronger or weaker against the U.S. dollar. In this pair, the Euro is the first of the quote called "EUR." The U.S. dollar is quoted as "USD." This quoting system is used for all currency pairs, with examples being Great British pound/Euro as GBP/EUR, US dollar/Swedish Krona as USD/SEK, and the Australian dollar/Japanese yen as AUD/JPY. In the example of EUR/USD, if a trader thought that the U.S. dollar was set to lose value against the Euro in the next few days, he would set up a trade by selling USD and buying EUR. This is exactly what is done when a trade is made in the currency markets. By the way, the easiest way to look up a current market quote of a currency pair is to list the two currencies followed by a "= X". In the case of a live Euro/U.S. dollar quote you would enter "EURUSD = X" in the "symbol lookup" screen of Yahoo Finance, Google Finance, Marketwatch.com, etc. Here is the link to the Euro/U.S. dollar quote on Yahoo Finance: http://finance.yahoo.com/q?s=EURUSD=X. Figure 1-2 shows an Australian dollar/U.S. dollar pair chart showing the huge gain of the AUD over the USD indicated by the large upward bar of the chart.

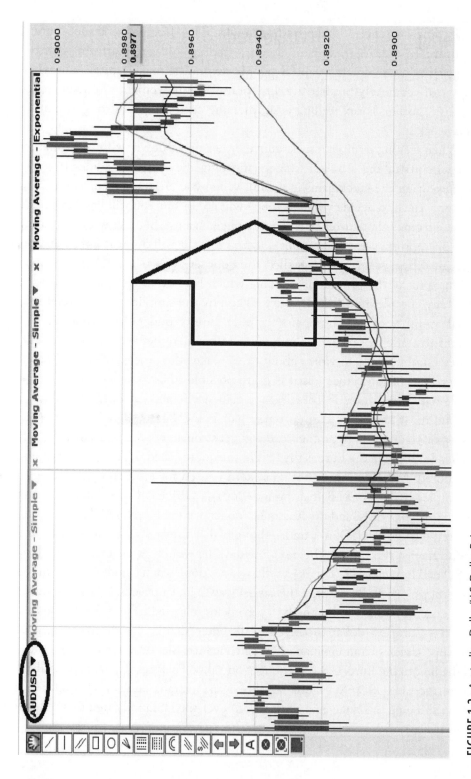

FIGURE 1-2 · Australian Dollar/U.S. Dollar Pair

Using Leverage and Gearing While Trading Forex

To break it down even further, a trader has a cash balance in his Forex brokerage account. He uses this cash balance for "gearing" or "leverage" to increase the buying power of his account from 10 to 50 times, and in some cases up to 500 times the amount in the account. Keep in mind that the actual multi-day movement in the EUR/USD pair may be in the neighborhood of 0.50%–1.25% in either direction, up or down, with either the Euro getting stronger against the U.S. dollar or the U.S. dollar getting stronger against the Euro. This means that if a Forex trader had a long EUR/USD trade on the books, and the Euro moved 1.0% stronger against the U.S. dollar (which is common in overnight trading) and the Forex trader had his Forex account set to trade at a 50:1 margin, the gains on the trade would be the 1.0% multiplied times 50. To put it another way, the gains that the Forex trader would experience would be 50% on this one trade. This serves as a very good example of the potential for return in the Forex market. Minimal percentage movements in the exchange rates between currency pairs can lead to maximum profits for your Forex account. It is clear that where a stock market trader can earn 1%, 3%, 5%, or even 10% per trade, the Forex trader can earn 30%–50% or more per trade.

With the right amount of risk management, diversification, and money management, a Forex trader can earn these large gains on a consistent basis. Another thing to keep in mind is that the currency markets are the deepest and most widely traded markets in the world, with hundreds of thousands of trades being placed 24 hours per day, 6 days per week. This means that a bet placed on a currency such as the Euro, dollar, yen, or even less-traded currencies such as the Swedish krona, will definitely move either up or down almost as soon as the trade is placed. The longer your trade will be on the books, or the longer your Forex trade is "live," the greater the chance for bigger and bigger movements. As an example, a one-hour long trade might move slightly, a few hundredths of a percent, and earn you just enough to pay for that night's pizza.

On the other hand, a larger move of 0.1%–1% or more would be expected for an overnight trade. With proper risk management, conservative position sizes, and automated profit taking, gains being in the neighborhood of 15%–20% of a Forex trader's total account balance can become the norm. It is not unusual to place a trade at dinner time and wake up the next morning to find that you have made so much overnight that you start to consider Forex trading full time! After a while you will discover trading opportunities come in two forms: good and really good. While it is not uncommon for Forex traders to be full-time professionals at mutual fund houses, banks, and hedge funds, it can be your goal to earn enough profits from Forex trading to make the payment on a new car, help pay your rent, or just simply add to your household's income.

With the right risk management, you can set up your trades so that they are able to withstand bad news. This allows you to have a Forex portfolio that is "impact resistant" to bad calls or mistakes, or just simply provides you the insulation to sit and wait out an unrealized loss until a reversal brings the trade into the profit range.

Higher Leverage Amounts than Stock Trading

One of the key advantages of Forex trading is the ability of the Forex trader to use large amounts of leverage. Most currency trading brokerage accounts allow for the use of leverage or margin in the range of 10:1 to 50:1. Some Forex brokerage accounts are domiciled in locations where it is possible for the owner of the Forex account to preset her leverage or "margin" to very high levels such as 250:1, 500:1, or even 1,000:1. As an example, if the trader had a balance of $100 U.S. in her account, and she had her leverage set to 50:1, she could buy $100 \times 50 = 5,000$, or $5,000 U.S. of currency. She could then take this purchasing power and sell the currency that she thinks will go down (similar to "shorting the market," as is done in equity or derivatives trading accounts) and use the proceeds of the sale of the shorted currency, in this case the USD, to buy the currency that she thinks will go up in value. In this case, the trader would sell or short USD and buy or go long EUR. It sounds complex, but the ratios, dollar amount of sales, and buying power in EURs is all calculated within moments by the trader's trading software, which is called a trading platform.

The different instantaneous exchange rates of the two currencies determine how much she can buy of the second currency. If the trader uses $1,500 of her available purchasing power to sell short USD, she will have created $1,500 worth of buying power to buy or go long EUR. If the exchange rate in the world's currency markets at the instant she places the trade is $1.25 USD to 1.00 EUR she will exchange her $1,500 USD for 1,200 EUR $(1,500/1.25 = 1,200)$.

The trader will make money in the trade when the price of the EUR rises higher than 1.00 EUR/1.25 USD. If the trader has predicted the market correctly, and if for example the world's currency markets, economies, stock markets, bond markets, and political news has changed in such a way that it has benefited the value of the Euro, and if that benefit has caused the value of the Euro to move to 1.35 EURs per USD, the trader will make money on the trade. Keep in mind that the gain in value of the long or bought currency can be very, very small and a trade can still be very, very profitable.

Deciding What Margin Amount to Use

Trading on margin or leverage is akin to trading with borrowed money. While it is true that when you trade with borrowed money in a normal brokerage account you may be responsible for paying back borrowed amounts or margined amounts that are equal to or even greater than the original borrowed (margined) amount, this is *not* the case with Forex.

When you set your margin to a certain level, you use the actual cash balance in your account to have a "buying power" that is a multiple of the margin level. If your margin is set to 20:1, you are able to buy 20 times the cash value of the account. Your preset margin amount (10:1, 50:1, 500:1, etc.) can determine how much value of currency you can trade. The thing to realize with higher levels of margin is that the percentage movements of the currency pairs will be amplified that much more. In other words, if you are trading at 50:1, you will experience the profit and loss (P&L) of your account moving at a rate that is 50 times the actual percentage movement of what currency pairs move daily. It is quite common for a currency pair such as the Australian dollar/U.S. dollar (AUD/USD) pair to move 0.75%–1.25% up and down from one trading day to the next. To put this into perspective, if your margin level was set to 50:1, the P&L of your trade would be moving 375%–625% of the cash value of the trade. While this percentage movement is good if your trade is gaining, it could also wipe out your entire account if you are in a losing trade due to the fact that your Forex brokerage firm might step in and make a forced margin call. A margin call is when your Forex losses are so great that your cash equity balance in your Forex account falls below a minimum.

Most of the time, your Forex equity can fall to very low levels before your Forex broker issues a margin call. If it happens, you will be required to close out your trades at a loss, or deposit more cash into the account to bring the cash equity balance back above the minimum level. If you fail to deposit the minimum cash, your Forex broker will force the close out all of your trades at an automatic loss. This is one of the disadvantages of high margin trading: rapid loss of account value and potential for total loss. Keep this in mind as you read further on about choosing how much of your total available margin to use with any position and at any one time.

Position Size Is Tied to Margin Levels

In order to prevent the chance for forced margin calls, professional Forex traders limit the size of each trade to a percentage of the total cash balance in the account. One of the best margin level/trade size ratios is to set your margin at 50:1 and then commit no more than one-third of your available margin to your entire open trades at any one time.

To put it simply, if you have a $250 USD cash balance, and you have your margin set at 50:1, you have a buying power of $250 USD × 50 = $12,500 worth of currency. This $12,500 is the *maximum* amount of usable margin value. While this is the maximum, most professional Forex traders will only use between 20% and 33.3% of this amount at any one time. This means that they will only have 20%–33.3% of their maximum purchasing power involved in all of their open trades. In this example, a professional trader would only commit $2,500 to $4,160 worth of his maximum margin ($12,500) to trading at any one time.

When this prescribed maximum level is adhered to, it can prevent accidental margin calls due to rapid swings in the percentage movements of the currency pairs that are being traded. This is due to the fact that the leftover available margin (80%–66.6%) can be used to absorb any swings of fortune, for example bad trades, in your account.

The Best Times to Trade Forex

The best trading times for Forex trading are those times of overlapping money center trading. This would be the time between 3 a.m. and 8 a.m. Eastern Time, due to the massive amounts of Forex that are being traded worldwide and the potential release of Forex news at these times. On the other hand, the best time to learn Forex trading is during the times the Asian markets are just starting to open, from 6 p.m. to 11 p.m. Eastern. This is because the markets will be much slower during these times, allowing you to have time to think through your Forex trades, your position sizes, and your diversification questions.

Most Forex traders will tell you that they needed time to learn how to trade in a slower market (and presumably with a smaller dollar amount in their Forex accounts) when they were just starting out, as it gave them time to get the hang of reading the market, digesting the economic news, looking at charts, and then moving on to actually placing a Forex trade. The late afternoon/early evening (4 p.m.–9 p.m. Eastern Time) can be the best time to learn. During these times the Forex markets are open, yet these are considered to be "off hours" between the close of the New York trading hours and the opening of the Sydney, Hong Kong, and Tokyo trading day.

The History of Forex

Before you get further into what it means to trade Forex, it would be best if you knew just a bit about the beginnings of the modern Forex and currency trading markets. Currency trading is and isn't a new thing. It has its foundation in the Renaissance during the late 1400s with the beginning of the international banks offering letters of credit, currency conversion, and currency value speculation. This was the real genesis of international banking as it is today. In the modern era, with major banks being involved in currency trading, and now with individual traders being able to open private Forex accounts and trade over the Internet, the current face of currency trading is relatively new.

During the last century and before the Forex trading of today, currencies were fixed in their exchange rates. What this means is that at any point in time between July 1944 and August 1971, each currency in world trade was convertible into another currency at a set exchange rate. In addition to this set exchange rate was the fact that the U.S. dollar would be fully convertible into gold at a predetermined conversion rate. The set Gold/U.S. dollar exchange rate (XAU/USD) had the effect of making the U.S. dollar the only currency in the world that was fully backed by gold. If a country such as Switzerland had a $5 million USD that they had in their treasury's reserves, they could make an arrangement to convert the $5 million USD in currency or book format directly into gold bullion. The set exchange rates of foreign currencies and the free exchangeability of the U.S. dollar into gold was a result of an economic summit by all of the victorious nations following World War II.

The goal of the economic summit, known as the Bretton Woods conference, was to create a stable economic environment in which the war-ravaged countries could build upon, and use to grow and strengthen their economies. The Bretton Woods Agreement was the formal agreement and plan that helped develop economically prosperous post–World War II countries. It had the effect of establishing the U.S. dollar as the dominant reserve currency of the world. This was due to the fact that many countries would then have U.S. dollars in their national currency reserves, mainly to help in the conversion of their home currencies into the U.S. dollar in order to then use that currency to buy goods and commodities that were only priced and sold in U.S. dollars in the international marketplaces and on the international exchanges.

As an example, if a Luxembourg-based steel manufacturer needed to purchase iron ore for its factories, it would first convert Luxembourg francs to U.S. dollars (at a set rate), and then use the U.S. dollars to go into the open market and purchase the iron ore. This converting and reconverting of various home currencies into and out of U.S. dollars had the effect of creating a huge need for U.S. dollars that were traded in the overseas market, outside of U.S. borders. In order to help the exchanges, and to insulate the Bretton Woods countries against economic hazard, the central banks of these countries built up and carried large reserves of U.S. dollars in their accounts at the Bank of International Settlements (http://www.bis.org/), at the International Monetary Fund (IMF; http://www.imf.org/), and in their own treasuries (http://www.bis.org/cbanks.htm).

U.S. Dollar Fully Convertible into Gold at a Set Price

Because one of the main features of Bretton Woods was the adoption of the U.S. dollar as the only currency that would be fully convertible into gold, the price of gold was fixed, leaving international dollar holders able to convert from dollars to gold and back again as required by their foreign currency reserve requirements (to be set by their treasury departments). During the era of the Bretton Woods Agreement (and the U.S. dollar's fully interchangeability into gold at a fixed price) many countries would buy and sell commodities such as crude oil, and food grains such as corn, wheat, and soy products with U.S. dollars. Because the world's necessary raw commodities such as crude oil and food commodities were priced in U.S. dollars, there had to be large amounts of U.S. dollars in circulation in order to allow the buying and selling of these commodities in the world market. Because the U.S. dollar had full interchangeability into gold, this meant that the countries could also have the opportunity to build up large surpluses of the U.S. dollar from international trade. In other words, they could choose to trade in U.S. dollars and therefore hold U.S. dollars in their reserves instead of gold. The inverse was also true: the countries with U.S. dollar surpluses had the option of taking a portion of this surplus, exchange it for gold, and diversify (or some would say strengthen) their treasury's currency reserves. This had the effect of diversifying the foreign country's currency reserves incrementally out of and away from the widely circulating U.S. dollar. One of the countries that took the most advantage of this opportunity to convert their dollar holdings into gold was France, under the leadership of Charles De Gaulle. The gold reserves of the major economies of the world are closely monitored today. When a country as big as Russia adds to its gold or a country as small as

Cyprus sells its gold, it makes the news. The World Bank keeps a listing of countries' current gold reserves at http://data.worldbank.org/indicator/FI.RES.TOTL.CD

U.S. Gold Reserves Become Depleted

The ability for nations to freely exchange their dollar holdings into gold at a set price was being exercised by a multitude of nations, and the U.S.'s gold holdings were being slowly depleted, reaching a very low level by the early 1970s. Because of the fact that the U.S. was exchanging gold at a record rate, and therefore subject to an ever-shrinking gold reserve, President Nixon issued an order that as of August 15, 1971, the "gold window" as it had been called, was to be closed. This meant that world nations could no longer exchange U.S. dollars for gold at a predetermined fixed rate. Countries such as France, the U.K., and Saudi Arabia that accumulated U.S. dollars from international trade could no longer expect to convert the U.S. dollars back into gold after the gold window closed. From this date on, the value of the U.S. dollar would "float" against the price of gold according to market demand.

The currency market as it is now did not get into full swing until the passing of the Jamaica Agreement in 1976, when it was determined that the world's currencies would float against each other without a predetermined rate. This meant that from this date on, the price of currency pairs would freely move up and down according to the market law of supply and demand. These days there are small retail traders and large institutional traders that are active in the Forex market. While today many countries' central banks are involved in the currency market for the management of their economies, it is the hedge funds, mutual funds, endowment funds, and individuals that are making the most out of the profits that can be made from trading in the Forex market. Asset managers that trade millions of dollars of currency daily use the same information and same basic ideas of currency trading as today's individual Forex trader. Prior to this time, Forex was mainly the business of central banks, large commercial banks, and banking centers. The small, private, retail Forex trader was locked out of the currency market due to contract sizes being very large and expensive and also the limited market for currencies.

Retail Forex trading as it is now didn't become possible until the development of high speed Internet, high capacity of personal computers, and the development of retail, private account Forex brokers. These three developments led to the further internationalization of the Forex business, with the regulatory bodies of some countries being very pro-Forex broker/account holder. This is why there are so many Forex dealers in places such as Switzerland, Cyprus, and the Isle of Man. These are money centers that have very pro-banking local environments while at the same time having very strong international Forex, banking, and trading regulatory bodies. Many jobs are created with banking, trading, and Forex, and the governments give tax incentives and other assistance to banking/brokerage related businesses there. Strong technological infrastructure and strong financial regulation has led to the availability of many on-shore and off-shore Forex dealers for today's Forex trader.

A Quick Background of Economic and Financial Policy

Starting in the 1960s, the U.S. central bank (also known as the Federal Reserve Bank, or simply the Fed) managed the economic policy by decreasing income tax, which left extra cash in their taxpayer's pockets. Because the typical taxpayer was spending much less in income taxes, the majority spent the extra money on goods and services instead of saving the money. When the people had extra money from tax savings and they spent it, the extra money then went to businesses and business owners, as well as to the suppliers and employees of these businesses. These businesses, suppliers, and employees also had more of their earnings to then spend, because they too were enjoying the same tax breaks. This extra money was then spent, which in turn was spent again. This spending again and again gives the effect of causing what is called a "velocity of money." In other words, not only is there a lot of money in the country, but it is moving from person to person very quickly. The result is an expanding economic climate.

At the same time as the tax-reduction fiscal policy, the Federal Reserve had begun lowering interest rates in the U.S., which in turn, had the effect of growing or expanding the money supply of the country. The overall effect was simple: There was more money from less taxes and it was easier to borrow money due to lower interest rates. The combined strategies had the total result of quickly and effectively improving the economy of the United States. The recovery was strong, and the economy prospered into the late 1960s.

The sluggish economic climate of the latter part of the 1950s had developed into a slowly overheating economic climate by the time the 1970s started. The economic stimulus policies of the 1960s caused the economy of the 1970s to become greatly inflationary. Prices of materials like precious metals, copper, and gasoline shot up to unprecedented level. In the case of crude oil, the Organization of Oil Exporting Providers (OPEC) added to the problem in 1973 by reducing the supply of oil in an attempt to increase prices, which would have the effect of increasing the oil producer's profits. This was called the OPEC oil embargo and it was a time when the world's suppliers of crude oil got together to cut back on production, limiting oil supply, and therefore forcing the price of a barrel of crude oil to rise substantially. The reduced availability of crude to the global economies triggered even greater inflationary activity as, while there was a large supply of U.S. dollars, there was at the same time a shrinking supply of one of the world's basic commodities, crude oil. This had the effect of causing widespread inflationary episodes in the U.S. and most of the European countries. (Remember, certain commodities such as crude oil were priced and traded in U.S. dollars only.) The end result was an inflationary climate in the U.S. in the middle of the 1970s which lasted well into the early 1980s. This inflation caused high increases in the prices of everyday goods, as nearly every product was tied to the overall inflationary pressure. Homes, cars, food, labor—inflation was felt everywhere and reflected in every component of goods and services.

Additional experimentation with economic and fiscal strategy was undertaken at the beginning of the 1980s. With the election of President Ronald Reagan, the new fiscal policy heralded the end of the tax breaks for the public. The Fed began to take an alternative approach by hiking up the interest rates of the country higher and higher until a slowing of the economy was achieved. Again, it was shown that interest rates act like a temperature control of the economy.

Today's Economic Climate

These days there has been a repeat of the inputs into the inflationary components of the world's economies. While it is true that inflation has yet to be determined, currency plays can be determined by looking forward to see which countries' economies will slow and which countries' economies will grow. To put it simply, if you determine that a country will grow its economy faster, you would go long or buy that currency and you would go short or sell the currency of the country with a slowing economy. Keep this in mind as you read further into how to spot what Forex trades will work out for you, and what Forex currency pairs to trade.

Increasing and Decreasing Money Supplies, Lowering and Raising Interest Rates

It is a known fact that it takes time for an economy such as the Euro zone, United States, or Japan to catch up with the addition of increased monetary supply. The path of lower interest rates leading to economic growth then leading to economic overheating is usually followed by a country's central bank then desiring to slow the economy by raising interest rates. This is the natural economic cycle and is the single basis for the change in the exchange rates between country's currencies.

For example, over time the strengthening of the Swedish currency against its trading partners' currency, the Euro, might be substantial. This is usually due to the perception of a current or future stronger Swedish versus European economy. This idea of the potential for a strong or getting stronger Swedish economy would catch the eye of Forex traders, who would then also go long the SEK. A Forex trader might learn through research that the Swedish economy is doing very well, and is in fact doing much better (or has the potential to be doing much better) than the mainland European economy. He would then take this information to short the Euro and go long the Swedish krona (Short EUR/SEK.) His trade would make money as the economy of Sweden does better and better compared to Europe. In fact, part of the function of the winning trade would be the fact that other Forex traders would also notice that the economy of Sweden is doing well, and that the Swedish central bank—The Riksbank— (http://www.riksbank.se/en/) might have to raise interest rates in the future. This would cause a widespread buying of SEK against EUR which would have the added supply/demand effect. By this time not only would the overall economy of Sweden be affected, but it could be affected negatively, as the exports of a country with a strong currency are not competitive. This would have a cause-and-effect relationship of perhaps helping the Riksbank to then begin thinking of lowering interest rates to reduce the exchange rate between the Swedish Krona and the Euro.

The effect of lowering the SEK interest rates would cause the exchange rate to soften, correct, and fall to a more manageable level. This is mainly due to the interest rate differentials of the two countries' currencies not being as attractive as they once were. At this point, many long SEK holders would simply close out their short EUR/SEK positions at a profit and call it a good run. Keep in mind that this whole process can take anywhere from years to as little as a few months—central bankers meet and decide on inflation targets and interest rate adjustments every six weeks or so. Additionally, market sentiment is a key factor in the daily values of one currency against another. While it may be true that the actual process takes six weeks or longer, the anticipation of what is actually happening with a country's economy is what makes a Forex trader go long or short that country's currency. If there is a general feeling that the world is doing better, Forex traders will also feel as though economically things are well in the world. They might then place trades that favor economies that they believe are set to grow at a faster rate. Good times mean fast growing economies and bad times are the times to make safer trades with slower growing economies.

So, what is Forex trading, plain and simple? Forex trading is electronically buying one country's currency while simultaneously selling another country's currency, with the hopes that the bought currency will gain in value against the sold currency sometime in the future.

If you don't get it now, keep reading. We'll go over it again and again throughout this book.

QUIZ

1. **If you think that one currency will get stronger than another one in the future you should:**
   A. Buy both and exchange them at the market value later
   B. Go long the currency that you think will get stronger
   C. Go short the currency that you think will get weaker
   D. Both B & C

2. **When you make a trade in your Forex account you are creating an IOU with the currency that is shorted.**
   A. True
   B. False

3. **When you use leverage in a Forex account you are able to:**
   A. Buy more currency than your cash balance
   B. Increase the ability to earn in your Forex account
   C. Increase the chance of losses and risk in your account
   D. All of the above

4. **The Forex market trades online worldwide:**
   A. 24 hours a day, 6 days a week
   B. 9 to 5, 7 days a week
   C. The same hours as the stock market
   D. 2:30 a.m. to 8:30 a.m. Eastern Time

5. **The Bretton Woods Agreement related to the:**
   A. Floating rate mechinism
   B. Gold reserves
   C. The U.S. dollar/gold exchange rate
   D. Both B & C

6. **Under the Bretton Woods Agreement, the U.S. dollar was:**
   A. The world's reserve currency
   B. Fully convertible into gold at a preset price
   C. Used to buy commonly traded commodities
   D. All of the above

7. **When a central bank holds gold in its vaults, they are called that country's:**
   A. Assets
   B. Bullion holdings
   C. Asset backed securities
   D. Gold reserves

8. **When the United State's gold reserves became depleted due to other countries' gold withdrawals:**
   A. The U.S. president stopped the sale of gold.
   B. The U.S. president stopped the foreign exchange market.
   C. The U.S. president didn't mind.
   D. The U.S. president no longer allowed U.S. dollars to directly convert into gold.

9. **When the U.S. president stopped the fixed U.S. dollar/gold exchange rate it was known as "closing the gold window."**
   A. True
   B. False

10. **Going long a currency means:**
    A. You will buy the currency.
    B. You will sell the currency.
    C. You will buy the currency while selling another currency.
    D. You will sell the currency while buying another currency.

Chapter **2**

Getting Ready to Trade

CHAPTER OBJECTIVES

In this chapter, you will learn the following:

- How to handle the emotions that come with trading Forex
- How to evaluate your risk tolerance
- The importance of trading support groups
- How to evaluate your available funds for Forex trading
- Where to look for and evaluate market information

Having a working knowledge on the basics of Forex is the first step to knowing if you are ready to trade. Thorough study of the market, knowledge of trading platforms, and time spent paper trading with a demo account will allow you to go a long way into your trading career and allow you a good chance to be successful. The next step should be to figure out if Forex trading is a good fit for you. Some of the things to consider about trading are the time commitments to learn a good system of trading, getting to know your way around the markets, economic indicators, etc. You should also think about how currencies markets and 24-hour trading will fit into your daily routine with your other personal obligations such as family and friends, and how to handle the ups and downs of your fortunes when trading. When you are just getting started with Forex trading it is best to remember that a solid backup plan will give you the reassurance and safety net you need to help get your trading business off the ground successfully and guide you through the rough spots.

Learning to Deal with the Emotions of Trading

Most jobs come with emotional stresses and strains, but Forex trading ties your income levels to an unpredictable market which can add significant amounts of stress to your day. The higher the stress levels, the stronger the emotions that can run through you in a moment, causing a chain reaction before you may realize it. For example if a foreign exchange (FX) trader is running on a highly profitable day, they can be on an emotional high and have a feeling that they are on top of the world. On the flip side, a losing day could darken your mood and help move you towards a negative losing pattern instead of making the "day-over" call and closing up shop for the day. Trading can also get you to the point where you are trading for the thrill of it and making money becomes secondary. In fact, some Forex traders purposely seek out the wild ride of the markets, enjoying the ups and crashing hard with the downs, much like the thrill of a roller coaster ride. If you find that this is you, that's fine, just trade with a smaller amount of cash that you are willing to risk to the fullest and not be afraid to lose. On the other hand, professional currency traders know how to stand back, take in the larger picture, and see the job of trading as just that: a job that produces income, has trading hours, requires risk management, etc., and have a life outside of the trading room.

Even though a professional horse trainer would be excited when a new client brings him a potential race winner or a temperamental thoroughbred racehorse, the horse trainer would still perform the same basic assessment to the horse including the vet checks, hot walks, grooming, shoeing, and warm-up gallops that are part of a professional trainer's daily routine. He would not be overly impressed by bloodline, breeding, or even a recent winning streak. A true pro knows how to get the best out of his skills on a daily basis and uses all his tools and experience to the best of his knowledge to maintain a sound training program, trusting in his long-term methods. A trainer won't stop feeding an animal if it doesn't perform as expected or tell an owner his horse can't run. Similarly, as an FX trader, you will be "training with" high performance, hot-blooded, extremely unpredictable Forex markets (the thoroughbred), and you will use every tool in your toolbox to do so.

Running your Forex trading accounts like a business is the key for a healthy, long-term trading career. Even if your emotions are tied to every trade, you can keep a cool head to strategically plan entry/exit points. Keep in mind that entry points are the points that you make your initial buy or sell of a currency pair. Exit points are where you close out the trade. Keeping a calm head with a sensible approach will help alleviate the wild emotional swings many new traders face. Forex traders share many stories of exciting market swings that make them instant wealth (on paper with unrealized gains) only to have their trade close out badly and lose the profits. These are the traders who you can learn from when they say "what was I thinking?" or "I should have taken the profits." These traders rode the wave, and even after seeing the crest, still failed to close out their trade because they sought an even higher wave. Good tools in your trading toolbox won't matter if you cannot master your emotions in the middle of a rocky moment. It is best to learn to harness the power of your emotions and you will be well on your way to a high-profit, low-emotion, successful Forex trading career.

The Time Commitment to Forex Trading

Next, consider your available time commitment to FX trading. Getting up to speed on market research, your trading preferences, and your personal market knowledge can take a few weeks to several year-long seasons. Give yourself time to learn, because just as any other new job has a learning curve, so will currency trading. Read financial magazines, websites, news feeds, and books aimed at day traders as much and as often as you can. The *Wall Street Journal* and *Financial Times* are excellent resources to find help getting acquainted with the structure and flow of the markets. The more information you have, the better your trades will be when you start making them.

Being a successful day trader is not about throwing good money after bad. The long-term, successful trader is always learning, always exploring markets and trends, and always thinking about ways to make his or her trades work for them. Many new traders hastily throw their hard-earned money into the market to follow the latest trend, only to lose it all very quickly when the day's hysteria blows over. Starting out slowly is a good idea when starting something new. No one expects to have flawless trades, a perfect portfolio hedge, and huge gains in the first day of learning how to trade. Keep your expectations realistic, and commit to what you can learn on a steady, daily pace to grow your knowledge base. For example, learn all you can about your specific trading platform software, run the demo, read the help notes, find out how to open and close trades, and practice with real-time data if the software allows.

Some traders are so new to the scene, they haven't figured out which button to hit to place a trade, or how to close it down on their trading screen. Take the time to slow down and learn your new software trading platform inside and out. You wouldn't drive a stick-shift car if you only knew automatic transmissions, so why try running an FX trading account when you don't know what your software does or doesn't do? Take the time to open an account, learn how to properly operate it, and find out what sort of trades interest you.

Keep in mind that it also requires a time investment on your part to sit down in front of the computer and to stay vigilant while the market moves up and down, in order for you to capture gains. Some markets can be traded overnight or in the evenings, while many of them are only open during the mornings and early afternoons. The best educated traders do their research before placing trades, so think about getting up earlier to stay on top of the news. It is still entirely possible to be a part-time trader. Trades can be made after regular work hours during the week or on Sunday afternoons. You may face a few limitations on what is available to trade at those hours; however, it is a great way to get up to speed on the markets with a reduced schedule of availability.

Risk Tolerance

What sort of risk taker are you? Can you live with a lot of uncertainty or are you a $5 cash in the hand is better than $20 in an hour type of person? There is always risk involved in Forex trading, some of which can be reduced. There are risks associated with everything, including a regular "day job"—you could be hit by a bus during your morning commute or your job might be transferred overseas at a moment's notice. For example, when an Emergency Room doctor has a bad day, he loses a patient and someone dies. But if a retail store cashier has a bad day and counts out the wrong change, he or she still goes home with a paycheck. Of course the ER doctor risks more every day and earns more in salary, but saving a life is a much larger reward to receive than a steady $8.00/hr paycheck the low-risk, low-gain cashier earns. However, most people would agree that risking their daily paycheck leaves them weak in the knees and shaky before the morning coffee break rolls around. "Opportunity risk" is the idea that the Forex trader who makes a successful living trading full time has passed up the opportunity to earn regular income from a lower stress job. This is not a one-size-fits-all type of career path. No one but you can make the assessment of whether it is right for you.

Any time you put your own money on the line to make a living, you invite risk. Forex trading involves a different level of risk that's not for everyone. Many low-risk careers offer steady jobs with convenient bi-weekly salaries and plenty of great benefits as well. There is no reliable paycheck in trading. Your net profits make you break even, or have far more or far less than when you started the day. Putting your hard-earned money into something that may or not be fruitful can be addictive or depressing, depending on what your attitude is. Taking on risk to gain rewards in the form of profit can tempt even the most sophisticated Forex trader to knock on potential's door more often. These traders are the ones who know that in order to gain more, you must risk more. Before you jump on a hot market tip or trend, decide what your acceptable risk level is. In other words, manage your risk ahead of time, so it doesn't manage you.

Develop your unique risk-level management with a good dose of common sense mixed with mathematics and market knowledge. This will help to shore up your risk levels and protect your assets by lowering the profit margins. While it is possible to hedge all of your risk away, you also may give up any real profit. Find a profitable balance between your risk comfort level and the profits you seek and you'll enjoy a long career as a skilled day trader.

Available Funds

As with any business, certain tools are required in the old toolbox. For Forex traders, this includes cash. You don't have to have thousands of dollars to get started. Some accounts can be opened with as little as $250, $100, or even $10. (Oanda www.oanda.com allows an account to be opened with $1!) While FX trading can be started with small balances, a good amount of learning, profit (in relation to the cash balance), and excitement can be had with a smaller cash deposit. Keep in mind that the typical Forex account offers up to a 50:1 margin, so this would mean a $12,500 to $500 available currency trading account.

In the beginning, a novice trader can get their feet wet in the market slowly. Perhaps you have the evenings free to read market news, study trends, and make small, quick trades while relaxing on the couch. Start out with the habit of taking the time to train and learn the basics before you involve a real cash balance. Some traders start out small to learn the ebb and flow of the market and also realize a tiny profit at the same time. Having an extra $20 to spend on lunch the next day, due to your small, practice trades from the night before can be a great feeling and will encourage you to keep trying. It also imprints how your trading platform software works, builds confidence, and prepares you for making larger trades in the future.

Small dollar amounts are not to be taken lightly. Don't fall for the idea that small cash accounts equal small profits and you should instead jump into higher risk levels for higher gains. Poor position size, bad margin management, and a couple of poorly placed trades can slam the door on any gains and close out even the tiniest accounts.

Getting used to the demo feature on your trading platform, doing a couple test trades, and getting into the habit of checking the news and resources, puts you in a better position to use real money. Get used to that winning feeling on the trades you researched, planned for, and added in the profit column of your balance sheet. Gradually, over time, you can build up your account and trade larger amounts. Eventually, when you're up to full-time trading, you'll be able to draw a salary from your account. In the meantime, be sure to use funds you can live without for a while and certainly not your rent money! Use your latte coffee money or brown bag your lunches to get that extra cash put aside for trading. It will be put to good use and eventually pay you back. Grow your account by plowing the profits you have made back into the trading account.

Can You Work Alone?

Now that you're confident in your ability to conquer your emotions, have established a solid risk tolerance, and have a small cash amount to trade with, the last part is learning how to work by yourself. Full-time or part-time, most Forex trading is done alone. Today's superfast computers, with easy-to-use software programs and trading platforms enable day traders to either work in the city or on the outskirts of town. Forex traders can have their home offices in the most rural part of Montana or in heavily populated New York City. Either way, the best part or Forex trading is that you can work from home, in your slippers if you want, taking breaks as needed, all the while keeping an eye on your trades. The downside is that it can get a bit lonely all by yourself, especially if you happen to be one of those types who prefer to be on the more social end of the office friendliness chart.

If you're one who likes to chat at lunch, tell jokes around the water cooler, or hang out with office buddies after work, you may miss the social interaction that a regular job offers. Being alone works great for extended periods of intense concentration, but has its drawbacks when you're looking for feedback on a trade or chitchat during some downtime. Other drawbacks of working alone include the lack of peer support as to whether or not to place a trade: "Is this a good trading opportunity?" "What do you think of today's labor report?" Or even, "What do you think of the EUR/SEK pair at this price?" These are some of the questions that can't easily be asked of your officemates. At a regular job there is also some sort of supervisor; it seems that everyone has a more experienced person to consult about a question or issue. When you work alone trading Forex, you will have to make your own decisions as to what is a good trade, when it is a good time to trade, how much to trade, and even when to take your profits. At the same time, once you get good at doing your own thing, you can take your profits of an overnight long AUD/USD trade by 8a.m. Eastern time and close up shop. In this case, you might have discovered that you knew the market well enough to make the right call without any help, and that you've made your daily wage by the time the day is just starting for most people.

This is one of the best parts of Forex trading: It can be run like a business, you can be your own boss, and you can pay the bills with the profits. There are tales of people learning to trade Forex and slowly building up enough experience and confidence to have a big enough balance to get to the point where they can make a 5% return on their cash balance very safely and very consistently. These returns can be made with only one or two safe trades a week. These traders keep a large balance in their accounts, and trade at a high margin. They look for only the best trades, and they make the money consistently. It is quite easy to make 20%–30% per month in returns by trading very infrequently (which is actually a very safe way to go about Forex trading). The money can then be rolled over and the account can build up over time, or the profits can be taken out at the end of the month, with the cash going directly into your checking account and then used to pay for the mortgage, rent, bills, car payment, or other necessities. This type of trading usually occurs after about a year or two of learning.

If you would like to get to this level of trading and consistecy, the best method is to trade trying out different styles at a variety of risk levels using a small amount of cash. This will allow you a really good opportunity to learn all there is to know about the business. With this method, you can get all the experience you need to see opportunities before they come up, as well as gain the knowledge as to when to take your profits. If this is your goal—to earn a consistent 20%–30% each trading month—then trade as often as you can, week after week, month after month. You will gain skills quickly, and you can build confidence and trade with bigger and bigger cash balances as you earn your successful trades.

Many Forex traders decide the issues related to working solo are not that bad. The list of advantages of successful Forex trading can be much longer than the list of disadvantages. However, the social isolation that comes from working with your trading account instead of in an office full of people can make or break the Forex trader and should be taken under serious consideration.

For example, you are the only one liable for the decisions about your trading choices and accounts. Your personal satisfaction is the only performance review you'll receive. Treat currency trading like a regular day job from day one and you'll be able to maintain a businesslike attitude regarding your trades much easier. Keep a regular work schedule, set regular reviews of your trading activity, wear business clothes if that helps enhance your performance. Be sure to set a quitting time as well, in order to create ownership of your time and know that the trading day ends eventually. Socialize with friends regularly and take a real vacation (away from your computer) just like you would at a normal Monday through Friday 9:00 to 5:00 job.

Being your own boss also means you get to decide when to promote yourself. Perhaps you'll reward your much larger portfolio by venturing into new, more exotic trading pairs. Or perhaps you'll promote yourself to "senior trader" and give yourself a bigger year-end bonus as a reward to yourself because of maintaining a profitable account for 6, 9, or 12 straight months.

Like-Minded Traders and Other Support Groups

The more experience you gain over time, the more ups and downs you will face in your trading. Sometimes, the market will seem to have a life of its own, roaring ahead like a runaway freight train and everyone and their brother is in up to their necks pitching trades and making money. Traders will see bad days too, with whole portfolios wiped out, grinding down the best seasoned pros to their wit's end with endless streams of bad-to-worse scenarios. It is enough to strain even the most experienced traders and also why a good support group is a key to staying with Forex trading.

Being a member of a large, impersonal group can offer enjoyment and a feeling of fitting in that many find comforting. The news outlets can combine to make a trader feel less alone—when they are reporting the market intensity is widespread and lasting, you get the feeling you're not so alone after all, but part of a much greater financial machine. Live footage and interviews from the world's trading pits can make your home office feel very connected and at the center of the fates and fortunes of a much larger community.

Feeling part of the financial community can make trading a very enjoyable experience. Perhaps you've dove into your technical analysis and take a break to catch a news story about the one of your currency pair's homeland news and economic conditions. Not only is it vital to stay on top of such relevant information, it can also bring a foreign country's finances into your backyard and shape a new picture of it in ways you never thought possible. Making that kind of deeper association or a big-picture connection offers a unique sense of belonging to something bigger than yourself and your office.

Don't rule out the periodicals that are available in print, too, for another source of support. The *Wall Street Journal* and other similar daily newspapers report the news like CNBC, but include more in-depth articles. Monthly trade publications such as *Futures Magazine* write for audiences of full- and part-time traders with content that features problems many day traders face, such as money management, "what went wrong" scenarios, seasonal trading, and more. From beginner to expert, all day traders can gain knowledge and great examples from these resources.

Try a professional network like LinkedIn to find other traders who can relate to you and your situation. A basic account at www.LinkedIn.com is free to sign up for and you can find groups, newsletters, and individuals with whom to network, chat, and receive advice from on trading, Forex, economics, risk management, and a multitude of other topics. There are foreign exchange trading groups, quantitative trading groups, hedge fund groups, and more.

After joining a group, you can view the listings of other members to single out those with whom you'd like to network. Be picky or be liberal with your connections. Then contribute regularly, read and learn through posting comments, review the forums, and keep up on the latest news with your new group.

Also, these groups can alert you to what others think in your profession, what they favor, and their overall impressions of the market. This information can be refreshing and enlightening as you combine your research with what others have posted on the groups and forums. Getting an e-mail from one of your online connections confirming your thoughts is helpful. Friends from online communities like LinkedIn allow you to connect with just about anyone the world over.

A close network of family and friends never hurts either. Being able to unwind over a weekend can bring relief to an otherwise crazy market run. Take advantage of those around you and take a break from the currency trading routine to get out of your head and your profit margins. Family and friends are an excellent source of fresh perspectives regardless of whether they follow the markets or have any idea what you do for a living.

Lastly, it's not as hard as you think to find other people discussing the market. Your farmer's market, your local gym, your doctor's waiting room, in the checkout line, on the train, or waiting for the bus are all excellent places for finding like-minded people who enjoy following the markets and the economy. Taking all things into consideration includes time, money, and risk-oriented responsibilities.

A key idea with Forex trading is that with additional responsibilities and restrictions on your time, money, and risk, FX trading becomes progressively more stressful. Try to keep it fun by reducing the dollar amount at risk during difficult or highly stressful periods of your life. If you find your life becoming too stressful, or feel your time is best devoted somewhere else for a period of time, or just that the currency market is not offering up any good trades, then trim down the balance in your FX account. Believe it or not, those types of days come more often than not, and the best way to deal with them is to treat these times as a lack of trading opportunity. During these periods, it might be best to withdraw some of the cash from your Forex account and enjoy the money in a more productive fashion. There is a saying in trading: Sell in May and go away. This usually means that the summer is a time to enjoy your winnings and your life beyond the computer screen and financial markets. It also means that many of the other traders in the world (including bond, equities, and commodities traders) will close out and take time off during the summer months as well. Because of this, trading is usually a bit more difficult, and profits may come a bit slower.

Time is short and even shorter when you have family or obligations that compete for your time. Raising a family with young children or perhaps providing care for an elderly family member can take up nearly your entire day, leaving you with small bits of time here and there to study the market and place trades. Perhaps in this case, you could start trading part-time in the afternoons. The FX market is open 24 hours a day from Sunday night until Friday afternoon. Research the markets during the day at baby's nap time or whenever you get a moment. The bits and pieces of knowledge you'll gain will add up over time to make a difference in your trading.

Maybe you've enjoyed learning about the markets and are very interested in taking the next step to post your first real-time trade. But perhaps you're very limited in the amount of cash to day trade with, or simply cannot assume the additional risks that FX trading brings. If so, try a free demo account offered through a brokerage. Start out the fund with an imaginary deposit and place real-time trades using the exact same software and trading platform as for a live account. Many brokers use demo accounts to test their trading platforms' functionality. Day traders can use the demos as a test for their latest tip or market theory to place live trades and see what happens in real time but with no risk. Using tools such as these can help refine a trading idea, test a theory, and practice using your market-trading knowledge.

Backup Plan

Having a designated fall-back plan, or backup plan, is an excellent way to alleviate the pain of ugly market trends, wild swings, and volatility. Many day traders include a backup plan that they will implement when they find it hard to make profitable trades within preferred risk-tolerance ranges. The summer of 2010 was a perfect example. European nations were overwhelmed with individual countries' debt and the Euro was losing value against the U.S. dollar for several weeks. On one weekend, UBS, a Swiss brokerage house and investment bank (http://www.ubs.com/), released an update that stated the Euro would fall even further in the upcoming six to nine months and the performance was "disappointing." Meanwhile, another news outlet, Market Watch (www.marketwatch.com), reported the upcoming week could prove to be very difficult for currency traders unless they were braced for extremely wild market swings.

Your backup plan can be put into place to cover just these types of situations. It will provide you with some form of riskless or low-risk activity to keep you out of high-risk scenarios such as these. A backup plan can include cushioning your account by other means, such as with a side job or other venture you can turn to as needed while the market sorts itself out.

Uncertain times like these also give you the opportunity to take some of your profits out of your account and spend them on a much-needed vacation or other enjoyable activity. Falling currency, a banking crisis, rocky economy stories, and a barrage of bad news can hype up the already swooning market even further. Forex trading does involve risk; however your money does not always have to be put at risk. You control your account, your trades, and your appropriate risk level. Knowing ahead of time that some days it is okay to sit out of an unpredictable market can make you a savvy day trader.

Listening to the Market

Every day, your skill level will increase as you learn how to find day-trading ideas by listening to the market. There are countless sources of information available to you as a Forex trader, some more reliable than others. Deciding how much information, the source, and the quality of the information are important issues to consider when reviewing news on the market. While your brokerage, cable TV, and Internet news feeds can provide a lot of data, the question you need to ask is how this information helps you make a better decision on what trades to analyze and set up.

How Much Information Is Enough?

In a perfect trade, the best scenario is when the market has priced a Forex pair too low or too high. This means that the market has too many or too few buyers or sellers of the trade, and during the short term (the trading cycle), there is an opportunity for other traders to move in. How market traders react to the too low or too high price can cause the markets to change course, even a small amount. This scenario is best considered for an immediate short-term time frame when evaluating such a situation. One of the best ways to seek out trading scenarios is when you can place a trade while the momentum goes in your direction, then plan to close out of it as soon as it proves profitable.

By using a wide variety of information to help interpret the market's levels, a Forex trader can find the best entry and exit points. If you are still working with a demo account and in training mode, you should first learn what Forex pairs are the best to trade, as well as when the best time is to place an order and the exit points. In order to get an overview of the entire market, a Forex trader needs to review and listen to as much daily market information as time permits.

When you are first learning how to trade, it is best to read, listen to, or watch four or five different news sources in order to get up to speed on the flow of the market before placing your first trade of the day. This process will help you to have the proper mindset for a profitable day of Forex trading, especially if you have been away from your trading desk for a few days.

Doing some due diligence work when you read and listen to market reports will help you focus on the facts and how specific FX pairs (and also economic zones) are doing. It will also come in handy when you need to put yourself in another trader's shoes to think about how she will react to the same market news. Role playing in your trades, or seeing it from a different perspective, will enable you to foresee the trading day ahead clearer and help you to avoid pitfalls. All public sources of information should be considered general insight into the market, but not the sole determining factor for your currency trading activity.

Of course, using your brokerage's reports and newsletters are a key to staying on top of the Forex news. Checking your 5-minute, 1-minute, and 30-second charts for the day's entry/exit points is the next step. Before you head into a trading session, try to have the market overview of which economic zones and currency pairs you would like to focus on during the session. Use your own individual ideas based on your trusted sources of information plus the technical analyses from the short time-frame charts.

Having a set routine for digesting the day's market information will also help you focus on the task at hand: analyzing the currency markets and economic news, looking for setups, and placing trades. Starting with the news feeds, review reports and long time-frame charts, then move on to short time-frame charts. This allows you to roll into the day's market with the proper pace and mood. You can decide to follow a single currency pair or you can watch several at one time. One of the best ways to learn how to trade is to get into the habit of watching a trade develop, as it happens, on a short time-frame chart and noting the movements. When you begin to observe a pattern, you can then begin to place your trades.

Where to Source Your Trading Ideas

Current information flows quickly in and out of the market. You'll begin to rely on your trusted sources (central banking websites, brokers' reports, well-known news feed sources) and general market chatter to get the best feel for trading suggestions. Reports and summaries present a logical view of the market and are typically based on mathematics, previous market activity, fundamentals, and technical indicators (as opposed to market chatter, which can be more opinion and sensationalism than fact). The more-detailed reports can be read when you're off and away from your trading desk. Reviewing them will give you a deeper understanding of the underlying dynamics of the market and the analyst's reasoning process.

Let's say, for example, a report comes across your desk that a more cautious stance will be observed in the market for the rest of the month. You might also find out that the S&P 500 moved into an overbought range. An overbought range means that the fundamentals are seeing the stocks in the range have reached a general high average P/E (price/earnings ratio), meaning the prices are too high versus the anticipated earnings of the companies. Add into that a report that the S&P is stuck at a resistance spot for over a week, and you can infer two things: One, the S&P is topping out, and two, it will probably linger there for a while and might stall out. Worse than a stall would be a correction (overvalued market is sold off to realistic levels). Knowing all this, you would realize that now is a good time to go to a "risk off" stance in your Forex portfolio. This is because when the market is overbought and ready for a correction, Forex trades that are more conservative will profit greatly when the market has a reversal of fortune.

When the world's stock indices, such as the DAX, CAC 40, FTSE 100, and S&P 500, move downwards during a trading day, Forex trades that are "risk off" will usually win big. Keep in mind that risk off Forex trades are trades that short the high-yielding currencies of high-growth countries and long the low-yielding currencies of lower-growth countries. Classic examples of risk off Forex trades would be a long EUR/SEK trade, a short AUD/USD trade, and a short NZD/JPY trade. As you can see, in each of these trade setups, the currency that is shorted is a currency that has traditionally been that of a high-growth economy. Sweden of late has had a much more stable and growth-oriented economy than mainland Europe.

Sweden's economy and the Swedish Krona (SEK) have long been associated with being a high-beta currency—a currency whose upward and downward movements closely track those of the stock market. Not only is the SEK known for following the stock market, but trades that are long the SEK are known to perform quite well when the market is moving up, and trades that are short the SEK are known to also perform quite well when the market is moving down (as shown in Figure 2-1).

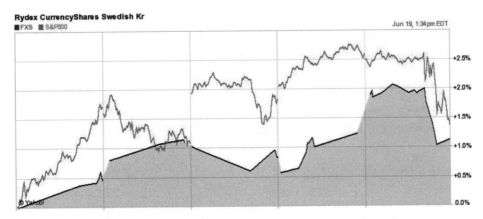

FIGURE 2-1 • Illustration Showing the Close Relationship of the USD/SEK Proxy Exchange Traded Fund (FXS) and the S&P 500

A really good way to trade Forex and win consistently is to do what is known as "trade risk." Trading risk is simple: If the signs of the market tell you that the market is moving or going to move up or down, set up your trades for risk or risk off. Trading risk can be one of the easiest ways to consistently win in the currency market. All it takes is to observe what currency pairs react well or not so well to up and down markets. Make some observations as to what is working in the current market. AUD, NZD, SEK are good consistent ways to trade risk. You can also get creative and have some of the more exotic high-growth, high-yield currencies work in your favor. Good trades to look for are short EUR/HUF, and short EUR/PLN, as the Hungarian and Polish economies are considered growing economies and are more on the risk side of their trading partner, the EUR. If you would like to split the vote, so to speak, you could place a short EUR/CZK, as the Czechoslovakian economy has been especially promising. Again, these trades would short the EUR in a good market, in order to capture the gain of the high-growth Eastern European countries. At the same time, the trade would be reversed, with a long EUR if the market was in a downturn, as historically the high-growth currencies would fall in value against the more conservative Euro.

Market chatter is a term used for short-term news reports on the marketplace. Don't forget, a lot of other people are using the exact same reports and reading the same information. The key is to read between the lines and understand the impact of the news itself on the herd mentality of the market. Experienced traders will know what to expect because they've seen more market reactions than a novice trader. Keep in mind that the general knowledge plus the long-term reports will indicate if a Forex pair is under or over prices. Your short-term reports, including wire reports with buy and sell points, are best thought of as a suggestion for what day traders are thinking in general. Most will be focused on the same buy/sell points because everyone is reading the same news. However, it is precisely because of this that you should never place your trades based only on these types of reports.

Cutting through the Noise

When you're in a crowded room, it can be hard to hear yourself think, let alone what your friend right next to you is saying. Shouting across the room to catch someone's attention doesn't work, so what can you do instead? Most people would raise a hand and start waving it to catch someone's eye. Flagging your attention by using the eyes instead of the ears sometimes works better to cut through the noise, so keep that in mind when you're reviewing tons of news reports and analysis. The answer might be staring you in the face. Market movement and predictions are not absolute sciences, but experience will help show you how best to see the market and any waving flags of opportunity.

Be highly selective when you choose an information source. When the market is running hot, you'll start to think of trading automatically during the day. Get to the point where you're the expert and you'll have an easier time of reducing the general market news to a degree of background chatter instead of a focal point. While you scan the *Wall Street Journal*, monitor CNBC, and read reports, you need to selectively find the points of vital information that are key to your customized trading system and use it to your best advantage.

The Emotional Market

The market is made up of rational, logical products that are sold in an easy-to-understand manner. Your information sources may be reliable and factual; however, investors and traders are combining money with emotions and greed, and this is always a tricky combination. The herd mentality of the market, along with a variety of trained investors making educated trades, can open the door to an emotional and illogical marketplace. Similar to counting cards in Vegas, breezing through the markets is a foolish venture, and relying on an information source to predict any type of accuracy is extremely unlikely to work. There are simply too many variables to account for in the marketplace. However, this is exactly what the big hedge funds and investment banks try to do. They utilize the best logic, statistics, and complex mathematics and try to apply them to an unpredictable market that is driven by underlying human emotion. The market is just like a difficult, hot-blooded thoroughbred—some days he'll run, some days he won't. Over time, a day trader will eliminate the noise of the outside chatter, find the key points she is looking for to get her individual plan in motion, and learn to recognize the view of the market from an insider's view of the traders' ideas and feelings.

What Should You Listen To?

As a Forex trader, you are in business for yourself. You are responsible for all issues surrounding your business, such as turnaround time, technical issues, software, market analysis, and functionality. It is essential that you identify your trusted sources of information.

Let's say you're a home builder and want to build a new home. However, you know your limitations. You're not an expert in architecture or plumbing or electricity, so you subcontract out these important functions so you can get high quality expertise. Perhaps you know people you trust to recommend sub-contractors to you or perhaps you look them up on the Internet to read reviews of what others say. You wouldn't just hire the first guy to knock on your door who gives you an estimate to put in plumbing. Nor would you buy a set of plans from the Internet and hope for the best when it came time to dig a foundation. Planning out your site, making a detailed survey, and checking for code restrictions and setback rules are important items you need to address before hauling in a cement mixer.

Still, when you go to pick out your new tile, and some other customers are talking about their tile guy, you'd like to listen in as much as possible, right? It suddenly matters to you what others are saying, even if it is not directed at you specifically. Friendly chatter can be informative and relevant for future use. But, the question remains, how likely are you to believe this information from random strangers?

Would you pay close attention to your hairstylist when they talk about how their contractor messed up their new roof? Or would you want to hear more from the other home builders who have had bad luck with a certain roofing contractor? You would want to avoid a sloppy roofer and save yourself time and money by finding a better one that does the job right. You will be more selective in choosing your preferred information sources after family and friends have fully exhausted themselves telling you horror stories of their contractor nightmares.

The same thing will happen when you selectively listen to preferred information sources for market research and tune the rest out. The horn blowers and worriers should be easy to peg, as will be the panic-prone types. As a trader, you'll recognize that investors and traders like talking about money quite a bit. People in the markets enjoy discussing their latest big deals, the huge profits they made, how much they have in their accounts (or how little), and even bragging about the major wins and how they did it. Everyone is full of good stories. You'll also find out everyone has an opinion and money has a unique way of evening the playing field as related to profits and losses.

Questions to Think About

It will come as no surprise that TV news fills time slots with advertising. What you may not realize is that they also add in stories to fill time on-air as well. Sometimes these fills offer details, sometimes they are simply a bridge to the next story, and sometimes they're just fluff. Periodicals and magazines sell full page ads for the same reasons. The question you need to ask is: Are they selling something or telling me something important that I need to apply to my trading needs? What is the source of the information? Is the publisher of this magazine known for fluff articles or is this serious reporting that is factual and objective? At the end of the trading day, it is your decision and your money. Learn, research, and grow your knowledge base and you'll enjoy the day trading system a lot more.

Internet Forums and TV

Internet forums and TV are two types of information sources that have the leading edge when it comes to updating their content quickly. Both can change what they decide to include in their news stories as events unfold. Online forums, such as news feeds, chat rooms, or market recommendation sites, and TV are often very reactionary to the day's news, and their writing styles skew toward sensationalized storytelling (meaning they make out stories to be more dramatic than they actually are). A great way to think of the fast-moving reporting style of Internet news and TV is like a giant shallow scoop. Hundreds of stories will run into the scoop and, while a few get filtered further down, most are just surface depth stories with a sound bite or two added in.

Driving the TV news and Internet forums is the basic information you need to follow. You'll want to keep up to speed on the overall market news, but keep it general. Do not rely on these outlets to provide a true, reliable prediction of a market trend or recommendation for trading activities. Basing your decisions to buy or sell on these news outlets' reports is not advised. In fact, some of the bigger full-service wealth management investment firms will flat out tell their clients to just turn off CNBC when the market raises or lowers significantly in a trading day.

Although the top priority in FX trading is preserving capital, your second goal should be capital gains. Each trading day should always be approached with the attitude that a cash position is the safest position. Any trading you wish to accomplish should be done only when you have a realistic prospect of a gain. Therefore, your trading business should be taking only selective risks relative to the would-be gain.

Now with the first part of your plan of capital preservation in place, you can enter trades with an idea of how the market will move in the near future with a reasonable amount of certainty. Let's say that the S&P 500 trends in one direction for three or four days and then backs down. A reasonable assumption is that if the S&P 500 is up for three days straight, then it (and most likely several similar risk-sensitive trades like USD/SEK, AUD/JPY) will be ripe for the sell off and allow you to begin profit taking. On closer observation, you may have noticed a large multiday run up in the market. Big gains at the close of the week make for very happy traders because they can enjoy their gains over the weekend and sell on Monday to ensure their profits. If this is the case, you would make a long position in risk adverse currency, or a risk-off trade.

Economic News Days

There is a great amount of anticipation and secrecy surrounding economic news reports. Predictions from leading brokerages, TV news anchors, and Internet forums will abound. Sometimes the news comes out and it is not what was expected. This can cause a ripple effect, with the market moving up or down according to how accurately the predictions were. On the flipside, if the predictions match the actual report, the market is already priced for what was expected, meaning the values of the trades had covered the prices. The market will sell off anyway, as everyone is aware of the actual numbers and profit taking occurs. A much more complicated trading day happens when multiple regions release economic news reports simultaneously, such as Asia, Europe, and the United States. The outcomes cannot be predicted with reasonable accuracy due to too many variables, and it is best to not have any trading positions in your account, especially any related to the sector the reports are highlighting. In other words, news days should be avoided if capital preservation is your top priority. The markets will still be there on the next day, and you have the option of trading after the news comes out.

So, what does it take to get ready to trade Forex, plain and simple? It takes knowing the skill levels, risk levels, and reward levels of Forex trading. If you don't get it now, keep reading. We'll go over it again and again throughout this book.

QUIZ

1. Trading in the Forex markets can lead to a "thrill-seeker" trading style.
   A. True
   B. False

2. The best way to get yourself ready to begin trading Forex is to:
   A. Jump right into it without any preparation
   B. Read this book
   C. Study all you can about the economy and learn as much as you can
   D. B & C

3. Before trading Forex it is best to know how well you know your:
   A. Technical knowledge
   B. Time management skills
   C. Market skills
   D. Risk tolerance
   E. B, C, & D

4. Interpersonal relationships will keep you fresh and able to take the stress of FX trading.
   A. True
   B. False

5. The best opportunity to trade Forex is when the market has mispriced the currencies. This is because:
   A. Mispriced currencies never happen
   B. Mispriced currencies are impossible to detect
   C. Other traders have overreacted to market news
   D. Other traders have either sold or bought a currency with emotion and not fact
   E. Both C & D

6. The newscaster on the market news channel CNBC says the world stock market indexes are all down over 2% for the day. You can conclude that the market is trading:
   A. In high volume
   B. Seasonally low
   C. Risk off
   D. Risk on
   E. High risk

7. **When looking at, listening to, or reading market chatter it is best to:**
    A. Take it all at face value
    B. Use it all because it is all very important
    C. Listen to none of it
    D. Evaluate it with the thought that you are the expert

8. **The combination of_____and_____can add up to a difficult Forex trading environment.**
    A. Logic and trust
    B. Knowledge and facts
    C. Goals and limits
    D. Emotions and greed

9. **Your Forex trading should only be done in a selective manner with the highest chance for gain.**
    A. True
    B. False

10. **Sometimes when market news comes out it has a far-reaching, widespread:**
    A. Ripple effect, causing markets worldwide to move
    B. Panic, causing markets to go risk off
    C. Feelings of well-being, causing markets to go risk on
    D. All of the above

How to Navigate the Online World of Forex Trading

CHAPTER OBJECTIVES

In this chapter, you will learn the following:

- The importance of a short-term trading perspective
- The basics of what Forex software tells traders
- How to use demo accounts for real practice
- The basic risk management technique of position pyramiding

Forex trading should be considered to have both short- and long-term perspectives. Give yourself plenty of time to learn the trading platform software inside and out to run your orders accurately. If your account offers a practice or demo account, try it out before you run live trades. Practicing before going live will boost your confidence levels. It also makes an ideal testing ground for new trading strategies and ideas.

Short- and Long-Term Perspectives

By definition, a short-term time frame runs from a few minutes to a few days depending on the holding length of the trade. The best part is you can run many short-term perspectives as you roll through your trading day. Keep in mind that while a trade is active and open, the risk does not end until you finalize or close out the trade. Keeping short-term perspectives on your trades helps you to assess each individual trade based on its own qualities, aside from the long-term outlooks that you assessed for the market in the beginning.

What you want to strive for is simple. Keep a long-term perspective as the ideal standard, or big picture, of what you want to accomplish but make the short-term outlooks work for you as well. It is best if you view your market and trading analysis with an ultra-short term outlook, a short-term outlook, and a long-term outlook. The ultra-short term outlook can last anywhere from one to fifteen minutes, the short-term outlook can last a few hours, overnight, or a few days, and the long-term outlook can be your thoughts on the direction that the market, economy, and currency pairs will take in three to six months. A trader needs to define and assess each individual trade in order to maintain a clear focus and to keep trading profitably. Table 3-1 shows the basics of taking a short-term perspective.

TABLE 3-1 The Five Basics of the Short-Term Perspective
1.   Everyday assessments of general market environment
2.   Instant assessments of available money and margin accounts
3.   Searching for specific trading ideas
4.   Assessing the risk of a possible trade
5.   Using ultra–short term outlook technical charts

Opposite the ultra-short term outlook is the long-term outlook which can run from three to six months. Long-term Forex traders put a lot of weight on the fundamental analysis and technical charts for a specific driver of an economy and how it relates to the price of a specific Forex pair. Such a combination can strengthen a position when it comes to overall market conditions for a particular sector. Let's say you receive a report from your brokerage that shows a high probability that commodities will be profitable for the next six months, but mainly in energy. Using that information, you could review what you currently know about the energy sector, including that Norway is a heavy producer of a type of crude oil called Brent North Sea Crude. You also know that Canada is a heavy producer of oil and oil shale. Next, combine your new knowledge with a long-term perspective to analyze the potential of the trades under a short-term time frame. This is the type of knowledge that would lead a Forex trader to be long the currency of oil producers. After seeing this news and reading these reports, the Forex trader would make sure to be long the CAD and the NOK against both the USD and the EUR.

Be sure to keep the worldwide picture in mind when you look to your long-term perspectives. Figure 3-1 shows a minute USD/NOK chart, whereas Figure 3-2 shows a daily USD/NOK chart, displaying the effect of a longer time period on the USD/NOK trading pair. The arrow in Figure 3-2 points to the part of the chart that is covered in the one minute USD/NOK chart in Figure 3-1.

An understanding of the world economies, market conditions, sovereign debt, foreign currency strength, and how the developing economies of the world interact takes time to learn and more time to apply to trading. These are vast subjects, covering a huge range of information, so don't plan on becoming a world economist overnight. Country, market, and sector fundamentals are combined into the 15-minute, one-hour, and one-day charts; however, a one-day chart at this broad level may cover the price movements for the previous two years.

Trading Software

Most trading platforms offer entry level accounts with easy access to news reports and charts with alternative time frames. They all also contain the same basic information, as shown in Table 3-2.

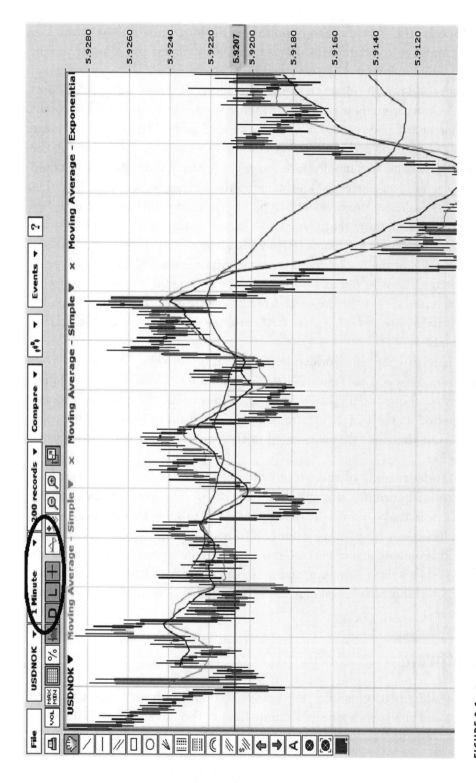

FIGURE 3-1 • One-Minute USD/NOK Chart

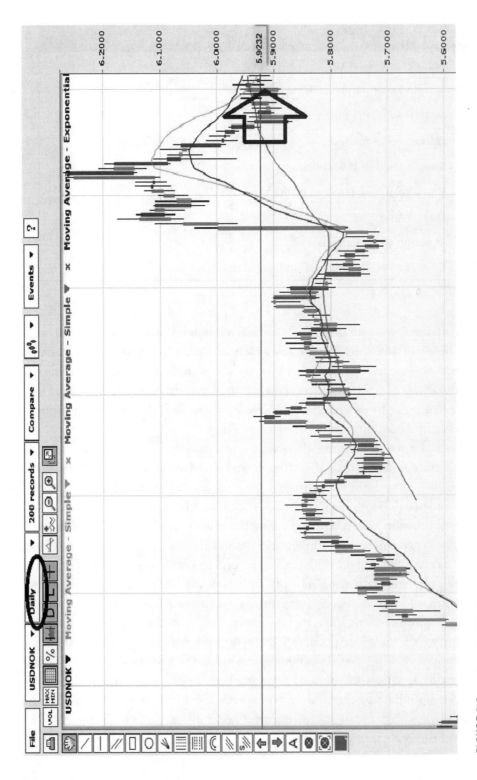

FIGURE 3-2 • Daily USD/NOK Chart

TABLE 3-2 The Nine Pieces of Trading Information on a Forex Trading Platform
1. Actual Cash Balance
2. Margin Percentage Available
3. Margin Available in U.S. Dollars
4. Margin Percent Used
5. Margin Used in U.S. Dollars
6. Unrealized and Realized Profit and Loss
7. Open Trades
8. Standing Open Orders
9. Gain or Loss Percentages on Open Trades

One part of your program may include a live feed of a news wire, plus the price boxes of your preferred items which will flash from green to red as the security increases or decreases in value. Most day trading can be easily done on a laptop using a single computer screen. Larger investment banking traders use multiple screens in order to simultaneously track each day trader's positions, occasionally updating as many as eight at a time.

Check the activity section of your trading program. This will show a history of cash flow in and out of the account and the daily interest amounts (if so equipped). As you progress through your trades during the day, the current open trades will be found in the trades section, where you can observe them from starting purchase point to entering the money-making area as the market changes. When running multiple trades, you can close them by using the close order box and holding off until the last second to gain a larger profit. The gains will then be added to your account automatically, showing in your realized profit/loss and increasing (or decreasing) your cash for the next trade.

The trading account software can easily show you the open positions and identify which trades are profitable and which are not. The charts can track an open trade and offer you a graphic representation of the trades' up and down movement. It will also show you the original entry point indicated on the chart. You can input lines on the chart to edit your exit (selling) point. Watching your chart track your trade as it creeps into a profitable zone will also give you a sense of the general market flow.

Another feature of the account is the hedged position. After you construct a hedged position, and it has worked out well, the software will indicate the total net trade profit in percentages and a dollar amount. When this occurs, you can simply close out all the parts of the hedged trades with a single click and lock in the profits. The trading system will show you the results of the hedged trade so that you can grade it for technique and efficiency for future hedged positions.

Imaginary Accounts Reveal Real Insights

Never underestimate the power of practicing. Skilled musicians practice upwards of six to eight hours a day to perform with a world-renowned orchestra, even after they're awarded the highly acclaimed position of First Chair. While seasoned day traders may scoff at the mere idea of "fake money" or playing games like a day trader, they won't argue that building your trading skills is a waste of time. Don't discount the value a demo account can offer a currency trader without any risk. By using the same program and software and using live trading data, a trader using a demo account can get the hang of how the trading platform works and how it will look. You can practice entering orders and closing out trades using actual data and market rates. Try out different leverage amounts, go ahead and use unfamiliar markets or sectors, test your skills at building hedge positions and turning them loose in the demo. You'll never know how the horse will run if it only stands in the stable looking pretty. You can check your trades, see what worked out and what didn't, evaluate your progress, and see how you feel after experiencing a real market's typical up and down lifecycle, all without risking a dime.

Plus, when you use a demo account, you can test your broker's knowledge too. Follow one of their recommendations, watch it rise or fall and see if it proves (or disproves) your broker's advice. Perhaps their trading advice is very solid but very conservative compared to your trading plans. You may want to test out one of your investment hunches and put it into play in the safety of the demo. When the market is entering a volatile period, for example, it may suit your needs to stay out of it temporarily and practice in demo mode until the tidal wave subsides.

Even imaginary gains you receive in a demo account will still enhance the positive feeling that your hard work is coming to fruition, that you're interpreting all the data correctly, and calling the shots on your own account. Using a practice account can sharpen your skill set quickly and is a tried-and-true method of testing the waters of unfamiliar trading scenarios.

Check with your brokerage firm about practice accounts. Some firms have demo accounts with time limits on them, such as 30 days, before they shut down. Others allow practice accounts to run for as long as you maintain an active trading account.

Trade Faster with Smoother Order Entry

Every trading platform has an order entry system that you need to fill out to place a live trade. Some have a lot of functionality, some are more streamlined and are simple to use. Gaining confidence that you've filled out the entry form properly is important, especially when timing the market on a live trade. In the middle of placing a trade, you don't want to stumble and input an incorrect number on your entry screen such as a short instead of a long, the wrong amount of money or units, or the incorrect stopping point. It is very important to get it right on the front end because it will make all the difference when it comes to closing out a winning or losing trade later.

Get the hang of using your order entry screen while in practice or demo mode by creating and loading the form until you are fully accustomed to it. A good way to practice your order entry training is to place scalping trades. Scalping is when a trader uses a 5- to 10-minute time frame and small amounts of cash in a trade. Try writing down the security or FX pairs and margin amounts you want to use first, before placing an order. Be sure to stop and think through the entire lifecycle of the trade before you hit the confirmation button to set the trade in motion. Speed is not important in the beginning. Accuracy is your top priority and you'll see yourself getting faster with each trade you pull together over time.

Stress and emotions run hot and cold during an average trading session. Help train your emotions by using the practice account when trading large amounts of money in a fast moving market. Getting used to the high-pressure climate of day trading with zero risk will be excellent practice when you're ready to put real funds on the line.

More Hints for the Beginner

Even trading for a brief time period each day will boost your confidence, not only in your order entry skills but also in your market skills. The more you go in and out of the market, the higher your confidence level will be. At first, you should plan on staying with one trade at a time, with round lots of even numbers to start. Then, after you get familiar with round number lots, you'll have a better chance of translating your trades to percentage numbers.

If the demo account allows it, use a smaller imaginary deposit to start the balance. If you use a huge balance to practice with, you could set yourself up for disappointment later when your real cash balance isn't so impressive. If you can't alter the imaginary balance to a smaller set amount, then try to ignore the temptation to place bigger monetary trades and don't use the account too often. In addition, only trade for a few rounds then take a break. When learning to trade, it can take a lot of concentration, and it will help to break it up into smaller time chunks to lessen fatigue. Holding your focus over several smaller size trades is tiring and you want to stay sharp during an active session. Don't plan on making one big trade for the day and close out. Just like in Vegas, you don't want to put all your money into the first poker table you find and get wiped out. It is better to enjoy the trip, visit the extravagant hotels and shops, and enjoy the fine dining in between your short gambling sessions.

No Risk, Real Emotions with the Demo Account

A rocky marketplace can be an emotional rollercoaster for a newly minted day trader. Even seasoned professional traders can turn green when the market roils and twists with no end in sight. This is when your practice account can really become an advantage. Even though you won't suffer the cash risks, you'll be right in the middle of the live trading activity, watching your trades develop, and observing the exponential gains or losses with everyone else. The demo account will put you in full swing and is essential to learn about success and failure combined with emotional control, which is a key element to being successful in day trading. Knowing ahead of time how it feels to lose big, or win even bigger, can help temper your emotional swings and keep your perspective fresh for more trading.

In addition to testing your emotional grip, a demo account can help you learn how to find setups, or ideal situations, for your preferred trading scenarios. It will help you manage your money and margins, and introduce you to how to use a pyramid process to alleviate your risk levels. Practicing with your account will give you time to learn the functions of the account, plus how to resist getting angry when closing out a losing trade. It will also teach you how to take profits but avoid greediness, and even how to use moving stops (an automatic trade closeout to lock in profits). Finally, you'll learn how to take a loss, which is vital in the market, to roll with the lows and run with the highs. Exploring the full range of emotions in the marketplace, knowing what your options are when making a series of profitable trades, and understanding your comfortable risk levels, will ensure a long, successful career as a day trader.

It is perfectly acceptable to lose profits while in demo training. All day traders should experience placing a big trade and losing it in a huge way. Learn from the experience and incorporate it into your methodology, but don't lose sight of the fact that mistakes (and losses) will still happen with your real account as well. If even one losing trade gets minimized because of your practice account efforts, it will have all been worth the time learning how to use it.

Pulling out as much information as you can from a demo account can go a long way to directly influencing how your real trading activity will go. Lessons learned from an imaginary account are cheap and have no risk to your cash balance. Plan on giving your demo account the same treatment you would as if it contained real money and use caution when making your trades. The more ownership and pride you create inside a demo account, the more it will pour over into your real cash balance later, paying you back not only in profits, but also in your enjoyment in the market.

Building a Position by Pyramiding

One of the best techniques to use when trading is the pyramiding technique. The pyramiding technique is a form of mini-dollar cost averaging. Wealth advisors such as Merrill Lynch, Morgan Stanley, and others will often recommend that their clients build a position in mutual funds over time, instead of investing a lump sum all at once. In other words, it is recommended that the client adds to his position in the same mutual fund by buying a set and consistent amount over a weekly, biweekly, or monthly period. With this method, the total price paid for each share of the mutual fund will be at an average price, neither high nor low, as the thought is that the market will be moving up and down during the entire acquisition period.

To take the analogy one step further, it works very well if you stage your buy-ins into a Forex pair in three, five, or seven different purchase points. This is true because it is nearly impossible to tell when it is the best time to buy, and when the currency pair is at its lowest or highest. Granted, it may be true that the price is very good at the time that you are first buying into the pair, but the chances of the price being the best are difficult to determine. The best procedure is to know ahead of time the dollar amount you would like to commit to the trade, and then divide by five. This new dollar amount should be the most you spend on that trade. It never seems to fail: The winning trade will turn against you as soon as you get into it. With this one-fifth entry amount, you will have adequate cash in your margin account to buy-in more when the price moves against your (which it will, no doubt!). Keep buying in as the price gets lower, and even as the price gets higher and your trade gets into the profit point. This is the key to Forex pyramiding—multiple entry points on the same trade.

To fully round out the idea of Forex pyramiding, sell off the position in the same manner in which it was bought. In this case, you are spreading around the cashing out of the position at multiple price points. Since it is never known if the price will become more in your favor, you will always be working with a bit more in reserve just in case there is more profit to be made. If the price moves against you, you have locked in some gains at the higher price. The net effect of getting into and out of trades with the pyramiding method can go a long way, acting as a risk management technique that is very easy to manage, control, and execute. A good Forex pyramiding technique will, on average, work to keep the most profits in your account while keeping losses to a minimum.

So, what does it take to know how to navigate the online world of Forex trading, plain and simple? It takes developing a short-term perspective, learning how to know Forex software, and getting Forex trading experience with a Forex demo account. If you don't get it now, keep reading. We'll go over it again and again throughout this book.

1. **When trading Forex, it is good to shift your perspective from long term to short term.**
   A. True
   B. False

2. **A long-term perspective in Forex trading can last from:**
   A. 3 to 6 weeks
   B. 3 to 6 months
   C. 6 to 12 weeks
   D. 6 to 12 months
   E. None of the above

3. **A computer program that is used for Internet-based Forex trading is called the:**
   A. Interface
   B. Trading desk
   C. Trading software
   D. Trading platform
   E. All of the above

4. **When the software allows for hedged positions, you are able to close out:**
   A. The winning positions
   B. The losing positions
   C. All of the positions
   D. None of the positions

5. **A good way to learn about how to predict a good Forex trade is to:**
   A. Place many trades randomly
   B. Keep a trade journal and record the facts of the trade
   C. Study and then follow broker's reports while entering into the recommended trade in a Forex demo account
   D. B & C

6. **Getting familiar with your Forex order entry and exit is best done by practicing with your demo account.**
   A. True
   B. False

7. **One of the best skills that you can develop from trading in a Forex demo account is to know the emotions that come from winning and losing trades.**
   A. True
   B. False

8. **Position pyramiding can be likened to a form of:**
   A. Dollar cost averaging
   B. Building a position
   C. Risk management
   D. All of the above

9. **Position pyramiding can be used for both building and selling off a position.**
   A. True
   B. False

10. **Position pyramiding can be done with either three or five separate equal-sized buy (or sell) orders.**
    A. True
    B. False

Chapter **4**

Currency Trading and Overall Investing: Will FX Fit My Investing Goals?

CHAPTER OBJECTIVES

In this chapter, you will learn the following:

- Forex trading can be for gains or income
- How to match your Forex trading with your investing goals
- The elements of Forex risk
- How to add Forex to your overall investment portfolio
- Basic high-risk/reward and low-risk/reward Forex strategies

As an investor, there are only two goals: capital gains and capital preservation. Capital preservation investment vehicles act as a way to store your money for future use. These types of investments are typically lower risk, safer investments, and as a result you as an investor are accepting a lower potential for gains and lower interest paid. The lower returns are acceptable because it is less important to have a significant return on the investment principal than it is to have the money available for consumption when necessary.

An investment strategy that has a goal of capital gain can be expected to fluctuate up and down over the course of time, with an overall gently upward path. You are expecting that the investment will be worth more in the future than at the time of investment. In contrast to a strategy of capital preservation, in this type of investment strategy you are willing to accept a higher level of risk because it is more important that you see an increase in your initial investment than having the principal available for consumption at a particular time. The risk that you run is that the investment may not be worth as much when you sell it as when you bought it. The unknown of the future price of the investment is the risk you accept in the hopes that the investment will pay a capital gain.

The very first question you should ask yourself when trying to determine your investment strategy is: "Do I want to put this money in an investment vehicle that offers a riskier, higher return, or into an investment vehicle that offers a smaller but safer return?" When it comes to currency trading, the question is: "Based on my investing goals, answered by the previous question, will opening a currency trading account and trading in the FX market help me meet those goals?"

Trading in the FX market can help you meet several goals. It will allow you to create a portfolio that keeps most of your assets in low-risk capital preservation investments. This security would then allow you to put a small percentage of your overall investment assets into an FX account to trade with higher risk strategies. Your FX strategies can allow you to enhance an otherwise low-risk capital preservation portfolio with some riskier investments.

Meeting Your Objectives with Different Trading Styles

It is possible for the Forex trader to pursue trading to meet her financial goals. If she is looking for the highest returns, she can aggressively go after trading with nightly setups—short-term high-leverage trading that will capture gains that add up quickly. This type of trading is scalping, overnight trading, or position trading.

FX Trading for Capital Gains

A good example of a long GBP/USD trade would be as follows:

- **Opening of long GBP/USD**   At the beginning of the trade, the exchange rate is 1.25 dollars per pound. When you place the trade, you would sell U.S. dollars and buy pounds. For every 1.25 U.S. dollar you sold, you would be able to buy 1 pound. Doing the math, you would have an IOU of 1 U.S. dollar, but own 0.80 pound.

- **Measuring the change in the long GBP/USD trade**   Say you called the trade right, and that the GBP got stronger against the USD (which is the same as saying that the USD got weaker than the GBP), and now the exchange rate is 1.30 U.S. dollars per pound.

- **Closing the long GBP/USD trade**   You would sell your GBP and convert them back into USD at the new rate of 1.30 USD per GBP. 1 GBP/1.30 = 1.04. Your 1.25 GBP are now worth 1.04 USD.

- **Taking the profit of a long GBP/USD trade**   You have now closed the trade and converted the 1.25 GBP back into USD, but this time you have used the new exchange rate of 1.30 GBP per dollar. The yield of the conversion is $1.04 U.S. You use the $1.04 to pay off your 1 USD IOU with the Forex brokerage firm. After this is done you are left with $0.04, which is your profit on the long GBP/USD trade.

The Right FX Account for Your Style

The great thing about currency trading is that you can build a currency account that fits your desired trading style. When building your desired trading system, you should keep in mind things like your risk tolerance, the assets, and the time you would like to invest in trading in the currency markets. No matter what your risk tolerance or desired reward is, you can build or find the FX trading system that will work for you.

The Elements of FX Risk

One of the basic principles of investing is that in order to have the potential for gain, your portfolio must also assume some risk. Investing wisdom says that the higher the assumed risk, the higher the potential for gain. In other words, a portfolio that is fully insulated from risk will also be fully insulated from reward and have zero yield.

Risk can be an uncomfortable thing, particularly when it comes to your money. In order to help yourself think more objectively about the risks that you are taking, you should try to think of yourself like a hedge fund manager, investment bank, or FX trading house. This will naturally make you think more professionally, so you will view risk as something you enter into and then exit out of at a later date. You will also reasonably expect to be compensated for taking that risk.

Asset transformation is the basis of the currency-trading risk/return relationship. In currency trading, as in any sort of investing, you must assume some risk in order to have a chance of a return. But there is a limited amount of return that can be made for the risk that you assume in your FX portfolio. Additionally, you should always monitor the quality of the risk you assume on any investment and be sure not to invest in risky or very risky investments and expect a return if the quality of risk is not good. Instead of putting your money in high-risk assets for the chance of getting high rewards, you should consider a strategy that will yield the maximum return for each unit of risk you assume.

There is an actual measurement that compares how well an investment or portfolio is performing compared to others. The Sharpe ratio is calculated by comparing an investment's daily rise and fall against its overall return. The higher the Sharpe ratio, the better the investment is performing and the more efficient the returns will be. By examining the Sharpe ratio of an investment, you can include investments that will give you the most return for the least amount of risk in your portfolio. In other words, the Sharpe ratio is a measurement of how much extra performance or return the investment earns for each unit of volatility. If an investment has a high volatility (meaning it moves up and down in value along an irregular path) but the investment offers an average return, the investment's Sharpe's ratio will be low. On the other hand, if the investment has low volatility (meaning less wild swings in value day to day) but offers the same return as the first example, the investment will have a higher Sharpe's ratio. An investment's Sharpe's ratio is a measure of the cost of the gains of an investment as measured in risk (or volatility.) The thought is that an investment with the highest return with the lowest amount of daily upward/downward movement (think "risk") in its price is the best. The higher the Sharpe's ratio, the less risky the investment is per unit of return.

Most investment systems are driven by the concept of getting more return for less risk. You should base your currency-trading system on the same idea. The best way to limit your risk and get a higher return on your investment is to know where the risk comes from in trading currencies. There are also ways to tweak your FX investments in order to make your portfolio a bit lower risk for more manageable trading.

Define Your Risk Tolerance

By determining your risk tolerance, you will be able to figure out what type of currency trading you want to try and what sort of system you should set up in order to keep you in the FX trading game. If you want to make a living though currency trading, you will not want to set up slow trades or let your trades go dormant. If you want to trade recreationally or to make a bit of money on the side, it doesn't make sense to set up a system that requires hours of your time every day.

As you ask yourself what you'd like to get out of currency trading, be sure you also ask yourself what things you are not willing to give up in order to meet your goals. This is also an important thing to consider as you work towards developing a trading system that works for you.

You can read every book in the world on currency trading and analysis, but all the knowledge in the world will not get you started trading until you are comfortable with what you are expecting from FX trading. Ask yourself, "What do I want from Forex?" Any answer is fine—from recreation, a specific monetary goal, adding additional returns to a conservative portfolio, or making a full-time living—as long as you are clear on what you want to achieve.

One of the best ways to figure out your risk tolerance is to look at your past history. If your previous investments have been in futures, options, or commodities, then you are likely a more risk-tolerant investor. If you typically invest in mutual funds or government bonds, then you are probably more adverse to risk.

Do not be afraid to ask yourself tough questions! As soon as you know what your goals are you will be able to see what the big picture of trading currencies looks like and where FX trading fits into that picture for you. If your goals tend toward a specific financial amount—say paying off a new car or a dream vacation—then most likely a smaller, lower-risk account and a conservative trading system are probably right for you. Similarly if you are looking to add some returns to an otherwise very conservative portfolio of bonds, you will probably also want a lower-risk, conservative currency trading strategy.

You will want to consider a higher-risk portfolio or trading strategy if you are hoping to make a larger profit, say to pay your mortgage or even live off your earnings. Before you start trading, you should determine how much you need to make each month. Depending on how large that number is, you will need to adjust the level of risk in your trading strategy. The more you need to make per month, the larger the risk you will need in your portfolio.

Forex Trading and Your Overall Portfolio of Assets

When you start thinking about what you expect to gain from currency trading, a good place to start is by looking at your overall portfolio investable assets. Many people make the mistake of only thinking about the amount of money they want or need to make. By approaching currency trading this way, you are only looking at the reward that you want to get, rather than considering the level of risk that you will need to expose yourself and your FX account to.

The very first question that you should ask yourself is: "How much money do I have to put into my account?" This applies if you are a student trying to earn a little money to start paying back your loans, a mother who wants to make a little extra money while the kids are at school, or a millionaire with most of your money in low-risk portfolios. First you need to figure out how much you have to invest.

To figure out how much money you need to invest, you must determine your overall investable assets. Especially when you are first starting out with FX trading, it is advisable to invest a smaller amount—say your "fun money." This will allow you to learn the ropes of FX and have some fun without having to worry about your financial security if your investing doesn't always go according to plan. Another way to keep currency trading stress-free and fun is to only trade with money you are willing to lose, similar in some ways to gambling! If you consider your trading money as money already spent, then you'll think of it as gone already and you can enjoy the process of taking risks and learning with your Forex account.

Now that you've determined how much money you want to put into your trading account, you should look at the list you've made of previous investing choices and figure out how risk adverse you are. If you want to earn a small amount of money for something like a car payment or a vacation, then you will want to follow a more conservative strategy. If your goal is to make mortgage payments or a living wage, then you will want a riskier strategy. After you have figured out how much risk you want to assume, then you can look at the size of your Forex account and see how realistic your goals are. For instance, if you have $500 or $1,000 to put into an account and are very risk tolerant, you likely will not be able to make enough to pay your mortgage, but you will likely be able to make enough for that car payment.

There are multiple factors that determine how much you can earn in trading currency. You must consider your goals, as well as your investable assets, your risk tolerance, and the size of your account. After considering all of these factors, you can figure out exactly what to expect from your trading system.

One way to determine how much money to invest in your currency trading account is by looking at your total investable assets. If your existing portfolio, perhaps a 401k, IRA, or retail account, contains traditional assets like stocks, bonds, or mutual funds, then you can look at your FX account as an alternative investment. Even though most of your assets are more traditionally or conservatively allocated, you can still designate a certain amount to your Forex account. This method can be a hedge against the overall returns of your portfolio.

Forex Trading Can Act as a Hedge Against a Traditional Portfolio

How does FX act as a hedge against a traditional portfolio? Stocks and bonds move up and down with the market, while the returns of your FX account may be completely unconnected to the fluctuations of the overall performance of the stock markets. Currencies fluctuate constantly, so you can go long or short on a currency pair, have long- and short-term time frames, or earn interest on a trade. If your portfolio is stock-heavy, then you can use your currency-trading portfolio as a hedge against your significant equity exposure. You may even create your currency portfolio with the intention of having it work against any downward movement your overall portfolio may experience.

With this option to hedge a stock-heavy portfolio with a smaller percentage currency trading account, it can be a good idea to have as much as 10%–20% of your investable assets in a currency trading account you are actively managing. This proportion is what is typically recommended by wealth management companies like Merrill Lynch and UBS as the percentage of your investments that should be in alternative assets.

As previously mentioned, currencies are not considered to be directly correlated with stock and bond markets, and so the returns of currency investments are not tied to the returns of the overall market. Hence, it is possible to use your currency trading as an alternative strategy and your Forex assets as alternative assets. Other examples of alternative strategies are investments in commodities like oil, or metals like silver and gold. Because gold, silver, and oil are priced and traded worldwide, investing in these metals or commodities is much like investing in currency itself. Therefore, a portfolio that is comprised of 10%–20% of investments in gold, silver, or oil can also be considered to be well-diversified.

Modern Portfolio Theory was established by Harry Markowitz in his 1952 paper "Portfolio Theory." Since that paper was published, nearly every money management professional has tried to follow Modern Portfolio Theory. The theory states that portfolio managers should attempt to produce the greatest portfolio returns for the smallest risk by limiting risk and maximizing return through portfolio diversification to include assets with returns uncorrelated with the other returns of the overall portfolio. A portfolio can contain uncorrelated assets in many ways, including having both stocks and bonds, having investments in precious metals or oil, or having another alternative asset like a Forex trading account. Currency trading, while potentially higher risk, can actually have the effect of protecting your portfolio from the fluctuations of the market.

As you consider starting your trading career, the amount of money you want or need to make can seem large. Rather than feeling overwhelmed or discouraged, first break down your goals to figure out how much money you need to make each day and week. For instance, say you need to make $550 a month for a car payment. If you estimate 20 trading days a month, that amounts to approximately $27 per day or $135 each week to make your goal of $550 for the month.

From this perspective, $550 per month suddenly seems much less intimidating and much more achievable. You could make $550 per month on a $1,000 account, traded at 10% value, making two 0.5% trades a day and using a 50:1 margin. Based on these numbers you could pretty easily trade two hours a day in order to make the money you need.

You should always trade with a goal in mind, that way you can make trades that will yield the returns that you need, making sure that you are not getting into trades that have higher levels of risk than you need or are comfortable with. This will be important as you encounter trades that offer a very high return but with high risk as well. You will be able to remind yourself that you are trying to make $550 per month and you should focus your intentions on that.

Keep in mind that there are a lot of people who infrequently trade currency and do so without a particular goal in mind. It is perfectly okay if you are this type of Forex trader. It means that you are most likely a recreational trader and are trading for fun and without the pressure of needing to make a certain amount of money each day.

"I want to earn as much as I can," is not an actual goal. It may sound like one, but if you consider it further you will see that the lack of a definite amount also creates a lack of rules. If you have no specific goal, you also will not have a way to determine if a trade is too risky. Because of this, you will inevitably take on riskier and riskier investments, and at some point, the risk will not pay off and you will lose big. Be sure that you always have a specific goal when FX trading.

While it is exciting to hear about the fund manager who made a 70% profit last year, people consider them to be a flash in the pan unless they can produce the same results again without risking the principal. Major news outlets always want to talk to the fund manager that earns 10% year-after-year regardless of how the economy is doing. Ten percent may sound like a low number, but if you have a specific goal, 10% can be more than enough to meet your goal.

FX Trading: Profit or Income

As discussed at the beginning of this chapter, there are two goals in currency trading: income and profit. Both of these goals will add to your overall returns at the end of the year. You make a profit when you buy a currency pair at one price and sell it later when the price of your pair has changed. "Later" could be anything from a few minutes to a few months from the time of purchase. This type of profit is referred to as capital gain, which we discussed at the beginning of this chapter. You can achieve these capital gains using the buy low/sell high strategy that is common in other types of trading.

In Forex trading, the majority of the profit will be made by buying and selling currency pairs at different prices. In FX trading you can trade as many as 50 times per session, so you can understand how you might be about to make the bulk of your capital gains in this fashion. The other type of gain you can achieve is called income.

In Figure 4-1, you can see a NZD/USD carry trade that has not only earned interest but has also had a large capital gain. The capital gain is shown by the movement of the NZD strengthening against the USD of 0.01 NZD or 1% NZD gain. This equates to a 50% gain in the trade if the Forex account was set to a 50:1 margin!

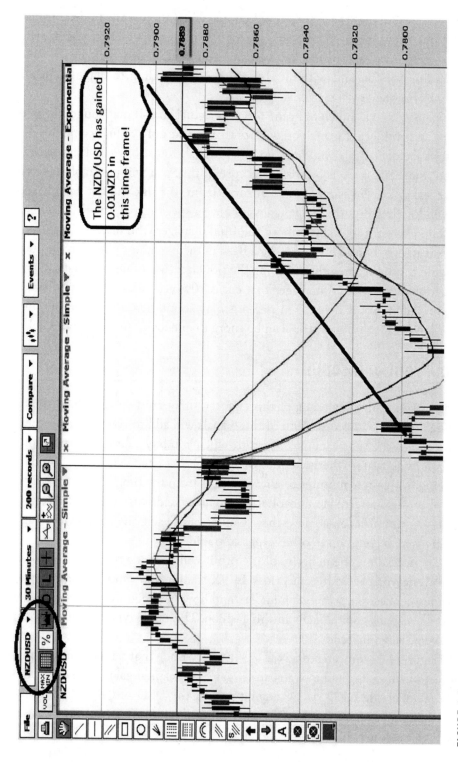

FIGURE 4-1 • NZD/USD Carry Trade

Most of the time, Forex income comes from what is known as a carry trade. A Forex carry trade is a long-term trade in which the long currency is a higher-yielding currency and the short currency is a very low-yielding currency. In the carry trade, the short currency will be funding the purchase of the long currency. This would leave the trade paying interest on the borrowed currency and earning interest on the long currency. Some of the typical carry trades would be a long New Zealand dollar/short U.S. dollar, where the short USD would "charge" a very low interest rate, and the NZD would "earn" a much higher interest rate. The amount of income earned from the trade is easily calculated by finding the difference between the NZD and the USD. If the USD charged 0.5% and the NZD paid 4.0%, the income on the trade would be 3.5% or 4.0%−0.5% = 3.5%. In order to estimate the income on a $500 Forex account, you would take the $500 × 33% (maximum margin used) = $165 × 50:1 gearing = $8,250 total trade value × 3.5% = approximately $288.50 interest earned per year. Keep in mind that the $288.50 is without compounding! This income relates to over 50% interest per year on the actual cash balance of the account ($288.50/$500 = 57.75%). As you think about considering carry trades, you should look for the difference between the high interest rate and the low interest rate. The other large factor to consider is the stability and the quality of the high interest rate currency. Just like risk, high-yielding currencies can differ.

With a rate of return like that you can set up a certificate of deposit that will generate income. A certificate of deposit, or CD is completely safe (risk-free) and some people choose to use them, and other low-risk investments like bond mutual funds, when income is a higher priority than growth for them.

To use currency trading as an income strategy is essentially just a long-term carry trade strategy. Bond mutual funds typically require a $1,000 minimum investment. When a bond fund is set up to generate income, they are often called high-yield funds. These high-yield funds can pay anywhere from 5%–9% per year, plus growth. If you took the $1,000 you would need to invest in a bond mutual fund and instead invested 20% of it in a carry trade like a long AUD/USD or long NZD/USD, you would earn the net interest difference.

All carry trades are calculated the same basic way: At the 50:1 margin previously discussed, the net interest difference would yield anywhere from a $400 to $650 a year return on your Forex investment. When you do the math, that turns into as much as a $54 per month return for a $1,000 investment. If you put the same amount in a high-yield bond fund, you could only expect up to $7.50 per month in returns. While the high-yield bonds are undeniably lower risk than FX trading, by planning carefully, you can create a portfolio that combines high-yield bonds and income-oriented carry trades to increase the monthly yield of your overall portfolio.

How to Keep the Risk Level Lower

Another trading style in day trading is a low-risk/low-reward account. The first step of this method is to understand the basics of your FX trading so as to use the right size account relative to your overall assets. Learning how to trade in a lower pressure style, plus the time you need to spend and what profit levels you should anticipate, are also important elements.

A lot of traders who enjoy sizzling markets don't like getting burned. They play it safe by using a low-risk/low-return style to make sure they never lose it all. They set up their accounts so that they only can lose the amount sitting in the account (losses never exceed the balance). Traders can make a profit on as little as $250 USD. Even $100 can still reward you with gains and the thrill of participating in a worldwide market.

A small cash balance in your trading account can be used for some rewarding and fun trades, done at your leisure in the evenings. Imagine gaining small profits—an average of $10 a day—from your tidy sum of $250, with only light trading in as few as three to four trades per night.

Forex trading doesn't have to be limited by a small bank account. Losing a dollar or two however, still stings, so take care to respect the market just as if you were trading thousands of dollars. Careless trading of $20 can wipe out a $250 account even faster than a $1,000 account.

Broke college kids are making money in the currency markets, believe it or not. They're the late nighters, holed up in dormitories eating last night's cold pizza for breakfast and they're setting up trades while studying or writing mid-term papers. When morning comes, they PayPal their earnings out and go get a double-shot latte at the corner shop.

College students aside, you won't have to trade all night long for your coffee cash or downsize to a single shot. Taking the time to fully appreciate your weekly and monthly earnings from trading is one of the upsides to part-time trading. Even nickel slots at the casinos can be fun to play with the right attitude, so take a page out of that book when you start thinking your pennies aren't enough. There are some Forex brokerage firms that allow account balances as low as one dollar. So, the lesson here is to simply find a comfortable winning stride, go at your own pace, and enjoy the market's ups.

A second element to a low-risk trading system is to invest at a smaller ratio to traditional assets compared to a more aggressive account. While an aggressive account will run to 20%–25% percent of your total investment portfolio, only 5% or less of the investable assets would be deposited into an active low-risk/low-reward account.

This plan means you can invest a small percentage of your money in an FX account, thus taking advantage of the swings in the market and gaining a higher percentage compared to your other conventional investments. Consider this: a 2.5% investment of $25,000 can net you $3,000 a year, which is an increase of 12% of your total investment portfolio. And, this very conservative number can be attained with approximately 10 days of trading per month, four to six trades a day from overnight carry trades and diversified short-term trades.

> Timing is everything to the part-time day traders. Perhaps when you have a free night and the market is chugging along, it might be a great time to engage in research and run your setups for trades for a couple of hours. Of course, there is no penalty for deciding time is too short and maybe next week will offer a better window of opportunity. The key is to know what it takes to make a good setup, and then just wait for the right FX setup to come along.

If enjoying what you do is more important than large profits, your smaller portfolio can be tied into safer assets. The smaller proportions will cause far less stress, with lower risk. Perhaps FX is an ideal forum for you to scratch that itch of experimenting in a new market, while the bulk of your investment is safely tucked aside in other assets. Forex can sometimes be the best when taken together with other investments. In fact, that is the best way to learn, and you will quickly see how certain currency pairs react in relation to other markets, including the commodities market, the gold and silver markets, and the stock and bond markets.

Trading is more aggressive in currencies than it is in stocks, and you may feel that currency trading is more exciting than other higher-return products like options. Options trading means you need to have a much larger account balance and far more involved knowledge of setting up profitable trades. By accepting much smaller account sizes and offering more simplified trading scenarios, an FX trading account can be up and running quickly.

When the pressure's off, the casual day trader can relax and enjoy the markets a lot more, making profits and learning without the fear and drama that a high-risk/high-reward program entails. A conservative, low-risk program will still offer far-reaching markets and lots of rewarding action that only live trading can offer.

No matter what the balance is in their accounts, all Forex traders can enjoy the ups and downs of the markets as they peruse the central bank websites, digest their reports, and use their fundamental knowledge to set up their next trades. A winning trade is a winning trade, whether it is for $50 or for $5 million. Rest assured, the same basic principles are involved in the transaction and there is a fair amount of pride in running winning trades. Staying up-to-date on the news and latest reports and incorporating the trends and charts into your trading plan will all help you to build up your expertise. The difference between a low-risk and a high-risk account is getting rid of the high-pressure intensity that aggressive trading presents.

> Many casual day traders seek to unwind after a day's hard work by doing some low-stress (low-risk) trading in the evening. By limiting your amount of time to trade, you will also reduce the money you risk and decrease the chance of losing in your trades as well.

Change how you play the market game to fit your rules in day trading. Reduce the risk, raise your enjoyment level, and you may find yourself truly enjoying a new hobby of day trading. If this sounds like something you'd like to try, keep it fun and stress-free. If the trades aren't setting up right, it's perfectly fine to close up for the day. If it was fun for a while but it starts feeling like a burden, take a break from the markets. They'll still be there in a week or month or two when you're fresh and ready to try it out again.

If a less risky approach to the market is appealing to you, then a tame trading session would be a good match. Tame trading follows the same general course as an aggressive type of trading, but at a much reduced dollar amount and fewer number of trades. The money you make in profits may be a smaller percentage than that earned by an aggressive Forex account, but this is the cost of having greater security.

Greater security on your investment has a price tag attached to it. There is a cost related to its safekeeping, such as tying up your money in a low-risk savings account or CD but only getting a tiny percentage of interest each month on your bank statement. This is exactly the same concept underlying a conservative Forex account. You give up greater gains and accept lower daily/yearly yields than if you were trading aggressively. This reduced yield is the price tag you pay to keep your money safe.

Starting out in Forex with a tame, low-risk/low-reward account will reward you with a low-risk, pleasant experience. For example, you may try long AUD/USD positions after work to get the upward movement in the Asian market. What you should keep in mind is that the basic trading ideas for low-risk trading are the same as those for high-risk trading, with just the hedging and smaller cash outlays combining for a slower, less-feverish pitch. Plus, the more comfortable the early trading sessions are for the beginner, the more the learned curve is enhanced. While the overall effect has a lower yield, a secondary effect is a greater chance of keeping you active in currency trading. Many traders feel that keeping their Forex account fully funded is a good reason to try out a trading system.

Also, never discount the chance to change tactics in the middle of setting up trades. Mentally, you would divert certain funds to an "in play" account leaving the rest "walled off" and not touched, giving yourself a specific time limit as to how much margin you use on each trade plus the type of risk management preferred to reduce risk. Professional traders often use this tactic during market upheavals. It is also used at the month end, when the bulk of trading and profits have already been made for the month and they wish to keep risk lower.

Once you've decided to use a low-risk/low-return FX system, you will not have to spend a lot of time to achieve your profit goal level. In fact, you can achieve very good profits and call it a successful day in just a few hours in the morning or evening a couple of days a week. Even better, you can create a trading program that only trades when the perfect setups are found, offering you the best chance for a profitable trade. You could spend more time on research than the actual trading.

This casual, low-risk/low-return system offers the most flexibility to your daily schedule. You could run your daytime routine, add in checking your markets and reports for the day, and then decide to actively trade or skip it entirely. However, if something comes across your early morning radar and it is looking good, it is easy to fire up the computer and enter into the trades as you see fit. For example, you could enter some long AUD/USD and short USD/SEK positions before the New York Stock Exchange even opens at 7:30 a.m. EST. By setting up the trades to buy at market level, then entering in a tight "take profit" point, you could continue getting ready for your day while the program automatically monitors the account.

Even better, you could check every half hour for your profit and losses, and once your position shows any profit, simply click on "close all positions" and proceed to close out your open positions. By checking every half hour, you will be able to clearly see the direction that the market is moving that will win or lose the trade. The key to this process is to be sure to close out your positions with a gain as frequently as possible.

A natural question comes to mind when you're hovering above the "close all positions" button. "Did I make enough on this trade?" The answer is always the same. "Yes!" You can't lose by closing positions that are showing an overall profit, this simply allows you to lock in the gains.

Let's say you're running five active trades but only two are profitable. Your trading data says your positions are net profitable, so you have gained a profit. This is the time to click on "close all open positions" and lock in your profits.

Now you're ready to put risk in its place. Traders do this by using a hedge. A successful hedge is when you have several trades active with just a few gains, but the overall value is up. Generally, you lose a bit of profit in the process as well, but you still end up ahead of where you started.

Therefore, when you check every 30 minutes on an open trade that you manually need to close, you set your internal clock to this time frame, helping you to stay on track for the rest of your day. The half-hour system forces a time restraint on you and makes your trades simpler by closing at the first sight of profit. Also, adding up your gains at the end of each month, instead of each day, will ensure you will have plenty of profits and avoid that doubting question, "Was it enough profit?"

A more conservative profile naturally reduces the amount of risk and time your Forex account is utilized. Lower usage rates means a lower chance of running a poor trade and losing profits, thus giving you a higher percentage of winning trades versus the total number of trades made. A conservative account running gains at 1% consistently, month over month, year over year, can add up to fantastic return on your money. Trading for a low-risk gain of 1%–2% is easy to accomplish with a good amount of safety. Compare this to the 7%–10% that the stock market runs at in a full year. Placing currency trades in a way to make gains consistently will grow your portfolio slowly but steadily.

Make a goal for a trading session to hit a 1%–3% gain each night or morning. After you hit your goal, close out of the trading platform for the rest of the day. This part-time approach suits a conservative approach well; do some research, make your profits, and then your regular life goes on.

Maintaining a conservative stance while you continue trading will keep you on track to help retain a higher rate of wins to losses. The wins may be small, but they are still profits and profits will add up over time, as your skills continue to grow.

At any rate, you can ensure your higher expectancy of win/loss ratios by activating smaller trades, diversifying, shortening the time in the trade, and making use of a tight take profit automated close point. Enhance your trading system by using a manual half-hour checkpoint to see if there were gains and closing out the trade at the first sign of profitability. Clean house, or close out all trades, and book the profits. A 1% gain is as much of a real win as a 3% gain. Currency trading is all about winning little amounts many times over to be successful, and you will be amazed at how quickly your profits add up over time.

Try the thirds method to help you divide your available margin. Take your current margin and divide by three. From this number, divide again by three. This final number is the maximum amount of margin that you should feel free to invest at any one time. The best way to diversify your cost basis in a currency pair is to trade three entries of the same currency pair, if you are not diversifying your Forex portfolio trades in any other way.

A case in point: If you're trading long on the New Zealand dollar against the U.S. dollar to capture the added risk sentiment of the world's traders, this position would let you gain if there are signals showing an increased-risk sentimentality throughout the world's markets. Indicators from Europe may show decent improvement in a sovereign debt issue or that China's growth numbers are better than anticipated.

Regardless, sensing an indicator of growth like this will open the trading doors for you to capture profits on the growth potential movement. The same could be done for a long SEK/USD or EUR or other traditional currency pairs like a long NOK and long AUD compared to the USD or EUR. A trader can use a wide array of currency pairs to capture this movement after researching his technical and fundamental analysis.

Let's assume a long NZD/USD that you can build a position by taking three-equally measured "bites" at the pair. Recent news reports indicate it is a good time to build a position to trade on, and you move to buy three "ins" every

30 to 45 minutes. However, if the reports came through in the morning, the U.S. markets have already reacted to it. You didn't place any trades into the FX market until well after lunch Eastern Standard Time, so you can go ahead and place the trades in 10 minutes apart. This shortened time is okay now because there is less movement in currency markets between 3 p.m. and 6 p.m. EST and it will not make much of a price point difference to set them in close together. After 7 p.m. EST, however, traders in Sydney, Hong Kong, and Tokyo are getting into work in the morning.

By reducing your trades into chunks of thirds, you will only risk one-third of your margin at any one time. Out of this one-third, three equally measured trades will position you into a form of dollar cost averaging, which is a method of buying more or less as the market fluctuates—a very useful method. Using dollar cost averaging, if the FX pair is cheaper, you buy more units for a fixed amount of your margin. Then, as the FX pair grows in price, you purchase less for the same fixed amount. This is the same method mutual fund managers use to buy into shares, only in this case, you're purchasing over a few hours instead of months or years as in a mutual fund.

A Typical Example of a Low-Risk Forex Trade

A typical example of a low-risk Forex trade would be to take 90% of your overall investment portfolio and invest that amount in very high quality bonds. You would then take the remaining 10% of the portfolio and use this money to trade Forex at a higher potential for return. While the 90% bond portion of the portfolio will be almost 100% safe (as a bond portfolio that is rated AA credit quality or better would be made out of only the highest quality government bonds such as U.S. T-bills, U.K. Gilts, German Bunds, etc.), the remaining 10% would be trading in a highly leveraged way that would amplify the gains of that part of the portfolio. Figure 4-2 shows the German Bund bonds, U.S. T-bills, and U.S. S&P 500, reflecting the stability of AA rated bonds versus the movement of an all-stock portfolio.

If you traded the Forex part of the portfolio with a 50:1 margin, and you used 33% of your Forex portfolio at any one time, and you only traded once a week, it would be quite possible to have returns of over $40,000 per year on a $100,000 bond/Forex portfolio. This represents a gain of 40% per year while putting only 10% of the portfolio at risk at any one time. In other words, for each 1 unit of risk that is taken, there is the potential for 4 units of return. To get a feel of how good this ratio is, the typical 60%/40% stock/bond portfolio has a return of 7% per year, while putting 60% of the portfolio at risk. This

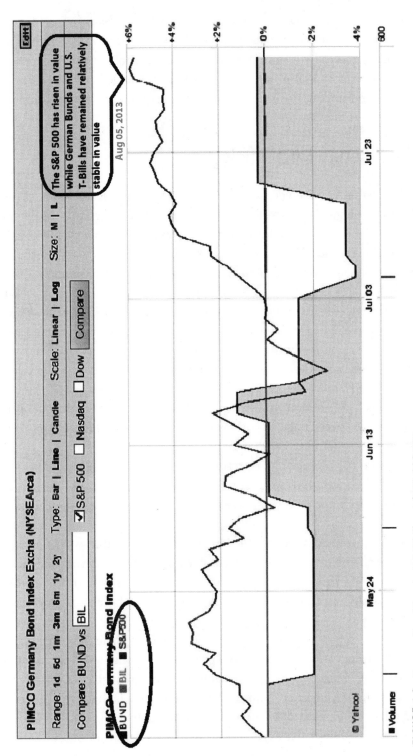

FIGURE 4-2 · German Bund Bonds, U.S. T-bills, and U.S. S&P 500

means that there are only 0.11 units of return per unit of risk (7% return/60% equity portion of portfolio). This method of valuing the risk/return of a portfolio is considered to be a simplified version of a complex trading concept of Value at Risk, or VaR. VaR is one of the methods that large hedge funds, investment banks, and trading firms use to measure the quality of their trading positions on a day-to-day basis.

High-Risk/High-Return Forex Trading

If you decide that you are very risk tolerant and would like to build a currency account that is high-risk/high-reward, there are a few things to consider first. A high-risk/high-reward account requires a certain amount of assets, more time to spend on Forex trading, and a tolerance for the high levels of stress associated with trading large amounts of heavily leveraged money. If you are willing to take on a higher risk in your currency portfolio for the chance of a higher return, you next need to determine if this type of account is possible for you. If you do have a greater amount of investable assets, then a high-risk currency trading account is perfectly reasonable, especially as it is likely that your stock and bond portfolio or other main assets will be holding their own and providing you with a steady, reliable return.

With the security of your lower-risk portfolio assets, you can feel confident putting a smaller percentage of your assets into a high-risk FX account. If you have enough assets available to put into that account, you will be able to trade and take more risks to get higher returns than a more conservative portfolio might yield. You might have your currency trading account make up 20%–25% of your portfolio. You can use your Forex account to trade aggressively and take more risks.

If you were to speak with a financial advisor at a firm that works primarily with private clients, you would find that many of them would recommend setting some money aside for riskier trading. Typically this would be put into a separate trading account, which in your case would be a currency trading account.

By creating a separate "at-will" account you can then trade more aggressively with your currency account to try to win big. With a higher-risk account you will need to take bigger risks in proportion to the account size. The reason it is important to have a larger account for high-risk trading is that you will be able to sustain larger swings into and out of profit range, enabling you to get bigger rewards for those bigger risks. Not all of your trades will work out, but a larger account means that you will then have a larger percentage of your account in cash, which will allow you to trade very aggressively with 10%–15% of your account. By proceeding this way, if any of your trades do not work out, you will have 85%–90% of your account available and will be able to avoid a margin call. The additional available cash will also give you more flexibility to keep a trade open longer than you otherwise might be able to afford, meaning you can wait until you can get out of the trade at a profit or a break even.

High-risk/high-reward trading can add to the pressure you will be under as well as the profits you can potentially make. To get the most out of your Forex account, you will need to be fully alert and ready to really work when you sit down to trade. If you are scalping and getting in and out of trades multiple times per trading day, your trading experience can become very stressful very quickly.

Having a large account can actually add to the pressure of high-risk trading because you have more to gain but also more to lose in currency trading. Additionally, if you are spending many hours a day trading, you increase your chances of mistakenly making a bad trade. Every trade you make puts your money at risk. As an example, if you trade three scalping positions every hour for six to eight hours each day you will be risking 25%–33% of your account 18 to 24 times each day. That is a lot of pressure, but it can also be very exciting!

Ask yourself how much money you are used to handling. If you have an account with $50,000 of investable assets, then you're most likely used to placing trade orders that fit in a $50,000 account. Maybe you also have an online brokerage account and are familiar with trading on margin. In that case you may have been placing trades of $5,000 or $10,000 per order. Trading a $50,000 account managed by a brokerage firm is very different from trading $50,000 in a currency account due to the huge amounts of margin available with Forex trading. Scalping and trading 33% of your currency account every day can be intensely stressful, especially if there are a few days when you are not showing a profit, or if you have a trade that goes bad for a while and you are stuck with a loss.

These kinds of situations are the sort that makes you question if you should keep trading so aggressively, or if you should stop trading currency entirely and invest in a safer money market account. If you start feeling this way, don't despair! If currency trading is running too hot for you, feel free to take a little time away from it. Take the rest of the week or the rest of the season, especially if you've started feeling like you don't have a knack for currency trading. To do this type of trading full-on can take a lot out of you, both mentally and physically. Tension can physically manifest itself as tightness in your neck and shoulders, or aching knees from so many hours at your desk. Mentally it can cause you to be short-tempered with friends and family over the smallest things. One way that professional currency traders deal with the high stress levels of high-risk/high-reward trading is by becoming avid athletes. They may deal with the stresses of good and bad days of currency trading by kick-boxing, running, or swimming. Whatever their sport of choice, they use athletics as an outlet for the day-to-day tensions of currency trading.

When you start experiencing these mental and physical stress signs, this can be a warning sign that you are overtrading your Forex account. Currency trading may have been fun when you started, but when friends and family have noted a change in your behavior, it is a good time to take a break.

Currency trading can be both fun and profitable. If you stop having fun with it for any length of time, no matter the reason, trading is causing you too much stress. This could potentially cause you to start making mistakes with your trades. You may even subconsciously make mistakes so you have to close down your account and stop trading. This is much more common than you might think, and is actually the reason so many people seem to fail at Forex trading when making a profit is not that difficult.

One reason currency trading may become less fun is if you are expecting too much profit. Another reason may be that you are not used to managing a margin account of this size. It may seem easy to place trades for $10,000, $25,000, or even $100,000 worth of currency, but that is a significant amount of money. You may even start to lean back towards more conservative strategies when trading, asking yourself what happens if you lose. When you start feeling this way, it is probably time to take a break.

You should remind yourself that the money is still there for you to use. Leave a small amount of money in the account, but have the rest sent to your bank account. Go on vacation, buy yourself a gift, or start that hobby of mountain biking, kayaking, or rock climbing to work off the tension. The break will also give you the opportunity to evaluate your trading system so you can come back to trading with fresh eyes.

It's probably an easier decision to move forward on trading currencies than it will be to actually find the time to do it. Life is busy no matter who you are or what you are doing, and finding the time to study, practice, and work never gets easier. It requires discipline, energy, and a lot of stubbornness just to make it through the learning curve by not quitting when the going gets rough.

If you're out of work, in between jobs, a college student, or an at-home parent, having flexible time on your hands is valuable for researching and investigating the broad market trading system. Keep in mind that if it were simple, then everyone would be doing it.

If your goal is to build up your portfolio with a high-risk/high-reward pattern, then plan on spending more time trading. The good news is that even full-time workers can still manage to squeeze in trading and researching. Perhaps you'll be a night owl, trading into the evening hours as a scalper, placing a few big trades over the course of the late, late show or a TV movie. Others may find the early hours are better suited to their trading habits, such as before the regular work day starts or the kids wake up. Just think of the Marines, who get more done before 6 a.m. than most people do all day long and you'll get the picture. Keep in mind that whatever your current responsibilities are, you'll need to carve out a chunk of time dedicated to learning about currency trading.

While it may only be two to three hours of actual trading per week, this short time frame is a good idea. You want to be fresh and excited about what you're learning. This plan is best suited for a "nearly normal" lifestyle, meaning you keep your regular day job, keep up with kids and homework, and still have some free time off. It is completely realistic to be an aggressive day trader and maintain a family friendly lifestyle.

A trader would plan for this trading schedule by spending the time he is not actually trading doing the researching, reviewing and finding setups. But this can be built around your normal day. Instead of watching YouTube videos on funny cats, you could surf over to the currency news websites and check out the latest updates. Bring your smartphone to the gym and listen to the day's reports as you sweat to the market news. When you're really dedicated, you'll switch your home page to CNBC.com, download the market apps to your phone, and keep your RSS feeds streaming with breaking news on the markets that interest you.

> Make whatever schedule you have work for you, not against you. If you know you're tied up between 9:00 and 5:00 Monday through Friday, then plan to dedicate a window of time just for researching. Switch up your usual out-of-the-office lunch break and sprinkle in your reading and research to find a good setup you can try out in the evening.

Researching the markets takes time, especially in the beginning when you don't know the USD from the CAD. The important thing is to keep moving forward with your studying because the goal is to eventually gain the skills to recognize a good trade before it happens. Think for a moment about a big, juicy fruit salad. You may know that a tomato is a considered a fruit (knowledge) but you also know that it does not belong in a fruit salad. Knowing to *not* put it into your fruit salad is wisdom. Having a broad range of information on the world market, economics, politics, and currencies is one thing. Knowing how it all ties together to affect the markets, then pulling the trigger on your particular trade, in your selected timeframe, that is wisdom. Confidence builds up only after a long period of time, covering many winning trades, losing trades, and figuring out your next setup. The more confidence you retain, the happier and less stressed you will be and the more gratifying your market trades will be.

Setting up and maintaining a working schedule is always hardest at the start. Given a few weeks, most traders fall into a reliable pattern of researching, reading, and updating reports so that when they sit down to actually trade, it is very enjoyable and low stress. Plus, the knowledge does build on itself, helping you digest additional reports faster with a shorter learning curve and enhancing your bottom line even more.

Regardless if you are trading frequently or irregularly, plan on putting in the time to learn the markets and avoid setting yourself up for failure. Trading with an aggressive plan can be stressful enough, so try to balance this by becoming well educated and knowledgeable in your preferred currency-trading sector. Over the long term, this will be time well spent.

Aggressive Forex Trading

Aggressive trading is hardwired for high risk, high returns and you will doing a lot more trades per session, hoping to capture a larger profit in each trade. There are many more trading choices to this aggressive style for FX trading versus a more conservative style.

Trading aggressively means you will be trading more, and with each trade comes another chance to win or lose. The higher number of trades can help you or hurt you. They can hurt you because each time you trade, you are risking money in the market. On the other hand, each time you trade you can use the methods shown in this book to search out trades with a high probability of winning while at the same time using tight risk-management techniques to eliminate loss when a bad trade happens. Bad trades do happen, and the more you trade, the more chances there are to make a mistake.

The higher the number of trades is designed ahead of time by your trading plan. Basic math can show you that if you trade for 6 or 10 hours a day, running trades of five or six per hour, then the number of losing trades can be disappointing. Think about a trainer walking through his stable full of racehorses. Each one has potential, and each one can win, but the majority of them won't win all on the same day.

The overall percentage of winners to losers is similar. By having a larger account, the dollar amount lost can seem steep. Remember to look at the losses by comparing them to the dollar amount of your gains. If you're winning big, you probably have a net gain in your account after it all balances out. A slow but steady increase is normal. As long as your winning trades outpace your losing ones, you are playing the right trading system.

It is also normal to feel much worse about losing a big dollar amount, thus making a poor situation even more negative. However, keep the perspective that if you've been trading high amounts, you are risking losing larger amounts too. The flipside of this, of course, is winning a bigger amount because it feels so much better. Keep in mind FX markets run hot and cold, dormant or active, so there may be a lot of trades to run or hardly any at all. Keep your winning trades 1% above your losing ones and you'll still be ahead.

Big money losses usually involve various amounts of emotional tumult or lingering doubt in some form. A big loss has psychological impacts as well as financial ones. However, if you're trading often and with larger sums of money, then you should realize it is even more likely you will hit losses just as big as your gains. The negative feelings that come with a big loss under an aggressive risk/reward account are also greatly magnified when you realize a big profit.

When you're ready to start making aggressive trades in your FX account, you'll need some aggressive strategies. Some traders align their account with the market's risk appetite. Others trade exotic currencies that are found in countries with big economic growth rates. Still others may trade the quasi-currencies such as gold, silver, or oil. The most important thing you need is a trade that will net you a higher return.

Many traders decide to trade the market's risk appetite by catching the low-risk currency gains and selling short on the high-risk ones.

Experienced traders know that when the world market has a reduced risk tolerance, it begins to shed risk assets. Such risk assets include selling off stocks and higher yielding currencies. Traders will then move into bonds and other safe havens. Most of the sell-offs occur because the traders all digest the same market news, draw the same conclusions, and jump out to protect their money.

> The world market can roll like an avalanche once a large number of traders begin selling off securities at the end of a major increase in the markets. Many traders jump out of the way to avoid being trampled. The U.S. markets have turned more unpredictable over the past few years. Wild swings and upheavals create opportunity for worldwide traders to gain profits.

Although sell-offs generally occur during upheavals, the opposite end swings through about three or four days after a big run-up in the market. For example, if the U.S. and European stock markets jumped 3% or 4% in the past three days, a lot of people will feel they've had a good run of it and start selling off their winning securities in order to lock in their profits.

By observing the markets and keeping a trading journal, you will be able to predict when the markets are ready to make a reversal due to the traders selling off. Noticing that a recent run-up has driven the market up 3%–5% could mean a ripe market turnaround. Check if the U.S. stock market's gains have been in the news a lot recently. If the media is noticing the upticks, this is a great way of predicting that now is the time to book some trades to prepare for the market correction. By the time the stock market makes the general news, like your typical 10 p.m. newscast, it is already "old" news and the markets have compensated.

Finding out the stock market has had a big day on your local news should pump up your trading gears and get you ready to put some trades together. The idea is that these trades should make money when the traders have had enough of risk assets, as when they are selling short the DOW 30, the CAC 40, and the Hang Sang. But if you have shorted risk, then you have bought safety and you will gain profits. Meanwhile, if the market has been sliding downwards for four or five days in a row and it makes the local news, you should consider this a good time to go long on risk and short on safety.

Selling Risk Short with Currency Trading

Another idea is to check on the DAX, the S&P 500, and the FTSE 100 for recent increases. If they are showing gains over several days, then you can set up trades to capture the risk aversion that will be coming up shortly. While it is human nature to think the markets will go up forever, the professional traders secretly wish for the typical investor to push up the indexes a lot higher after the initial rise. Then the pros will know when it is time to take their profits and cash out. They know when to reverse their positions, take the cash out, and close up trading. New investors should follow the same rule. By understanding the cyclical nature of the market time frames, traders can capture gains that the increased risk aversion has caused after a big run-up. Traders can catch the ride back down as the market reverts. Remember, the value of the currencies is tied into the growth of the country's economics. With a perception of slowing or stagnation in the economy, the risk of growth-oriented currencies will drop as compared to safer currencies.

A favorite way to capture safety and growth is the shorting of the Swedish krona against the EUR and USD. Sweden relies on its exports of industrial and consumer goods to its European neighbors, so it is a safe bet that long USD/SEK and EUR/SEK positions will gain when stock markets fall.

As traders begin to dismantle their SEK positions, this pushes the movement up on the USD and the EUR. In addition, the USD is considered a "safe-haven" currency during times of economic turmoil. Keep that in mind when considering a long USD/SEK position.

Another pair that will most likely move in sync is the euro and Swiss franc. Favored for its predictability, professional traders chose the EUR/CHF pair when times are challenging, shorting the EUR against the CHF. The flow of money from the euro into the Swiss franc will dramatically increase at the tiniest hint that the economic picture is deteriorating in Europe. This is due in part to the fact that neighboring countries such as Belgium and France, who use the euro, see the Swiss franc as much stronger. The Swiss National Bank is also highly regarded as a well-run banking system and very conservative, which boosts the franc even more.

A short EUR/CHF allows a trader to capture the influx of high-risk assets (EUR) into the lower-risk assets (CHF). This fruitful combination of going long the USD and the Swiss franc, while shorting on the EUR and the krona will help keep you protected and profitable.

Developing Countries/Exotic Currencies

Now that you've learned how to trade risk sentiment by going long and then shorting the safe-haven currencies, it is time to take some of your margin and test the exotic currency waters. While developing economies' currencies can be profitable, they typically carry a high-interest rate and are suitable for carry trades. As their returns can be outside the traditional money centers, they can act/react independently of the better or worsening market conditions of the international powerhouses like the United States, United Kingdom, Germany, or Japan.

For example, capturing the growth rate difference between the United States and Brazil is similar to the way traders gain the interest rate difference on AUD/USD. Actually, you could capture a huge interest differential by borrowing USD at 0.5% and using it to buy Brazil, earning 10% or more. Trades such as this allow simultaneous capture of growth and carry trade of the currencies. Brazil could go up higher still and you would benefit from rate hikes, which would widen the differences of the USD/BLR boosting the carry trade higher.

> Look for currency pairs your Forex broker offers first. Check the symbols on the Internet and see what pairs are available. Do your research into those countries' central bank websites and dig up the behind-the-scenes story to see if the trades will make profits. Broker's reports are an excellent stepping-stone for getting started on finding currency pairs.

Many bullish traders also use euros to buy Polish zloty. A strong industrial and agricultural nation, Poland trades mainly with nearby European countries. In the past few years, the PLN has grown over 20% against the euro. Poland continues to seek membership into the euro zone and it remains a currency favorite for brokers in relation to other still-developing economies. The PLN strikes a good balance between currency trades, stability, and economic growth, and its desire to enter the European Union is a bonus.

A third resource to consider for exotics would be to go long on the Czech koruna (CZK) against the euro. Historically, the Czech National Bank has excelled at keeping inflation around 2% and has done so by raising interest rates. Also, some brokers foresee that the normalization of the monetary policy (after the 2008–2009 banking crisis) will occur. Additionally, the Czech Republic is entering a deficit-reduction period, which, combined with the other factors, make the short EUR/long CZK trade very appealing in the future.

As with any long position, it is best to consult your broker's reports for an indication as to price levels for entry. The developing countries' FX trades typically run longer term, so it is best to wait until the ideal price point comes up to ensure that a long exposure will not cause a problem.

Gold and Silver Act Like a Currency

A high-risk/high-reward portfolio should consider adding gold and silver as another strategy. These precious metals are priced in USD to be traded in identical amounts worldwide.

Also, many FX brokerage accounts allow you to go long and short and will spot gold and silver on the same platform as regular FX trades. Electronic spot trading can help bridge the gap between futures and physical metal.

Profits on trading large lots (100 ounces of gold/1,000 ounces of silver) of this size as currency can be enormous. At times, gold can go as high as 1%–3% percent against the USD, with silver ranging from 3%–5% percent against the USD, tagging along on the same days that gold moves up.

Let's say you want to go long, using 20% of your portfolio in a long silver/USD position and triple the size of your account during a strong run-up. Silver can go up over 100% in a single year. This would equate to a 5,000% return on the actual dollars you have invested in a silver trade at 50:1. If you had $10,000 in your account, with leverage set to 50:1 and you place just 20% of margin in a silver/USD trade, your account balance would be over $200,000 at year's end: $10,000 × 20% = $2,000 × 50 = $100,000 × 2 (100% growth) = $200,000.

> While a broker might offer a Forex leverage setting of 20:1 or 50:1, most will not offer leverage on gold or silver trading and will automatically convert to a 1:1 level each time you enter a long or short gold or silver spot trade. Be sure to verify with your broker before entering into these trades, because they can skew your profit estimates.

Going long on gold/USD can mirror the long on an AUD/USD position. It also captures the movement of a strong AUD. At the same time, having a long gold position as a safe haven matches the same interplay on the Swiss franc and short Swedish krona position. Today, a long gold position is a strong favorite hedge position in the markets as gold has taken center stage.

Gold being center stage or in the "front seat" is due to several reasons, like added risk aversion and additional money supply in the United States and Europe. The future may harbor increasing favoritism for gold and silver, and they may still hit even higher record-breaking price levels and returns.

While the future is not crystal clear, it won't hurt to have a long gold/USD and a long silver/USD position in your FX trades to add some glitter. Gold and silver remain under consideration as an alternative to the paper-based fiat currencies in the world. Leading central banks including Russia, Europe, and the United States keep gold as a hedge against their printed paper currency holdings. Visit the central banks' websites for details on the percentage of gold they hold.

A good example of a well-managed central bank can be found in the Swiss National Bank (www.snb.ch/). The Swiss National Bank has 270 billion CHF in assets, and almost 50 billion CHF in gold reserves, and 200 billion CHF in foreign exchange reserves, maintaining a 1:5 ratio of physical gold to foreign currency assets. As recently as early 2013, South Korea increased its gold reserves by 20 tons, valued at nearly 1.03 billion USD, and resulting in an increase of their gold holdings by 24% from 2012. If world banks are taking gold back into consideration, a day trader should take note and apply this when actively managing a high-risk/high-reward account.

Aggressive portfolio trading can also be done by trading "naked." The key is to wait until market activity is very light, such as between 6 p.m. and 7 p.m. EST, and limited orders of any size will have a big impact on the market. Fewer traders are running at this time—New York is closed and Hong Kong traders are just getting in—so a little trading during this sweet spot of time can go far. Put your skills and margin into play with scalping and overnight trading to advance your portfolio considerably in a short span of time.

The best time to do this sort of trading is during a major market reversal. As Asian markets deflate, see if the S&P 500 futures are matching it. Watch for the Asian markets to fall by 1%. At that point, it's time to jump in and clear your trades out and free up your margin.

Grab your calculator and split your margins into tenths. Here is how you'll work it: place four trades in the next two hours that will total 40% of your margin. Now, these trades are "at the market," which means they are purchased at the current price for that time. Moving ahead two hours, the markets will fire up. Traders in places like Hong Kong, Tokyo, and Sydney will dump risk-oriented trades. Early risers in Europe will have similar thoughts, as will fellow U.S. traders finishing up their dinner and making trades.

Using a traditional scenario of shorting, an example of a great currency pair that harnesses the contraction in the stock market is AUD/USD. This pair is a preferred choice of traders who seek to gain large, anticipated profits in a market decline. Traders make the first one-tenth margin trade, and then wait. Over the ensuing half hour, the pair will move and you'll find yourself gaining profits. Now, you'll enter a sell order, and then wait another 30 minutes before entering the next trade. After this point, you should see some direction to the market and you can verify it by viewing a five-minute chart. Entry points will be clearly marked on the five-minute chart. In addition, you'll see the chart move further downwards, which gives you the chance to gain more profits. Put in the final four trades by 8 p.m. EST.

> Naked trading is one of the most aggressive forms of trading for your FX account. Naked trades are riskier because they have no stop losses and no take-profit point. Heightened risks bring increased profits, but it also opens up the trader to the biggest potential losses.

Trades are considered "naked" because there is no risk hedge, and no take-profit point entered into the trading system. You're in free fall, assuming all risk of the market and all gains and losses as well. You do not have a take-profit point because you are uncertain as to how far the markets will drop or for how long (hours, days, etc.). At times, the market is primed, (or set) for a fall, and trades like these may run active for days on end, scooping up huge profits.

Walk away from your computer when this situation comes up. Shut off your computer, turn off the TV, news reports, and the market analytics and go out for a walk, for dinner, or a coffee and don't check the news for the rest of the night. You'll close out the trades later, when the time is right. Also, it is a good idea to *not* check your platform in the morning. Instead, program your iPad or smartphone to following the Australian dollar currency ETF Currency Shares Australian dollar trust "FXA" to see how poorly the AUD is progressing.

The AUD drops in percentage terms from the previous day with this ETF FXA. After you see a dramatic drop in the movement of the AUD, then you may go back to your trading platform. This is the time to check your trades and see what profits you've made. It is also a perfect time to close them out, count up your profits, and skip trading for the rest of the week.

Trading ahead of the news is another extremely aggressive trading method. However, you will be pressed to utilize all your skills, market knowledge, and analysis to make it work in your favor. On busy news days, the majority of traders skip the markets. Some will merely hold the positions they are in already or possibly hedge a few trades.

An aggressive trading style can take advantage of these situations to build up your FX position. However, if the market was a mess the day before and the S&P 500 futures are off by more than 2.5%, it is a good time to pause and reflect if the market has already fully absorbed the price shifts.

> Using technical charts can help you figure out if risky trades are correctly priced. Knowing this information can help you trade ahead of the news. Rock-bottom or top-of-cycle pricing is critical information to have on hand when deciding when is the best time to enter a trade to capture the market's rebound.

Experience and observation over long-term market trends will help you to better predict if the AUD/USD or EUR/SEK pairs will go even lower during an expected bad day for the market. Keep in mind that once the European markets have struggled with a round of bad numbers, a lot of traders turn to fire-sale or bargain-hunters mode. Multiple buyers coming in now will help form the bottom of the market, eventually stopping the price free fall, and setting the market up for another rise.

Again, timing is everything in the FX market. If the European markets dropped, and the U.S. S&P 500 futures are looking down, plan on the bulk of the FX trading already being in place by 6 a.m. EST, nearly an hour before the U.S. New York market opens. The heaviest time of FX trading is when time zones overlap in the U.S. and European markets. Traders may also conclude that taking some long positions on the more reactive of the currency pairs may be their next step since the new pricing has already been built-in by the U.S. market's lower opening.

You've explored the concept of trading ahead of the news with a rocky market. Usually, FX traders will have a good idea of the direction their favored pairs will be heading over the week. Difficulties may arise when bad news is expected from central banks and various resources. Be cautious in your trading during these rough spots. Use your predictive estimates, technical charts, and analysis and you may find strong profits by running longer, higher-risk trades as the market rebounds.

Building Up Forex Trading Confidence

New investors can dip a toe into the trading market waters slowly, first by reviewing markets as an overview, then watching how analytics, charts, and fundamentals play out together. The next step is to put your trades into real-time action under a demo/training account, before finally graduating to the big leagues and handling real cash and live trades. Reading about trading in a book like this is not the same as making live trades in the real market.

The same rules still apply, whether you are using a demo account or a live account, and traders must develop confidence to meet the challenges of risky trades. But earning their sea legs or gaining the professional confidence required, means that a new trader will, in the end, just have to jump in and learn to dog paddle until they realize they aren't sinking. Trading is different with real money, and while you may splash around a bit in the beginning, accidently swallowing a giant gulp of sea water will teach you more than just how to keep your mouth closed.

> Trading with real money in your account can truly bring you to life. Knowing you are trading with other international investors and winning can make your little piece of the world a lot brighter. Most people never know how far they can go until pushed there, and a little successful FX trading can up the ante.

It is absolutely not true that you have to be loaded down with barrels of cash in your account before learning how to handle entering winning currency trades. Quite the opposite is true and everything outlined here can be accomplished with a very small balance. With just $30 in your account, you can enjoy the challenging experience of setting up a hedged directional FX trade. ONADA, a Forex brokerage firm, allows low balances and odd lot sizes that help you to expand your skills without risking big sums of cash.

Any money you place in the account would still be at a higher risk than your other earmarked investment funds. This particular bundle of cash would be worked hard; you would trade aggressively in a quick pattern that increases your percentage gains exactly as it would with a much larger account balance. Plus, you can trade a $30 dollar balance, under the new principals and ideas discussed in the High-Risk/High-Rewards sections, and still reap great results.

Trying out double-trading volatile currency pairs. trading risk sentiment, and trading exotic currencies can add to your bottom line and your experience level, as well as your enjoyment of the markets. The key is to closely monitor the percentage gain on your trades. Say you move $20 from your debit card to your Forex currency trading account, and then spend the early evening running your calculator and laying out a few trades. You'll find out quickly just what skills and techniques work best in an aggressive trading session. Turn your computer on in the morning and you're up $0.75 cents. A lot of people would say, "All that work for less than a buck?" What they don't see is that you're not just ahead, having made winning trades; your percentage of gain is 3.75% overnight, which, if done every night for the next year, equates to *over 900% returns*, not including compounding!

Remember, building up skills and experience required for Forex trading with an aggressive style gives you a chance to start with very small sums and makes an excellent starting point. Always remember, look to your percentages, not the actual money you are gaining. Larger sums of money can come later, but first figure out how to dog paddle in the crashing waves with your mouth closed.

Pitfalls of Overconfidence

A successful trainee can be a mentor's worst nightmare. Gaining rapid successes early on with apparent ease can make a new trader overconfident. Let's say the new trader has made some wins, had mostly gains and a few tiny losses. This is a wonderful boost to confidence, not to mention a source of pride to the newly minted trader. Perhaps they've begun hedging positions and had some success with other complex trades. The whammy only comes when they're riding high, and rest assured, it happens to every trader at some point.

Traders never plan on taking that last trade that wipes them out completely. If they had really thought about it from a short-term perspective, they would have easily recognized the dangerous waters that they were wading through. "But it looked just like a log," is what the antelope thinks as the hidden crocodile suddenly chomps down on him and pulls him under. That is exactly what a day trader will experience when his or her confidence level puts them on top of the world and then the bottom drops out. Watch out for those logs!

If you played it smart (or were just lucky) the log will not wipe you out, but it may knock some sense back into your head. Use your first major loss as a stepping stone back to a realistic approach to the market. No trader "knows" their trades are "all good." Actually, most FX traders have early successful runs and then a massive loss. Get to know yourself, understand you're only human and subjected to the exact same failings as the next person, because you *are* the next person. Better yet, plan the trades out as if each one could turn instantly into a croc and you had to jump or be eaten. Do you jump blindly to another log, or find out too late it's not what you thought? Find out where your confidence level sits, but don't forget to plan out your bail-out measures.

When you're feeling cocky or overconfident and all your trades are good, be wary that you are not paying enough respect to an untamed market. Anything as fluid and complex as a free open market cannot be fully predicted, no matter what sort of superstar trader you might be six months into it. Respect the FX market's complexity and hold true to the training, charts, analytics, and fundamentals you've learned along the way. People wiser than you will read brokers' reports and check central banks' websites for research. Seasoned traders skip out for extended vacations during especially volatile market news. Hold yourself accountable to your training and you will receive the bigger benefits and life-changing effects of running trades in an international marketplace. You might even earn a percentage or two and keep going for another day of trading on your net profits. Either way, you'll never look at a log the same way again.

So, what does it take to know if Forex trading meets your investing goals, plain and simple? It takes matching your Forex trading style with your investment trading objectives. If you don't get it now, keep reading. We'll go over it again and again throughout this book.

QUIZ

1. **The two different Forex trading objectives are:**
   A. Long-term and short-term gains
   B. Long-term and short-term goals
   C. Long-term and short-term interest rates
   D. Capital gains and interest income

2. **One of the best ways to determine your risk tolerance is to:**
   A. Take a quiz
   B. Ask your broker
   C. Let your friends tell you
   D. Determine for yourself by looking at your past investing history

3. **One of the best ways to keep your Forex trading fun, safe, and interesting is to:**
   A. Trade with large amounts of cash
   B. Trade with borrowed money from a credit card
   C. Trade with small amounts, and only what you can afford to lose
   D. None of the above

4. **Forex trading can act as an excellent hedge against what type of trading?**
   A. Stock trading
   B. Bond trading
   C. Mutual fund trading
   D. Penny stock trading
   E. All of the above

5. **Limiting the number of trades and dollar amount in your Forex account is a good way to:**
   A. Keep the risk of the Forex account low
   B. Keep the risk of the Forex account high
   C. Keep the risk of the Forex account balanced
   D. The adjustment has no effect on the risk of the Forex account

6. **One well-known investment system is a portfolio of 90%____ and 10%____.**
   A. Stocks, bonds
   B. Stocks, mutual funds
   C. Mutual funds, cash
   D. Bonds, Forex

7. **Even with high-risk, high-frequency trading, it is best to keep your Forex trading:**
   A. On your schedule
   B. Within your risk limits
   C. Using only margin amounts you can handle
   D. All of above

8. **When trading aggressively:**
   A. The number of trades will be higher
   B. The number of successful trades will be higher
   C. The number of trades will be lower
   D. The number of successful trades will be lower
   E. A & B
   F. A & D

9. **Trading the _____ is one of the best ways to capture predictable gains.**
   A. Market's volatility
   B. Market's good feeling
   C. Market's bad feeling
   D. Market's risk sentiment
   E. All of the above

10. **One of the best indicators of market risk sentiment is:**
    A. The market chatter about the strength of the market
    B. The market chatter about the weakness of the market
    C. The percentage gains in the market indexes
    D. The percentage losses of the market indexes
    E. All of the above
    F. C & D

Chapter **5**

More Tips on Forex Trading

CHAPTER OBJECTIVES

In this chapter, you will learn the following:

- How to diversify your Forex portfolio
- The best way to close out a profitable trade
- The best time to keep a trade open
- How to trade long-term Forex trends

Low-risk profiles have various options to help fine tune your portfolio, including diversification, when to unwind a position, and when to roll winnings into a new currency pair direction. The key to a successful Forex account is building your profits to get some real money flowing out of it on a daily or weekly basis.

Diversification Is Critical

When aligning your FX account to a low-risk profile, think about the appropriate amount of diversification under your one-third margin that is being used at any one time. Using one-third of your available margin, for example, you can divide it again by thirds to place trades into three different currency pairs.

Figure 5-1 compares the EUR/USD, USD/SEK, CAD/USD, and the AUD/USD. Note that diversification is key in Forex trading because these currency pairs have moved in different directions against the USD in a one-year time frame.

We've used real trading results to show exactly what happens in this example. Let's say you start in the middle of a trading week with zero in your account and you add $225 of funds. While this seems like a small amount, using three well-thought-out trades can capture the market movement to make a large percentage gain, help you learn the process, and get accustomed to closing trades using a smartphone or iPad.

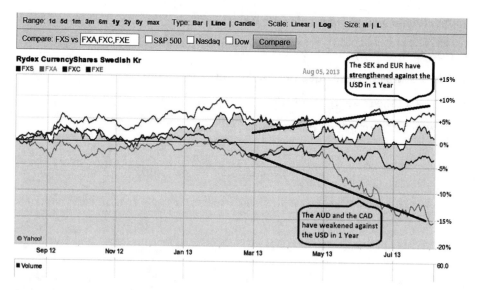

FIGURE 5-1 • Currency Pairs Comparison

Next, a quick scan of the day's news shows a major story breaking from Europe, sending the risk levels of the European currencies and others on a decline. Details from your brokerage report confirms this and reveals that traders around the world have begun selling stocks in place of bonds, causing a downward pressure on the U.S. and European stock markets.

Now you have a game plan, which is to dive in to the market as a bargain hunter or "bottom feeder" to snap up the deals that the other traders have abandoned in their haste to vacate a risk position. By using just one-third of your margin, you enter in three equally placed trades that are well diversified. The overall trades will capture the upcoming rebound; they will still be diversified across industries.

In this example, you can set up the first trade pair as a sell order for 133 units of EUR/SEK at 9.22618. This is because the EUR has been underperforming against the USD under this bad news, and the SEK is sensitive to risk appetite, therefore it will be likely to gain versus the EUR when good news comes back.

For the second trade pair, put in a sell at the market cost of 133 units of USD/NOK at 5.67152. This is because the NOK is tied to Norway's main export, crude oil, and is a well-run currency, and this commodity has been tied to risk sentiment recently. World traders are linking the growth of oil-producing economies such as Canada and Norway to the price and the demand for oil.

A great many trades in Forex accounts are performed with currencies that tie into the value of commodities. The correlation of commodity consumption and growing economies is always at the forefront of a trader's analysis. When a country is growing, they use more commodities, driving up the price of the commodity-producing countries' currencies in the process of an economic boom.

Traders who think the world's economies are shrinking or slowing will wait to see if the falling price of oil matches the downward trend. This is the reasoning for your long NOK exposure because it is set up to capture any anticipated increases in the price of crude oil.

Next, the final trade is to buy into the AUD by selling the USD. You might notice that the AUD/USD pair has been down recently due to negative perceptions in the markets. You go long AUD/USD for 100 units at 1.02359. In this case, the AUD/USD will gain when there are thoughts that the economies of the Asian developing nations are going to be getting stronger, and in particular when it is thought that the economy of China is going to be getting stronger. This is mainly due to the fact that the value of the Australian dollar is tied to the value of the exports of Australia. The exports of Australia are mainly the raw materials that are used in growing industrialized nations. These raw materials include iron ore, nickel, and other metals that are used in the production of industrial products and capital goods. Also, Australia has a gold and silver mining industry that greatly benefits when economies such as China and India are doing well. This is due to what is known as the "wealth effect." When the people of those nations are better off financially (due to a stronger economy), they have a tendency to buy precious metals such as silver and gold. All of this creates a strong demand for the AUD in times of good economic growth in both the Asian countries and the rest of the world.

Back to the example trade in the discussion. Now, the three trades (EUR/EK, USD/NOK, and AUD/USD) total to about one-third of your available margin. Be sure to leave two-thirds of your margin free to insure your account can handle any big downward swings in the market. Keeping back two-thirds is absolutely vital to this trading strategy, as it allows for breathing room and offers space on margin calls until the FX pairs turn in your favor. Review and record your trades, make copious notes on the trades you made in your journal, then shut off the computer and walk away.

Dismantling a Profitable Trade

It can be hard, at first, to walk away from your trades, but babysitting your computer as the market churns away will only raise your blood pressure and increase your stress level. Feeling anxious about something outside your immediate control is a normal reaction, and trying to ignore it will be challenging, like an itch you have to scratch. But, let's say you've been pretty good, staying off the computer all last night and doing your usual morning routine. You finished your workout, have a cup of coffee in hand, and you take a peek at CNBC. Whew! The markets are still there! And look at that ... they've gone up a tiny bit.

Now is the time to scratch that itch using a computer, or by using your Forex broker's app on your iPad or smartphone (which can be pretty handy if you would like to view your trades along with the ability to use buy/sell commands). The app won't show a complete platform, but just what you need to see—the balance of the net for your trades. This is the bit of information that you want to focus on. In our example—and this is quite common for the markets to react with this much percentage gain—the balance shows that it is up $42.10 since last night, about an 18% return on your $225 balance, and a good profit for the day.

Now, you can use your buy/sell commands via the app to go to the close order page, close out each of the three trades, and list your profits. In this example you close out the USD/NOK trade at 5.58817, the EUR/SEK at 9.16278, and the AUD/USD at 1.03203. Congratulations! Your new balance has gone up from $225 to $262.10, a nice gain! Keep that gain in mind as you forget about the rest of the markets, relax and walk away from the trading platforms, and stick to your regular routine for the morning. Knowing when to walk away from the markets after a big win is just as important as learning how to set up a big win in the first place. Remember, you just made an over 18% gain in less than one day, and that, compared to a CD (at 2%–4% per *year*) or the stock market (at 7%–10% per *year*), the gain is huge! Also, the perceived values of the currency pairs will most likely be a bit off due to the gains, all which have the effect of making it very difficult to jump back into the market in such a short time frame.

Instead of taking the profits and churning them into another trade right away, what you should do is, later in the day, go over what exactly happened to your trades in greater detail. Grab your trading journal and look over your notes for some clues. You might ask yourself, "Why did the NOK and SEK move so much more than the obvious choice of the long AUD/USD?" Check your broker's statements and you'll see that China's growth numbers came in (while you slept) and they had slightly slower than anticipated growth for the consumer raw materials. Therefore, since Australia provides much of the raw materials for China, this means a slower rate of growth of Australia's export of raw materials.

You've gotten your answer, now be sure to make a note of this in your trading journal for future reference and keep an eye on the AUD/USD pair. On your broker's report, you see that they have recommended accumulating any AUD/USD priced at near parity or 1:1, and that the pair will face a rough road to get above 1.045. So, for the near term, plan on getting into the AUD at this level. This trade, however, is still considered a good carry trade and the pair still reacts well to positive trading news; it was simply a one-off that the overnight's news slowed its upward momentum.

This is a great time to use the apps on mobile technology to get you out of the house (or office) and still keep an eye on your trades. These devices are handy, and can be an adequate replacement for a full computer to manage trades after a full day of trading. Walking away from the office and getting a fresh perspective can actually work to your financial advantage, especially if you have the tendency to overtrade your Forex account.

Keeping the Profits Rolling

After checking your notes and updating your trading journal, you'll need to decide what to do with your profits. As the recent action has rolled through the U.S., European, and Asian markets, now is a good time to look in a different place to make some money this afternoon or by tomorrow morning. Going back through your broker's reports, you see a news piece from last weekend concerning the GBP/USD pair. Heighted inflation in the United Kingdom was reported and the broker's analysis suggested building long GBP/USD positions anywhere under 1.60.

Figure 5-2 shows the rapid rise in value of the GBP/USD FX pair, and then a settling of the price in a range after the initial strengthening of the GBP.

When you switch your technical chart over to a one-hour time frame, you see that the GBP had no visible benefit from the recent gains in the market that the SEK, NOK, and AUD had. Then you check and see that the GBP/USD pair is at 1.587 and you decide to buy the pair at this level.

Once again, you take your account balance divided into thirds, and then take three even chunks out to buy pairs. But this time, all your trades will be in GBP. Your first trade will be at 1,500 units of GBP/USD. You make this trade, then close out your trading screen and get on with your regular day. About 45 minutes later, you take a moment to see how the pair has fared and see it has slid downward slightly and your position is down $3.00.

Realizing that it is mid-afternoon New York time, you are not likely to see any big price swings in either direction, you go ahead and buy in your next third at this price point. Now for your final trade, you need a little help from automation. Your plan is to buy the final third at a preset price, so you set up a limit order to be filled only if that specific price level is met. The best part is you will not have to wait around checking your screens for this price; the trading platform will automatically do it for you. You decide to set the price to be the same

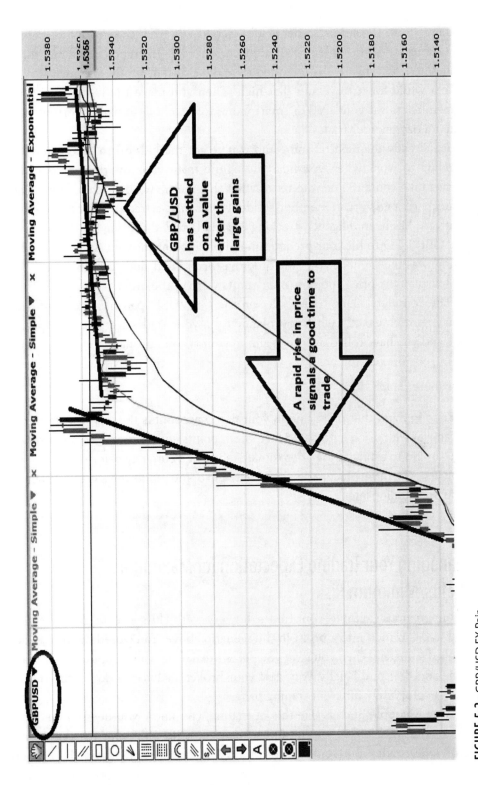

FIGURE 5-2 · GBP/USD FX Pair

distance from the second order as the second was from the first. Now, before you submit the limit order, you first place your take-profit position for all three trades at 1.63. This rate is intended to make a decent profit, although it may take a while for it to get up that high. Then you place the trade order. You remember to set your iPad or smartphone for "Audible Order Reporting" and call it a day on your trades.

It's already the next morning and you've got the kids off to school and are heading to work when you hear the chime from your smartphone or iPad. It may take you a moment to recall what that chime was for again, but as you scan the details, you remember suddenly you had a trade running. Your FX platform has been diligently tracking the markets and waiting for the price of the GBP/USD to hit your predetermined price point for your limit order. The chime was the reminder that the order has been filled, and your phone or iPad will display the price and how many units were in the order.

The completed long-trade order on the GBP/USD pair has been fulfilled. You've gotten exactly what you planned for, your trades were evenly spaced out, and you have rolled over the gains in your account using investment advice from your broker. You are set!

> Keep in mind that practicing in your demo account is the best way to get familiar with using automated take-profit points and automated stop losses. Learning to estimate the approximate range of a currency pair can be tricky at first. The more practice you have with it in demo mode, the easier it will be for real trading later.

Managing Your Trading Expectation for Maximum Profits/Minimum Risk

In the previous example, your trades did very well. Three evenly sized, diversified trades turned into a profit in the scenario above. You closed them out and booked gains, and then you gave yourself a break from the computer after realizing an 18% gain. Finally, you used your broker's advice to do another trade with a completely different trading pair.

After a couple of days like this in trading, you know you need to take the rest of the week off, so you set up automated profit points for the three long GBP/USD trades. But come dinner time, you start thinking again about your active trades. This is a good time to check, as the FX market is usually slow at this time of day. Although you set an automatic fill order to a take-profit point of 1.63, you'd be thrilled with any profit before the end of the week. You could close out all of your trades and head into a weekend at 100% cash.

But in our scenario, the week falls flat. There was no real movement in any direction of the currency pair you chose. Now you have to make the decision: The weekend is nearly here, do you carry the trade over the whole weekend or close out and go into the safety of 100% cash?

Perhaps there is no movement in the FX markets or stock markets due to an upcoming report on the U.S. economy next week. Or there might have been a run-up or downturn in the stocks that traders are taking a rest from. Still, you need to decide to stay open or close your positions and you do this by reviewing your original trading plan. If going long on the GBP/USD pair was a good idea from the beginning, then chances are good that it still is a good idea and it can work out fine. In this particular case, you know that the GBP/USD pair often makes it up to 1.63, which places it within a normal price range for your profit point.

Quality review of your trades is essential to your trading plan, as well as keeping you focused on the motivation and logic behind a trade. Reminding yourself of the underlying reasons for the trade can help ensure you make better trades when you are considering doing the exact opposite.

The scenario above calls for waiting on the long GBP/USD trade to come around and make a profit. As tempting as it may be to close the trade while flat (and break even), a review of your notes can lead you to stay put and wait it out for the 1.63 to arrive. Patience could reward you for well-placed and well-thought-out trades with very large gains. Gains from smart trades such as these can go a very long way in keeping your account profitable.

Buying into Long-Term Trends

Low-risk/low-return traders need to seek out longer-term trends for more trading ideas. The longer terms usually mean sluggish currency price movements that can build up positions over a length of time. While building up your position over several weeks, try buying into smaller chunks of your currency pair.

Let's say your currency broker suggests you build up long positions in GBP/USD at a price point below 1.60, as shown previously. You know that the GBP/USD might not move much at all for weeks or even months, but you could still accumulate the pair by a dual method.

First, begin with a current margin balance, divided by thirds. You'll want to limit the total exposure of the long GBP/USD account to only one-third of your full margin. Previously, you've taken these thirds and split them again into thirds. This time, however, you'll change it to six equal parts that will be entered into the markets over a period of weeks.

Long-term trades such as these are slow and small, so whereas you would be buying into a trade in minutes or hours before, these trades are ones you buy every two to three days. By buying in over a span of days or weeks, you will get a smoother, more average cost basis. The average price of your long GBP/USD will be divided over a much longer time period, thus giving you a wider price variance. The wider the variance, the greater the chance of buying more on the lows because the pair's price moves along a bigger range in proportion to the amount of time covered.

The second and final part of the dual method to build your long GBP/USD position is adding new money to your account over the weeks and months. Many traders feel uneasy about trading with a large balance in your FX account. One way to dispel this uneasiness is to gradually build up a position over the weeks using the six parts of the one-third method, while simultaneously transferring more funds to your account. Some people set up an automatic deposit to be delivered into their FX account each week, such as $25.00 added each Friday before the closing bell of the markets.

Once you've gotten the new influx of funds, divide your total margin balance again by thirds. The new balance is the target number you want to have invested in the GBP/USD over a long time period. While you're injecting more money into your FX account, you will be combining that with the build-up of the long positions, creating a financial moving target that you aim to hit by additional purchases of the GBP/USD pair over a period of six to eight weeks. In the end, your account is diversified but also hedged on exposure because you bought into the pairs over an extended upward scale.

Playing the Interest Rate Differentials

Another trading strategy that works well in a low-risk scenario is playing the carry trade. If you can go for a six-month or longer trade, this type of trade can work out well. First, you need to locate a funding currency and an interest earning currency to make your pair. Choose a good funding currency that you can short a very low-yielding currency, like the USD, JPY or Swiss franc, which all have historically low interest rates.

After selecting your low-yield funding currency, check the stats on those paying a high interest rate. Great examples of commodity-based currencies are Australian, New Zealand, and Canadian dollars. Classic high-yielding currencies also include the South African rand and Norwegian kroner.

Remember, the idea is to short the low-yielding currency and go long on the high-yielding currency. On the backside, you're paying interest on the shorted currency (as a loan) and earning interest on the higher interest-bearing long currency (as an investment). Traders know that this is basically how all currency pairs are funded, but you don't notice the interest earned because the currency trades typically last only minutes, hours, or days.

> Even though you may be in an FX trade as a carry trade, do not feel obligated to wait longer on it. When it shows a profit, close it down, even if it hasn't been the taken as long as you expexted. Keep in mind that Forex pairs in carry trades can go up fast. A carry trade can turn out to be a capital gain when it turns to out to be low-hanging fruit, too tempting to pass up.

Of course, keep in mind that a carry trade earns interest over a much longer time period. Those weeks and months can be a lucrative sweet spot for your portfolio if you're willing to go the long haul. As the currency pairs gain and fall, you earn the difference of interest from the low-yielding versus the higher-yielding currency. On top of that, you earn interest that accumulates with daily payouts. In other words, the compound interest of a carry trade can add up fast.

In general, carry trades are thought to be very low risk and, if set up correctly, they can run for an extended amount of time. Earned interest rates can run to 5% or higher. Trading one-third of your account at 50:1, the interest earned is over 80% of your total account balance. For example, if your account balance was at $1,000, the earned interest is $800 per year (if the interest rate difference was 5%).

Adding this type of ultra-long-term trading to your carrying trade strategies can bolster your account over the very long term. Patience is essential, however, when placing your trades spread out over the proper ins. When you are waiting for the prices to fall in the world market, it means you're waiting for the bad times to hit stock prices. However, the lows of the market will mean you are making buys at the lowest point possible, making trade bargains.

When the Market Corrects

Now you've spent a considerable amount of time creating a well-planned position that is fundamentally sound and technically ideal. All that is left is to sit back and wait for the trade to play out and earn you profits. Although it is a great feeling to hop in and out of the market with short, snappy trades in a few minutes' time, the majority of big money gains are done in the long term—having a plan, sticking to it and trusting the trade to work for you.

Make sure you plan on the longer term trades taking an extended time to work out fully to your benefit. It will seem, from time to time, that all the world traders are homing in on a currency pair that seems really on fire and it's not yours. This is not the time to jump ship because another pair has fancier sails. Other times, all the other currency pairs are pulling out ahead of yours and yours are seemingly drifting aimlessly about. Just like checkout lines in the grocery store, you feel like you have chosen poorly, your line is never going to move, and some price check on zucchini will tie you up too long. Other times you're in the shortest line, but the guy in front of you has five kids and two carts to check out, so you hope he doesn't have coupons or tries to write a personal check with no ID. The markets can be just as unpredictable!

Markets have lulls—periods of time in which not much happens—usually around holidays and such. Market swings, just like the grocery lines, are things outside of your direct control. There is no sense in panicking after a carry trade has been made, as long as it has been made with a well-thought-out plan. Use the time you're holding the trade to reassure yourself you've made a wise choice by reviewing your trading journal and focusing on your logic.

After you've let the anxiety subside and you know your ideas still hold up, go and set up a take-profit point that is one-third away from the stop-loss point. By setting up your stops in this way, you can ride out triple the amount of market downward trends as upward trends. Basically, your automated program will be set to win one-third as much as you lose. This way, you'll average out a win three times as often as you will a loss.

> Keep in mind that it is hard to stick to anything that doesn't directly interest you. Expand beyond currency trading, gain a new hobby or skill, and you might find yourself enjoying the markets from a whole new perspective while having trades still churning away elsewhere.

While this idea may not seem logical because it appears to want to set your wins to be three times your losses, it still makes sense. By following this plan for stops, it takes three times for the movement to finally close the trade out and put profits in your bank account. Meanwhile, you are booking losses three times that of booked wins. But remember, a win is not a win until it is realized or when the profit gets posted to your account. Of course, a loss also becomes a loss only when the trade is finalized or closed out and the loss is put on your account.

Finding yourself in a situation where your trade is not moving at all, or worse, losing, is the time to make the call to close out or wait. Waiting would mean hoping for a correction in the market. As happens often with currency pairs, they swing back and forth, from winning to losing and back. Often this occurs while you are not at your computer or watching your positions. This is why is it vital to use the automated stops, or properly placed take-profit and stop-loss points. Using these points wisely will help you avoid large downturns and be ready to profit as soon as the trade turns around.

Automated Forex Trading Systems

Automated Forex trading is a method of using a computer program to manage the daily buying and selling in your currency account. These trading systems use state-of-the-art neural network artificial intelligence technology to analyze Forex market trading conditions and automatically place trades in your Forex account. These automated Forex trading systems are programmed to perform many mathematical and statistical calculations per second, exceeding the capacities of even the most seasoned human trader.

Automated Forex trading systems are designed by their programmers to analyze a variety of technical indicators simultaneously. Some of the common built-in technical analyses include Fibonacci retracements, pivot points, volume analysis, statistical correlation, and volatility analysis.

Once automated systems are set up and installed properly, they will run with a "human-hands-off" method of control. Forex market data will be input into the system live. The system will then continually analyze that data for the best trading opportunities.

Preprogrammed "Win-Rates"

There are usually different levels of risk associated with each automated Forex trading system. Most programmers of these systems have built in a level of win-rate.

This win-rate is determined by programming the automated trading system to analyze the market data at all times, yet only place trades with a mathematical probability of winning that trade of a certain percentage or more. If the automated trading system has a preprogrammed win-rate set at 95%, the amounts of trades made per month may be limited to a smaller number, usually to between 20 and 50 automatic trades per month.

In addition to the benefit of the built-in market data analysis, some automated trading systems allow the trader to add additional technical data to be analyzed for trading opportunities. This allows for the set-up of a semi-custom automatic trading system that is best suited for the trader.

Around the Clock Automated Trading

While Forex automated trading systems can be single- or multiple-currency pair based, they are all designed to perform their technical analysis and search for high-winning-probability trades on a 24-hour/6-day-a-week schedule. This means that once the automated system is installed, it will run during the entire Forex trading week. In this way, these powerful mathematical artificial intelligence systems will be looking for trading opportunities during all Forex market hours and peak trading center trading times.

Some systems can be set to offer e-mail and SMS notifications in order to let the trader know when the trading system has determined a trading opportunity and has placed a trade. Once the trade has been closed out, a second e-mail or SMS notification will be sent informing the trader that the closing trade has been made, along with the profit made on that trade.

Testing

In order to insure that the Forex automated trading system will work in future market conditions, the systems are back-tested during product development. This back-testing is the process of taking the system and running it through years of actual historical market data. While in back-test mode, corrections and fine tuning to the system's ability to analyze and detect winning trades are made. The result of proper and thorough back-testing is a solid, sound system that has been tested under real market conditions. Other testing methods include real-time testing, which is the running of a current system alongside of a Beta-version, allowing for continuous improvements to the programming. With this in mind, it is best to seek out an automated trading system that has been thoroughly back-tested with real data and continues to undergo an improvement process. Additionally, keep in mind that a provider of automated trading systems should offer access to software updates for the life of the product.

Automated Trading System Requirements

Most automated trading systems will work on personal computers, laptops, and netbooks. Some systems require a Windows-based operating system and are not compatible with Apple computers. Other system requirements include a minimum amount of available RAM (usually 512 MB or higher) and an Internet connection of 36.6 KB/s or faster. Most users do not find these requirements an issue, as modern computing well exceeds these minimums.

These automated trading systems can be easy to set up and install onto your existing trading platform. Since automated trading systems are usually designed to run on the MT4 trading platform (through Expert Advisors, or EA), there may be some difficulty finding a system that is compatible with other Forex trading platforms.

Semi-Automated Trading Systems

In addition to the fully automated approach to trading, some automated Forex trading system providers will offer a semi-automatic version. These semi-automatic versions will use the same artificial intelligence programming to perform mathematically based technical analysis of the Forex market.

While the fully automatic versions will take control when it comes time to place an FX trade, the semi-automatic version will send an e-mail, SMS, or on-screen notification that an optimal condition is present to make a statistically significant winning trade. After the notification goes out, it is then up to the trader to place the suggested trade or not.

Some traders find these semi-automatic Forex trading systems more suited to their needs. Benefits include the added flexibility of using more Forex major and cross pairs (some systems offering up to 20 FX pairs), as some fully automatic systems are programmed for only one pair, such as the EUR/USD. As with the fully automatic versions, semi-automatic Forex trading systems will suggest profit and stop-loss orders, as well as when to exit a trade and take profits.

While most fully automatic Forex trading systems have only one time frame built into their programming, some semi-automatic Forex trading systems offer the flexibility of switching time frames between short, medium, and long. This also adds to traders' flexibility when searching for profit opportunities.

Mathematics-Based Trading, Free of Emotion

The usage of a well-designed and programmed automated Forex trading system can greatly add to the profitability of currency trading. These automated systems use a rules-based approach and mathematics to determine the best time to place a trade with the best chance of winning. Users of these systems can trade using mathematical logic, free of emotional ties to the Forex market, 24 hours a day.

So what does it take to know how to best manage your Forex portfolio, plain and simple? It takes knowing how to diversify your Forex trading portfolio and how to buy and sell Forex positions in smaller parts, among other things. If you don't get it now, keep reading. We'll go over it again and again throughout the book.

QUIZ

1. **One of the key elements in Forex trading is to keep your trading portfolio:**
   A. Trading at all times
   B. At high risk at all times
   C. In concentrated positions at all times
   D. Diversified as much as possible at all times

2. **You can diversify your Forex portfolio:**
   A. Across geography
   B. Across economic areas
   C. Across industry
   D. Across commodity production

3. **Once you have a good trade it is best to know how to:**
   A. Dismantle the trade in sections
   B. Get out of a trade with enough profit
   C. Lock in profits while eliminating risk
   D. Sell the trade all at once
   E. A, B, & C

4. **One of the best ways to dismantle a trade is to sell it off in thirds.**
   A. True
   B. False

5. **Mobile apps on cell phones and tablets can add to your ability to monitor your trades.**
   A. True
   B. False

6. **Low-risk traders need to look for:**
   A. Fast-acting news
   B. Slow-acting news
   C. Quick profits
   D. Long-term trends

7. **Buying into long-term trends means that you look at what the currency's value will be in 3 to 6 months.**
   A. True
   B. False

8. **A well-proven strategy is to go long a high-yielding currency and short a low-yielding currency.**
   A. Yes, known as a carry trade
   B. Yes, known as long/short strategy
   C. Yes, known as playing the interest rate differential
   D. A & C
   E. None of the above

9. **If you are in a carry trade for the long term, but the currency moves up fast, it is OK to sell and lock in your profits.**
   A. True
   B. False

10. **Carry trades work by earning a high rate of interest while paying a low rate of interest.**
    A. True
    B. False

Chapter **6**

Using Research for Better Forex Trading

In this chapter, you will learn the following:

- What fundamental research is
- How to use fundamental research to make trades
- What technical research is
- How to use technical research to make trades
- How research leads to spotting good Forex setups

Before executing your initial currency trade, you will need to have a solid understanding of the basics, which is called doing fundamental research. After gaining robust knowledge of this, you can then start independently reviewing central bank websites and comparing your own research with the news and brokers' reports.

Next, you can take these combined ideas and utilize them in a plan to trade currency pairs.

Fundamental Research 101

One key component for currency trading when finding setups is good research. Without it, you may just be tossing your money around in trades without an understanding of what is a good trade and what's not. It may seem fun to first act with abandon when trading currency, but you should remember you are doing so for pleasure and to make money. This is why it's important to conduct good research for a currency pair. You will also have to realize that determining which direction the currency pairs will go in the future is important and that studying economic indicators, brokers' reports, central bank websites, and news information is a good thing. All of this combined information is referred to as fundamental information, while the study of it has been named fundamental analysis.

Once you undergo these activities, then it is time to trade your currency pairs and place your order on the FX trading platform. Anything before this time could become too risky; you can forget about having any fun, as you'll see your funds will quickly disappear instead of profits showing up.

Fundamental analysis may be defined as the process of reviewing one country's inflation rate, growth rate, current account surplus/deficit, and additional information. On occasion, it is necessary to undergo a separate study of economics to see the big picture after gathering all of this fundamental analysis that has been culled from the website of a central bank.

You'll soon learn that fundamental analysis is vital for a thorough and organized trading system. By taking the time to learn fundamentals, you are allowing yourself to see the big picture. This may come after reviewing central bank websites from countries including the United States, Hungary, Sweden, and Switzerland—just to name a few—as sources for possible suggestions regarding the current state of the country's economic health. It may also be achieved by reviewing the central bank's website's economic reports and announcements for nuggets of information on whether or not its economy is improving; the country's economy may also be undergoing a growth phase or a slowdown. Then you could look at the signs and compare the hints and possible suggestions of the opposing currency you are interested in trading. An example will make this easier to understand.

Let's say you're interested in a currency cross for the Swiss franc versus the Hungarian forint (CHF/HUF). You could begin by reviewing the websites of the Swiss National Bank and the Hungarian Central Bank to gather information through reading previous news announcements and any content from those banks that have discussed the economy using terms such as "overheating," "on course," or "stagnant." By seeing these keywords, you can determine what the central bank for each country thinks regarding its economy, such as whether it is growing too slow, too fast, or is steady. If you saw a suggestion that the economy is growing fast, then you may believe there's a potential future interest rate hike coming. On the other hand, if an economy is slowing down, then you may think there could be either a cut or loosening of interest rates on the way.

Why? The majority of central banks will standardize their home country's economic growth through either increasing or decreasing interest rates. If you have a decelerating economy, then the bank would cut rates to increase lending, with spending moving toward growth. For a fast economy, you would expect the central bank to put on the brakes by increasing rates as a means to halt lending, which would slow down growth. Once you have gleaned this economic information, it's time to take it to the next step. You should review your broker's report and see if she also mentioned the same information, such as changes in rate direction or the market's sentiment regarding the direction of interest rates. Are they going up or going down?

There are a few news services that could also aid you in your research, as they will show similar information. These include DailyFX and FXstreet. When reviewing all of this pertinent information, don't forget that what you look for in one currency, you will need to do the same for the other currency in your pair.

You will need to find out if, for the currency that has an interest rate that will be increasing, the other currency's interest rate will be declining. On occasion, if you have an expectation for the currencies' interest rates to go against one another, then this could be a good enough indicator that you will have a solid FX trade. Remember, if the market believes interest rates (and each currency's relative value versus the other) will change, then FX market participants will be ready to make trades, and around the world, many traders will help move the currency pair in that particular direction.

Studying the world's currencies on their central bank websites is just a start for studying fundamentals of the currency pairs that you may be interested in trading. This could encompass pairings such as EUR/CHF, EUR/NOK, the EUR/SEK, or really any currency combination. Given these combinations, you would go to the websites of the European Central Bank, the Norges Bank, the Riksbank, and the Swiss National Bank and study their information. Take your time, as there will be a wealth of information. Get to know each bank's publications and economists. You can also sign up for updates from news announcements, research, and newsletters.

To find a list of the world's central and national banks, please visit the Bank of International Settlements (BIS) website. You will find a wealth of information on this site, such as gauging money movement across the world's banks and research reports including ones on inflation.

Now that you have spent time developing a picture of a country's economy from their respective central bank's website, it is time to dig even deeper in your quest to find information for your currency trading. It is time to look at some present and future economic indicators and a key source to review this is the U.S. Economics and Statistics Administration's website. Table 6-1 shows a few other websites that will have lists of key economic indicators that you will want to keep an eye on while you are participating in currency trading.

Here's just a note of caution. You'll find these economic indicators may be complex to understand and translate into information that you can use for your trading. Don't panic and become overwhelmed by the volume of numbers.

TABLE 6-1   Fundamental Indicators and U.S.-based Economic Information Websites

Economic Indicator	Website Link
Advance Monthly Retail Sales	http://www.census.gov/retail/
Advance Report on Durable Goods	http://www.census.gov/manufacturing/m3/
Current Account Balance	http://www.bea.gov/newsreleases/international/
New Home Sales	http://www.census.gov/const/
Personal Income and Spending	http://www.bea.gov/newsreleases/national/pi/
U.S. Trade Balance	http://www.bea.gov/international/

Keep your eye on the prize and remember that you want to find information that shows if a country's economy appears to be quickly growing, slowing down, or is just steady. After reviewing all of this information, as well as the details from the central bank website published out of other countries, you can expand your knowledge regarding expectations for interest rate directions in that currency from its present and predicted growth rates.

Using economic indicators is universally done to predict the direction of where a country is headed financially. A large number of financial professionals use this information, such as economists and a variety of traders (equity, fixed income, and currency). Not all economic indicators are created equally. Some will frame a picture of what has already happened; these are referred to as lagging indicators. Some will discuss the direction of where an economy will be in the future. These are called leading indicators. From these indicators you can gain a wealth of information. At any time, you can reference information you obtain with other sources. This could include referencing a news nugget from a currency news website with a piece of information from a broker's report that you received from your news feed on your trading platform.

If you haven't already done so, you should be keeping a daily trading journal. You can add the different bits of information from these varied sources into the journal. This could be the date of the information, where you obtained it and when (such as time and day), and when you noticed the suggestion that the trade will become a good setup. This could very well already be in the works. As you can see, fundamental information takes time to build; it is a process, but it gleans information you can use in the long-term. It can also represent more of a medium- or long-term analysis of where a currency and a currency pair are headed.

Many times, your broker may have shared a current price and a medium- and long-term range for a specific currency pair. What he is actually doing is conducting a currency analysis through a review of a currency's fundamentals, and then comparing it against a counter-currency's fundamentals.

Let's take for an example a currency analysis for NZD/USD for a potential trade: An FX analyst from an investment bank may compile a report for you including a compilation of written reports from the Reserve Bank of New Zealand for any indicators suggesting slowing, growth, or steady economic developments. These developments could precipitate a change for the bank's currency interest rates, with its currency expected to show either growth or the lack of it. The analyst would also review information available on the website regarding possible money flows either into or out of the country, as well as additional statistics.

In addition, he would compile this information and then compare it against the same details from the U.S. central bank's website. The information would then be matched against observations of the NZD/USD technical indicators to determine a stance—whether it is a long one, short, or neutral. He will then decide if there is either a broadening or convergence of interest rates for the two currencies.

One scenario is that the NZD will increase interest rates while the USD will either be steady or lower interest rates; a long NZD/USD buy signal would be listed in the report. This means you would sell the USD and use its proceeds to purchase NZD. You will make money from the trade when the NZD rises in value versus the USD as other traders push the price to increase.

This occurs as FX traders worldwide participate in the practice of carry trades, or making money by selling short a low-interest currency (in this example, the USD) and using the proceeds to then invest in a high-interest currency (the NZD).

More information for the entry and exit points of this NZD/USD trade would be provided and a senior banker would review this. Then an NZD/USD report would be widely distributed to the broker's clients and customers.

Interest Rates and Forex Trading

Keep in mind, the interest rates for the two currencies in an FX pair valuation represent the most important information. You need to understand that forecasts of change in the difference of interest rates for two currencies are vital for successfully trading and gaining profits.

From your direction estimates for the currency pair's interest rates, you can make your decision as to which is the ideal way to trade this duo, whether it is to go short or long. Remember, if you believe a currency pair will have widening interest rates, you should buy the currency that has rising interest rates and sell the currency that is remaining the same or cutting rates.

In FX trading, money can be made in two ways. One is via capital gains when you buy low and sell high. The second comes from interest when traders enter into a carry trade. This includes a low-yielding currency, which will fund a purchase for a high-yielding currency.

Traders worldwide are increasingly making bets using carry trades. As these trades are made by worldwide FX traders, the spread will widen further and further until the growth becomes unsustainable. At this time is will seem as if all traders will close their carry trades at once, which can cause the currency pair to quickly and dramatically tumble in value.

For the trade, a trader will pay interest for lower-yielding borrowed currency (ranging annually between 0.25% and 0.50%) and then invest the funds at a higher rate (historically, 0.75% to almost 7.25%). Money is just pouring in, thanks to the interest rate differential.

Say you borrowed USD at a 0.75% rate and then used the funds to purchase NZD at 7.25%. You would make a yield of 7.25% interest earned minus the 0.75% interest paid, resulting in a gain of 6.50% because of the interest rate differential.

You would also have an investment with the leveraged amount at 10:1 to 50:1. If your account was set with a leverage amount at the highest level of 50:1, you would make a 325% annual interest (6.50% × 50). In addition, the majority of FX trading platforms will offer repeated compounding and a daily payout for accumulated interest.

Keep in mind, you can add this money to your position and then see an additional compounding effect. In addition, having an idea of where the currency pair's interest rates may be headed, it will be advantageous for you to enter your trades early to seize the movement of this pair. Along with this estimate, you should also include all the information that you have previously gathered from your resources such as broker reports, websites, and from trader talk, which has sometimes proven to be invaluable.

Trader talk has been termed "word on the street," referring to all the chatter that comes from business news sources including CNBC and Bloomberg, whether it is on the Internet or TV shows. This can provide you with an additional source of information for where currency interest rates are headed and assist you in making a trade.

Along with all the information you can gather on currencies, there are also three forms of currency management that a central bank will utilize for regulating and controlling the home currency. One is linking the home currency value to one of a sturdier currency. This is referred to as "pegging" and is typically done for developing countries in Latin America and Asia.

Pegging one currency to another results in a fixed exchange rate. In addition, the volume of money currently in circulation and its growth rate may also have a relationship to the economy of the other country. This is because the pegged currency will also have its interest rate tied to the interest rate of the other currency. For example, if the Hong Kong dollar is pegged to the U.S. dollar at 7:1, the HKD will exchange into the USD at a fixed rate of seven HKD to one USD. Next, if the EUR/USD exchange rate is 1.5, then the USD exchanges into the EUR at 1.5 USD per EUR. Because the HKD is pegged to the USD the EUR/HKD exchange rate is $7 \times 1.5 = 10.5$ HKD per EUR. The same goes for interest rates. If the US Federal Reserve has set the USD interest rate at 0.5% to stimulate growth during a recession, the USD's exchange rate will be affected, and because of the peg, the HKD will be affected in lock-step.

Let's look at the example of China, whose currency exchange rate has been attached to the U.S. dollar for a very long time. In other words, the Chinese yuan has its exchange rate pegged for a specific amount of U.S. dollars. With this fixed value, as the USD sees its value go down versus the EUR, the Chinese yuan's value will also decline by the same percentage.

This pegging has worked out well for China's economy, in part because the USD is defined as the largest traded currency by volume worldwide (in 2010, more than 62% of trades were made in USD), according to the Bank of International Settlements website. In addition, many also believe this has worked for China's economy for all these years because, historically, this peg has been set at a falsely low rate, further assisting China to be competitive around the globe.

Some currencies are managed by utilizing a float/peg-like system. This differs from the Chinese yuan/USD relationship, as the currency value is consistently changed to the home country's benefit. A committee makes this up and down exchange rate adjustment depending on the needs of the home country. This has been referred to as a "dirty float."

In a second method for monetary management, central banks will utilize a technique called dollarization. This is defined as the central bank of one country ceding control for its currency by adopting another nation's currency. It is typically the home country that adopts a neighbor's currency—usually a strong trading partner or one that historically has shown economic stability. Examples for these types of relationships include the Caribbean Netherlands utilizing the U.S. dollar, the Cook Islands looking to use the New Zealand dollar, and Liechtenstein using the Swiss franc.

Dollarization offers the highest stability to these economic entities, but it cuts the home country's central bank's control of their own country's economy to almost nothing. They are at the mercy of the other country's currency, interest rates, growth of money supply, and shrinkage by that country's central bank. Even so, this can work effectively for either small countries or ones that have direct ties to the neighboring country.

The third and final method is called the floating rate system. This one may cause concern when you are looking for evolving FX trades. Before reviewing this technique, let's first take a look at the history and development of the gold standard 150 years ago. The gold standard had been the method of monetary management first developed and then adopted in the middle of the 1800s by the Bank of England. The system represented a definite face-value amount of paper money that would be exchanged directly for a specific amount of gold. The paper money's face value had virtually been fixed to a gold amount that been defined by the gold's fineness and weight.

All around the world, counties would issue gold coins to use for various reasons. For some, the gold coins had only been used for transferring wealth; it had not been utilized as a form of payment for everyday needs. There was an array of gold coins, including the following: German marks, Swiss 20 francs, Dutch guilders, etc. While each of these coins were different in fineness and weight, they were exchanged into each other by the gold content of each type of coin. For example, a larger Dutch Guilder had 0.1947 ounces of pure gold, while a Swiss 20 franc had .01867 ounces of pure gold. The conversion was simple: 1042 Swiss 20 francs would exchange into 1000 Dutch Guilders.

In 1944, the world adopted an international gold standard based on the convertibility for European currencies to the U.S. dollar; at the time, this had been pegged to a specific gold weight and fineness. It was simple: convertibility was $35 per ounce when the gold was 99.5% pure.

This evolved from the simple idea that rather than having gold coins circulated all over Europe as well as traded worldwide, the coins would be melted and formed into 400 ounce bars. All over the world, bars would then be stored in different vaults. The countries would have their gold on deposit, but could convert their gold holdings into dollars at a set rate, which would allow them to trade in dollars (much more convenient then moving heavy gold bars back and forth!). This evolved into a U.S. dollar/gold standard.

This currency management system was referred to as the Bretton Woods Agreement. It developed in response to the high indebtedness incurred by the different countries that had fought World War II. The system worked for a while, but when more gold flowed from the U.S. Treasury than into to it, flaws in the system became apparent. Gold had been flowing out so fast, that on August 15, 1971, U.S. President Nixon ended this U.S. dollar/gold standard by stopping the conversion of U.S. dollars to gold. Gold shipments from U.S. reserves also stopped.

After Nixon shut down the gold window and put an end to the Bretton Woods Agreement, dominant currencies around the world started to then move against one another as determined by supply and demand. This less-managed system has been named the floating rate system.

This method can be defined as the exchange rates not only between currencies, but the currency pair prices as they have been set by the central banks. Central bankers from the home countries could have a set amount that they desire to trade the currency at, but central banks utilizing this floating rate system typically do not go into the open Forex market or use other means to forcibly change the exchange rate of their currency. What this means, for example, is that the AUD and the NZD rates will be determined by the currency markets, along with the goods and services demand between New Zealand and Australia. This could also apply to countries including Europe, the United States, and many more.

Most times it is trade factors—the market forces, including supply and demand between two countries—that determines the market price of a currencies against one another. On occasion, a central bank may purchase and sell its own currency in the FX marketplace as a means to alter its currency pairs in relation to its trading partner. This type of activity took place late in 2010 through the middle of 2011 in Switzerland. The Swiss National Bank (SNB) had been utilizing reserves to purchase massive quantities of the euro in the open marketplace. Large amounts of Swiss francs were being sold by the SNB to buy up large amounts of Euros. This caused less Euros to be on the market, making the price of EUR to go up (remember: supply/demand) at the same time more Swiss francs were flooding the market, making the price of CHF to go down in relation to the price of the gaining EUR. The net effect was a lowering of the Swiss franc against the Euro. Other methods used by the SNB included using derivative agreements, to lower the price of its Swiss franc against the Euro. The SNB took these actions after the Swiss franc rose dramatically against the Euro when Euro block countries including Spain, Greece, and Ireland were having severe sovereign debt problems.

FX traders responded by looking at safe but low-yielding currencies, including the USD and the JPY but these didn't appear to be the best alternatives. In the end, the Swiss franc did become the best currency for a safe haven, and some news sources have said that CHF is as "safe as paper gold." While safe currencies may be a good thing, they do come with low yields worldwide. This stems from the notion that a lower-yield currency will typically equal a lower market price. Furthermore, if a currency already carries a low price, it also carries a lower opportunity to decline versus the currencies with higher yields.

During this time in Switzerland, there was a large rise in the EUR/CHF exchange rate, which favored the Swiss franc. The Swiss National Bank used its power, as well as its reserves, and brought its franc to a better-managed price level. The bank's methods did work for some time, as the franc's price dropped versus the euro, but pressure became high and SNB ended the battle.

This is a unique process and is referred to as intervening in the markets. Trading in a FX pair as a central bank is overriding the markets is not a good trading idea, as these actions are all encompassing and unexpected. Just the thought of a central bank going into the markets should be a red flag to stay away from that country's currency until notice has been given that the intervention has ended. Most of the time currencies in a floating rate currency system will move with market fluctuations, going higher or lower as the market does. These are the currencies to trade, as there is smooth movement and they may be predicted and tracked via fundamental analysis.

Technical Analysis

Technical analysis can be defined as studying currency pairs through graphs. By reviewing charts as well as utilizing the trading platform to both plot and create simple technical indicators, you are one step closer to creating a solid trading system.

As you saw earlier, fundamental analysis includes reading charts and market trading indicators, and then determining the right time to enter into currency pairs. Many times, you will use them for reviewing short-term trading patterns.

After you have done this for a while and you're comfortable, you'll start to get a feel for the right time to initiate and close the trades that you determine through fundamental analysis.

Technical analysis also includes using statistics and regression analysis as a way to look at the current market and trades. This comes from reviewing charts and graphs that enable you to view the market and trade pairs graphically. Traders skilled in technical analysis feel that trading decisions should be made from the analysis of charts and graphs, ignoring what the fundamental analysis indicates. Experienced traders or those with technical analysis certifications believe in this system based on three foundational ideas found in the Table 6-2.

TABLE 6-2 Three Theories Behind Technical Analysis	
Theory Name	**Description of Theory**
Crowd psychology	Crowds move in the same direction
Efficient market hypothesis	All information is reflected in the pair's exchange rate
Pairs revert to the mean	History repeats itself

The first of these is that information from currency trading includes loud chatter and if you listen too closely, you could end up going down the wrong road and making a bad trade even when you think you're on track to make the right one. Technical analysis enables you to use charts and graphs as well as fundamentals to screen the noise, and allows you to see clearly what to trade and when to do so. If you find yourself using technical information and producing technical analysis, you may want to consider applying for and studying for the Chartered Market Technician (CMT) designation and qualification. To qualify for this, three technical analysis exams need to be completed.

The Basics of Technical Indicators

This section covers the basics of technical indicators. Adding technical analysis to your trading can add a certain level of mathematics and science to an otherwise emotional trading environment. Read on to get into the basics of technical trading with technical analysis and technical indicators.

Support and Resistance Basics

Prices in the financial markets are affected by the number of buyers and sellers or supply and demand. When prices are at an equal place, they are referred to as support and resistance points. During times when more sellers than buyers are in the market, prices will decline. Switch this around, and with more buyers than sellers prices will rise.

And just to confuse you with a third situation, when market prices remain stagnant, this is called "price consolidation." You may also hear this referred to as a "pause" since buyers and sellers really aren't doing anything. Why this happens is due to different reasons but it doesn't mean there's a lack of opportunities to profit in this condition. Let's take a closer look at a pause by using these two instances: the present trend will continue or it will reverse. These are called support and resistance levels, with support defined as the place lower than present trading and resistance as a higher level than the present one.

These levels are often called power zones, as support and resistance levels become interchangeable terms.

A Look at Proactive/Reactive Support and Resistance

You can use support and resistance levels to aid your trading. This can be split into two areas: proactive support or reactive support.

Proactive support and resistance methods may be called anticipatory, as they suggest places that a price has not been yet. This comes from looking at present prices and then conducting analysis that will predict future prices. You may have heard of some of the methods that utilize proactive support and resistance procedures. You'll learn more about these later in this chapter.

You have the opposite scenario for reactive support and resistance procedures, which comes from action in either prices or changes in volume. This has been termed initial balance, OHLC (Open-high-low-close) open gaps, price swing lows/highs, and volume profile.

When to Use Power Zones

It's best to step back and revisit power zones. They can be utilized in numerous ways to help with your trading. This includes when to close either all or part of your current trading position. A power zone breakout can also be employed to either open a new trading position or add to a current one. Looking at a price as it goes into the power zone may help you decide on a new position or choosing the status quo. You may have a strategy that suggests it's time to buy as the price is under the zone; however, you may want to hold off after looking at the price's reaction to the zone of resistance. During this time, there are still different trading scenarios to implement in power zones.

Using some version of support and resistance in trading is the basis for the most profitable strategies that use technical analysis. You should add this strategy to your toolbox for trading; however, when you go ahead and employ it, you may face challenges as there are voluminous amounts of information and numerous available trading techniques that use support and resistance methods.

Take a deep breath, as we'll go through the information that will help you feel less overwhelmed by all the options. Luckily, you can keep on top of daily trading information.

Using Support and Resistance Indicators in Your Toolbox

Support and resistance methods enter all traders' toolboxes at some time or another, regardless of their experience level. In the past, maybe you're heard the statement on TV or read in the business pages that the market has hit a 50% resistance level, or resistance looks like a double top. You've also probably heard of moving averages and Elliott Waves—just to name a few—as ways to note support and resistance levels.

Should you use any or all of these indicators? The answer is most likely all of them and you can decide by asking yourself a few questions.

Power Zones and Your Marketplace Personality

Traders know markets have their peaks and valleys, with some phases having a lot of volatility or less, a bull market or a bear market, or interesting combinations from all of this. This can lead to a lot of frustration, as you may be scratching your head on which strategy to use. Something may have worked in one market condition but not in the next.

How do power zones factor into this scenario? It's similar to using different strategies. One support and resistance method may work for one market "personality" and other times a different one will need to be used.

So, here's your answer: Confluence.

This means that power zones are comprised of numerous mathematical methodologies for support and resistance that may sound a little foreign to you. These include calculated pivots, Elliot Wave, Fibonacci retracements/extensions and clusters, Initial Balance, intraday/prior day/week/month swing highs and lows, market profiles, moving averages, naked VPOCs (Volume Point of Control), OHLC, open gaps, trend lines, volume profiles, and VWAP (Volume Weighted Average Price).

Looking at Statistics

While putting together these methods to create a successful support and resistance recipe, let's take it one level higher with testing the use of statistics. Some of your research may include reviewing statistical calculations such as regression analysis to determine which methods to use at any one time, depending on what's happening in the current market.

Suppose the market is currently trending and your statistical testing suggests that volume profile levels may outperform in different methods. In this phase, the volume profile support and resistance method will carry greater weight in your analysis, no matter you trading time length.

By combining different methods of probability, you can produce unique support and resistance levels that will do best in the present market. This will help in your trading performance. At this point, you should also be able to see that numbers are combined not randomly but in an organized way. Keep in mind that markets will have their own unique personalities and phases. Just like trying to combine different people, some methods will work better for some than others.

What's the Market Profile?

The idea behind market profile comes from the knowledge that markets are organized by price, time, and volume. Every day, the market will see a range and value which is a new point for the day with equal numbers of buyers and sellers in the market. In the trading arena, prices will not remain stationary but instead they are consistently changing. A market profile can put together records of this activity and enable traders to review this information and make sense of it.

Component of Market Profile: Initial Balance

The Initial Balance is a measurement utilizing market profile; it represents the highs and lows from trading in its inaugural hour. You may find this statistical nugget interesting. In more than 68% of the time over the previous five years, a trading day's high or low has been determined in the time frame of the first hour of trading. Traders find it useful not only for the present day but also as a reference tool for the next day of trading.

What About the Volume Profile?

Let's put the market profile aside for a moment and talk about the volume profile. This means that the Point of Control (POC), Volume Average High (VAH), and Volume Average Low (VAL), and Volume Point of Control (VPOC) will remain pivotal points.

The volume profile is derived from aggregate volume versus price. The peaks and valleys represent the highs and lows of volume. They are likely to represent support and resistance levels with prices to represent to the levels from large volume amounts traded through time.

More Volume Profile through Naked Volume Points of Control (VPOC)

Naked VPOCs (or naked volume points of control) is produced from prior trading day numbers of the volume profile. VPOC may be defined as the price from the greatest number in volume for that trading day, while naked VPOC means the VPOC's price hasn't gone back to where it had originated from. This raises the potential for it to have heavy trading near that level with price movements of the future.

Volume Weighted Average Price (VWAP)–Measuring Average Price

VWAP is like a moving average, as it defines a ratio of the value traded against total volume traded over a specific period of time. This is commonly one trading day and the VWAP measures the average price of a product trading during that time.

Calculated Pivot Points

Pivot points mathematically come from support and resistance levels and the OHLC from the prior trading day. They use a number of formulas with names such as Camarilla, DeMark, Floor, Standard, and Woodie.

Standard Pivot Point Calculation

Standard pivots are calculated from the following formulas utilizing a range of time frames range including daily, weekly, and monthly time periods:

$$R4 = R3 + (H - L)$$
$$R3 = R2 + (H - L)$$
$$R2 = PP + (H - L)$$
$$R1 = (2 \times PP) - LOW$$
$$PP = (HIGH + LOW + CLOSE) / 3$$
$$S1 = (2 \times PP) - HIGH$$
$$S2 = PP - (H - L)$$
$$S3 = S2 - (H - L)$$
$$S4 = S3 - (H - L)$$

where H and L represent high and low, respectively; R1–R4 denotes resistance levels; PP indicates the pivot point; and, S1–S4 represent support levels.

Camarilla–A Pivot Point Calculation

Camarilla pivots are calculated using the following formulas with the same time frame ranges and the aforementioned abbreviations. The authentic Camarilla number set excludes a PP in the calculation while including the Close (C):

$R4 = (H - L) \times 1.1/2 + C$

$R3 = (H - L) \times 1.1/4 + C$

$R2 = (H - L) \times 1.1/6 + C$

$R1 = (H - L) \times 1.1/12 + C$

$S1 = C - (H - L) \times 1.1/12$

$S2 = C - (H - L) \times 1.1/6$

$S3 = C - (H - L) \times 1.1/4$

$S4 = C - (H - L) \times 1.1/2$

Woodie Pivot Point Calculation

Woodie pivots may be calculated from the following formulas using the afore-mentioned time frame and abbreviations from the standard pivot point along with the addition of the Open (O):

$R4 = R3 + (H - L)$

$R3 = H + 2 \times (PP - L)$

$R2 = PP + (H - L)$

$R1 = (2 \times PP) - LOW$

$PP = (HIGH + LOW + (OPEN \times 2)) / 4$

$S1 = (2 \times PP) - HIGH$

$S2 = PP - (H - L)$

$S3 = L - 2 \times (H - PP)$

$S4 = S3 - (H - L)$

A Calculation for Floor Pivot Point

Floor pivots may be calculated from the following formulas with the aforementioned abbreviations including support levels at S1–S3:

$R3 = (P - S1) + R2$

$R2 = (P - S1) + R1$

$R1 = (2 \times P) - L$

$PP = (H + L + C)/3$

$S1 = (2 \times P) - H$

$S2 = P - (R1 - S1)$

$S3 = P - (R2 - S1)$

Calculation for DeMark Pivot Point

The DeMark pivots formulas are shown below but differ from the aforementioned calculations in structure. PP is not a certified DeMark number but needs to be included to calculate these formulas:

The value for X depends on where the market closed.

If Close < Open then $X = (H + (L \times 2) + C)$

If Close > Open then $X = ((H \times 2) + L + C)$

If Close = Open then $X = (H + L + (C \times 2))$

$R1 = X/2 - L$

$PP = X/4$

$S1 = X/2 - H$

Technical analysis uses numerous charts and indicators such as a candlestick chart, Elliott wave principles, moving averages, regression analysis, and resistance levels. All of them employ the same ideas: taking the mathematics behind the currency pairs and either drawing lines or using statistics to create estimates for a good time to place trades. Some of these charts can be created from your FX trading platform. To do so, log in to your account and go to the section named Technical Indicators. Select the indicators you want to use and they will be included in your chart. Figure 6-1 shows Fibonacci series lines on a USD/SEK chart along with a 20/50 moving averages line. The Fibonacci series lines begin at the lowest point of the chart, which is the weakest point for the currency pair as evidenced by a fan-like gathering of the three lines. The chart has again gone up just by touching Fibonacci bottom line. Fibonacci lines are based upon a mathematical sequence of events. While complex to figure out for yourself, most trading software will have built in programs that allows the calculation of the formula just by placing your cursor at the bottom most point of a series of lines on a bar chart–in this way, the technical analysis software will calculate the ups and downs of the price of the currency pair in that time frame and then automatically calculate the three Fibonacci series lines.

These Fibonacci lines will then give a graphic representation of three levels (high, medium, and low) of support and resistance for that currency pair. This information can then be used to time your trades: for example, when a resistance is breeched (as shown by a Fibonacci line), there might be a breakout carrying the price of the currency pair well past that level. Traders use Fibonacci lines to quickly spot support and resistance points on their charts.

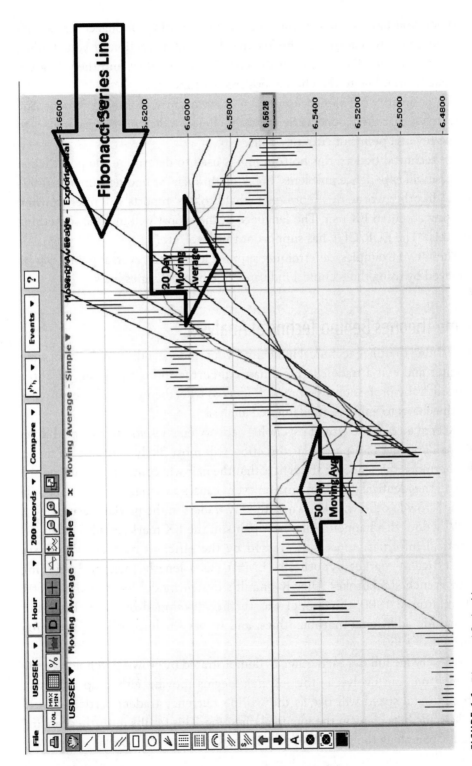

FIGURE 6-1 • Fibonacci Series Lines

When you have a chance, you can practice creating Fibonacci series lines on your charts by clicking in the Technical Indicators section of your trading platform software. Drop a pin in the chart's lowest valley, and then drag the Fibonacci series line to the chart's most recent time.

The popularity of Fibonacci series lines have occurred for many reasons, one of which is that the Fibonacci Series is a technical indicator used by traders to define reversal points of currency pairs.

For technical traders, this bottom line is used to determine the point when the pair will experience problems "breaking through" or finding "support at this level." In other words, this represents what brokers' reports will refer to when advising about an FX pair. The language in the report will include something like this: "The EUR/CHF has support at this level, etc."

These two examples, determining support levels and reversal points can be achieved by using the technical indicator of Fibonacci series lines.

Some Theories Behind Technical Analysis

By learning to utilize technical indicators, your understanding of the right time to enter and exit a trade can be enhanced. Furthermore, by seeing the three basic ideas by professional technical traders as true, then you will accept reading the charts to enhance fundamental analysis.

Acceptance of the crowd psychology theory enables you to accept that an FX pair moving in a particular direction will most likely continue to do so. Furthermore, the school of thought is that the pair will continue moving on the path in the identical direction until an event causes a change of ideas by people in the "crowd," otherwise known as the FX traders in the marketplace.

Why does this happen? All participants in the FX marketplace can access identical information, as is expressed by the efficient market hypothesis. The efficient market hypothesis (EMH) has a lengthy history, beginning with French stockbroker Jules Regnault's design model back in the 1860s. Then, around 1900, this model was further developed by Louis Bachelier to include additional mathemathics, and it was finalized by Eugene Fama during the 1960s.

As everyone follows each other, as demonstrated by crowd psychology, a big momentum can evolve as the FX pair begins moving either up or down. Strength and speed will rise as the world's currency traders participate and make trade bets going in the identical direction. This results in further moving the FX pair along the same direction, strengthening the number of same trades made by the world's FX traders. More and more traders will add on currency bets for the direction of that pair, until the point where a change in the crowd's sentiment occurs. This change could be based on either technical or fundamental information.

The crowd will develop the identical idea to change course all at the same time, and the direction of the FX pair will also start to change. This is the basis of the idea of the pairs revert to the mean theory. Momentum for the change in course will start to build and the direction of the FX pair will then move in the opposite direction. This change will continue until the process repeats itself. And once again, the crowd will go to the opposing direction.

By combining portions of theories and technical charts you can create a little bit of magic with your FX trading. This can help you decide about entering a trade—perhaps if and when to do so. This can also help to determine when this trade could begin to reverse, as well as help you decide when it is a good time to grab profits and quickly run prior to the crowd moving its sentiment toward a currency pair that you are currently trading.

At the time you start building an FX technical chart, you select a currency pair to trade. Let's use the example of seeking indicators for a EUR/CHF pairing.

You have already read broker reports and completed the studying of fundamentals. Now you will be able to have fundamental indicators assist you when determining a long EUR/CHF position coming from a review of the Swiss National Bank's website and reading news reports from DailyFX's website (www.dailyfx.com). You have also determined a large appreciation of the Swiss franc against the euro as well as a short-term regaining of strength by the euro.

Now it's time to look at this EUR/CHF currency pair on a chart but you will first have to draw one. One way to do this is through your Forex trading platform which will enable to you produce either a bar chart or a candlestick chart. Occasionally some of them will let you do both. If so, you can then go back and forth between the two by just clicking a mouse. Then you will be able to determine which of the two will work best for you in this scenario.

Let's review the two charts, beginning with a review of a candlestick chart, which has also been called a Japanese candlestick chart. It includes numerous vertical lines on a graph. These represent prices on the vertical lines while the times of day sit at the bottom (horizontal) part of the chart.

Maybe you will create a chart that has a 15-minute EUR/CHF. Your trading platform software will presents the pair's prices up on the chart, while the time of numerous days in 15-minute increments will appear at the chart's bottom. In addition, the EUR/CHF pair's actual price will appear for each trading period lasting 15 minutes.

You will see red and green lines. These are small and they will suggest the pair's price for every 15 minutes, but the trading range will also be indicated by the length of the green and red lines. A red line will suggest a downward movement, while a green line means the pair has risen during the 15-minute interval. Take a step back and review the time frame ranges in your charts. This can be helpful to you if you use a chart containing one day's worth of information. The chart will enable you to see a view of the currency's direction. You can also change to a shorter time frame review than 15 minutes. This could be helpful, and could include going to as short of a time span as 30 seconds. This chart can assist you with timing your FX trade more precisely.

Line Charts

You will likely find line charts easier to use than the candlestick chart, as well as being more intuitive. From a 15-minute line chart, the close and open for these time increments will be presented a by a left and right notch for the taller vertical line.

Should the currency pair go up and down on the open's price, then the line will display its ranges through either a shorter or longer line to cover the pair's prices during that 15-minute time frame. At its end, the close price will be shown by a notch on this line on the right for the longest vertical line.

When you view this on either a 15- or 17-inch laptop screen, a 15-minute chart line will be between one-half to one centimeter in length; this indicates the pair's movement (including EUR/CHF) during that period of time. Every 15-minute range line is near another one, and its effect will be a semi-smooth line going across the screen, exemplifying a chart of the price changes of EUR/CHF across time.

Timing Trades with Moving Averages

You have already used software from your trading platform to create a bar chart for the EUR/CHF currency pair. Now the next technical indicator to use is a 50-day moving average and a 200-day moving average. These averages will use statistical formulas from closing, openings, and even EUR/CHF pair averages from the previous 50 or 200 days on a rolling basis.

In other words, a 200-day moving average uses the last 200 days prices to calculate the average. In the next day, the average will be recalculated by dropping off the original first day of the 200-day's worth of prices (now 199 days of prices) and then adding yesterday's price (now 199-day prices plus yesterday's price = 200 days of prices) to be used to calculate the new 200-day moving average. In this way, the moving average is always "moving" with each new day's price. In addition, this is a rolling chart as defined by time. Meaning, if you create a one-hour chart, 200 days times 24 hours will be looked at and then in an hour, the 199 days added to 23 hours will be included as well as the last hour from the week of trading. The same holds true when using the 50-day moving average.

After you have your time frame determined, whether it is 15 minutes or another period of time, a bar chart can be created on your trading platform. This can easily be done by using the drop-down boxes labeled "Technical Indicators" from your software's commands. You will probably notice a command series from the drop down titled "Add Technical Indicators." Choose the one named "Moving Average." Now draw your chart by using your choice of day numbers.

You can first select 200-day in a thick-colored line, and then use a second thick line in a different color to create the 50-day moving average. For example, Figure 6-2 shows the setting and application of a 50-day moving average technical indicator.

In this example, using a one-hour time frame, two lines are created and the 50-day and 200-day moving averages are displayed, the lines will kind of follow the curve of the one-hour bar chart. A 50-day moving average reacts more sensitively to price changes and it will follow the bar chart more closely. This is illustrated in the above example by the lighter line.

The 200-day moving average will have less sensitivity and will move in a greater, slower almost more gently rolling pattern of of a line. This average is represented by the darker of the two lines. After creating a 50-day and a 200-day moving average chart as well as a one-hour chart from your trading platform, you can now use moving averages as your indicators. An easy way to do so is to create the 50-day and the 200-day and see their crossing points. You can see from the example, they do cross in three situations. The 50-day line is indicated and the 200-day line is the line running just along side of it—what you are looking for is points where the two lines intersect, or cross. Where the 50-day and the 200-day moving averages lines cross, technical analysis tells us that the Forex pair direction is changing and that new direction is likely to continue for a period of time.

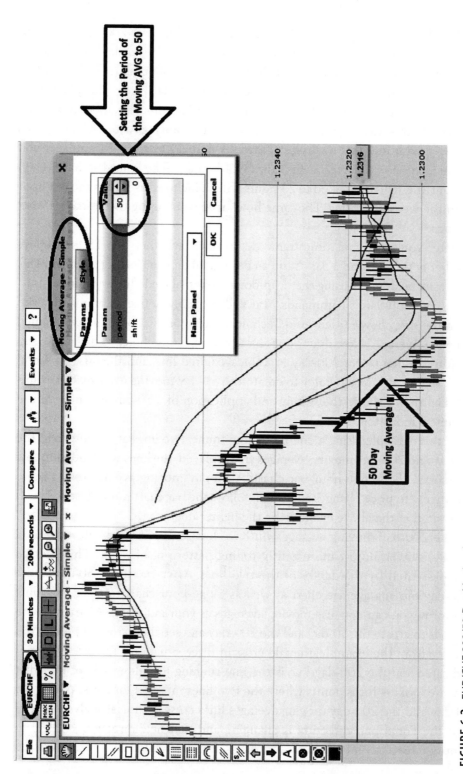

FIGURE 6-2 · EUR/CHF 200/50-Day Moving Average

After you've seen this cross-over point for the 50-day and 200-day moving averages, now it's time to support these observations by finding cross-over points for a 20-day moving average and a 100-day moving average. If this comparison creates the identical story, it is a good thing, as a trend is now developing. By looking at this example, you can now say this theory is true: a direction change is represented when two moving averages such as the 50- and 200-day averages cross. You will notice at the chart's end that the 50- and the 200-day moving averages are again starting to converge. If you enable your chart to go "live," and then set the 50 and 200 days to go along with the chart as time advances, you will see at some point that the 50- and 200-day moving averages again will converge.

At the time this occurs, you should review your fundamental information, such as broker's reports, interest rate expectations, and economics—to name a few—and then determine if you want to change the direction for your bets. Should the fundamentals confirm your decision and the technical indicators from the 50-day and 200-day indicators paint a similar picture, this represents a solid signal that the currency pair's direction is now changing. This currency pair's direction may only change for a day or two but you know that it only takes just a few days of movement to bring home a week's salary from currency trading.

Support/Resistance Indicators

You can use additional set indicators referred to as support and resistance indicators. They suggest a statistical and mathematical level for all currency pairs that are challenging to pass through. "Passing Through" or "Breaking Through" a resistance or support level is when the price of the security builds up enough momentum to go beyond the resistance or support level.

Getting to this point can sometimes be a major challenge as these levels are psychologically important, and the majority of traders worldwide will be avoiding placing their trades above or below the breakout point. The majority of brokerage firms will provide information for mid- and upper-support and resistance levels of the FX pairs that they cover.

By using either a broker's report or news services including DailyFX or FXStreet, you can quickly find data for these support and resistance indicators.

Support and resistances may be defined as price levels that are challenging to pass through as well as act as psychological indicators for traders. The indicators come from mathematical calculations for a certain currency pair to organically cease movement, whether it is in a downward (support) or an upward (resistance) direction. The lines represent estimates culled from the historical closes of the prior months, psychological significant levels (perhaps exceptionally good market news happened or bad market news happened near the support or resistance level) and the graphic lines called Fibonacci lines.

It is key to know how the support and resistance lines are created, as opposed to understanding how to create them on your own. Should you understand their basic meaning, then by all means go ahead and jump in to immediately use them within your personal trade plan. On occasion, it is good for you to know how to utilize either a statistical or technical indicator as opposed to spending lots of time attempting to run numerous scenarios and then trying to develop independently "fresh" information.

This idea may be similar to either understanding how to drive a car or first knowing how to design one. In the end, should you really desire to be somewhere, all you need to do is turn the car key and leave. It doesn't require a mechanical engineering degree when you just want to go to the store in your own car!

You will discover that some Forex news feed services will provide great quality technical analysis, but it will typically come at a price to gain access for these types of reports. However, if you pay for these top products, the information will assist you when you trade FX, or will at least help you back-up the technical analysis you have conducted yourself.

You can also say this about support and resistance lines: Because almost every broker's report, news feed, and FX trading website will publish the first and second support and resistance lines for each currency pair, you should spend time learning to utilize this information and not how to create it. After becoming familiar with using this means of technical information to help time the trades that you make, you can think about studying and reading to learn how you can create your own independent data. Meanwhile, you should utilize the information sources that you have at your fingertips.

Technical analysis may be considered a science and most professionals who conduct this analysis will create identical information, which will be published with the same identical support and resistance levels for consumers of this information. This is an advantage you'll find from a subscription to a high-end news services. With access to brokers' reports, most of the work has been done.

Fibonacci lines are derived from the theory of three levels from a currency pair's own peaks and valleys. These lines are created with the lowest point to the highest one during a time frame. Then, three levels are drawn at statistically key levels that have been preset. Exit and entry points are determined from these vital levels.

FX technical analysts will utilize software to create lines on their trading platform charts. Levels are viewed by worldwide currency traders, which gives credence that support and resistance levels do have significance. Around the globe, traders know if a level has been broken, then other traders will see it and react either in a positive or negative manner. This is an example of "crowd psychology" mentioned earlier in this chapter. This will be determined by their positions' directions.

Once a level has broken, theoretically, a breach will soon take place for the next level. After this, fast movement will then take place until the third level is reached. The swift movements in the levels are real for support and resistance: the level's breaching is what's important as opposed to the direction. Yes, some will win from this while others will lose for up or down movement of a currency pair.

When you begin understanding and using support and resistance indicators with your own trading, you will be on a path to utilizing a strong technical indicator to assist with the fundamental research that you conduct.

Here's a little background on Fibonacci lines theory and the three resistance levels. They are based on the "golden ratio." Fibonacci (originally called Leonardo of Pisa) initially introduced this concept in his book, written in 1202, entitled *Liber Abaci,* or *Book of Calculation.*

On your software from your trading platform, you can use the key technical indicators and create charts. This includes learning to utilize candlestick and bar charts to create a graphic visual of a currency pair's past and its future. You may also use a chart to view the FX pair move down and up through time; then you can select both short- and long-term time frames. Longer-term time horizons, including a one-hour or a single-day chart, can paint a picture of what's going on with a currency pair. Short time frames like those shown on 1-, 5-, or 15-minute charts, can assist to strategically decide the instant timing for a decent point to enter into a trade.

After you have drawn a basic chart, then you can expand to utilizing moving averages. This can be achieved by using your own software to create 50-day and 200-day moving averages employing various colors. Keep in mind to pay attention to where movement occurs in the average line crossing, as this is likely the direction where the FX pair will change its direction either up or down.

You can use this information and then utilize it against the information that has accumulated in your daily trading journal. Make notes in the journal when you predict the 50-day and 200-day moving averages will again cross. Some brokerage's trading platforms enable you to make free-form lines within your personal chart.

If you can do this through a broker's software, then choose the option to draw lines and derive an estimate for when the 50-day and 200-day moving averages will cross again sometime in the future. Now create a line across, then down. Make notes for the time and price this crossover point is likely to occur. You can utilize your software and place a pin on this point within the chart.

Don't forget to note this in your journal!

This represents a method of actively seeking entry and exit points by utilizing a little math as well as logic. It is good to be proactive when trading, not reactive. You should keep an eye on the success of your predictions. If you are improving at this predictive-type of analysis, then go ahead and move to the next level and start placing either the suitable long or short trades through a demo/practice account. Now, observe again and make notes as to the market's reaction at the time and price for this FX pair.

You can also learn about using technical indicators as a means of science to increase your observations in conjunction with fundamental information. By combining this type of learning via strategic observation and then making mock trades through a demo account, as well as marrying this with fundamental analysis, you can develop a robust trading system. This will let you predict and become proactive with your FX trades.

As you have learned throughout this chapter, a solid trading system will become a foundation to keep your active FX trading account in a profitable range over the ensuing trading days. It will also allow you to stay in the game and productively trade Forex.

QUIZ

1. **Fundamental research uses what elements to determine Forex values?**
   A. Interest rates
   B. Growth rates
   C. Economic indicators
   D. All of the above

2. **A country's growth rate and inflation rate is on its:**
   A. Public website
   B. National newspaper website
   C. Media sources, like CNBC
   D. Central bank website

3. **When looking for a potential trade keep in mind that:**
   A. All currencies are different
   B. All currencies are the same
   C. You'll need to compare two currencies
   D. It is best to take into consideration growth rates, interest rates, and central bank bias
   E. C & D

4. **Technical research uses:**
   A. Computers and the Internet
   B. Complex programs
   C. Charts and mathematical indicators
   D. All of the above

5. **A moving average is a measure of a Forex pair's previous closings.**
   A. True
   B. False

6. **One of the most effective ways to use moving averages is to combine time frames such as the:**
   A. Highest and lowest
   B. Fastest and slowest
   C. Biggest and littlest
   D. 200 day and 50 day

7. **Most Forex platforms allow the building of technical charts and indicators.**
   A. True
   B. False

8. **One of the best ways to trade is to combine:**
   A. Fundamental and basic research
   B. A trading journal and a trading calendar
   C. Fundamental and technical research
   D. B & C
   E. All of the above

9. **Pivot points come from support and resistance levels.**
   A. True
   B. False

10. **It is best to use similar time frame (200/50- and 100/20-day) moving averages when combining them.**
    A. True
    B. False

Chapter **7**

How to Make Trading Ideas Work

In this chapter, you will learn the following:

- How to build a conservative FX portfolio for income
- How to trade currency exchange-traded funds (ETFs)
- More about the FX demo account
- The importance of recordkeeping for tax time
- Ideas of how to build up your Forex account

Ready to limit your risk and get some fresh ideas on trades? This chapter covers using currency trading in a 90/10 bond/FX portfolio. The chapter also covers using currency ETFs in conservative trading for proxy. Finally, this we'll reveal how to put it all together and run your FX account just like a small business.

Enhance Your Existing Income with FX

Most people seek the greatest gains in the shortest amount of time in their FX accounts. However, there is a more conservative goal for some investors. These investors share an alternate view of the Forex account as an extended savings account with interest earnings. The capital gains which result are a secondary part of their investment strategy. These investors use a type of strategy called investing for total return, by combining both the interest and capital gains.

Some investors use their FX portfolio as an account for total returns. In this way, the currency balance sits in cash for up to 80% of the time The active trades only comprise 20% of the time the account is used. In the meantime, a trader seeks to spend 10% of his or her time finding extremely good trades. They trade only to pick up the maximum of capital gains, using one-third of their total margin, and subsequently dividing the trades into three trades/three time frames to buy into the select pairs.

Using this strategy, a trader closes out every trade at the slightest hint of a minimum gain. Trading like this means you hit the "close order" button the moment the trade goes "green" on the P&L chart. Remember, trades like this can be closed at a few tenths of a percent of a gain. The idea is to create regular interest in the account in a short time frame. Even these tiny tenths of a percent will accumulate in the account as an interest bearing function.

Traders understand that the longer the amount of time you are involved in a specific trade, the risks increase. Trades that go overnight or over a weekend have huge amounts of risk involved versus closing out a trade with a bare minimum of the smallest percentage of a return.

FX accounts pay continuously compounding interest that is calculated every second, thus giving you a much better rate of return than if you parked the money in a traditional savings account. Total return investing will enhance an FX portfolio, even if the gains are miniscule.

This method of trading is excellent for investors seeking safety and who are not concerned about maxing out profits. Keeping an account sitting tight on cash for the majority of time and then only actively trading when the trades are highly profitable, will allow investors to earn 5% to 10% from accrued interest and gains year over year. Ideally, a trader would only have to work on trades a few days a month, with only one or two hours of trading at a time to get the absolute minimum of trades completed for this strategy.

In addition, a trader using this very conservative method could reduce further his risk by using just one-tenth of his full margin at each trade, instead of the usual one-third. Using a smaller amount further decreases the risk involved and makes any possible losses very, very tiny. However, trading this way requires more hands-on involvement, more than the simple or automated trading done in more aggressive trading systems. One of the best times to trade with this method is in the early afternoon, when the markets are generally slow. Having a slow market gives a trader more time to react when a price moves up or down. Traders of this strategy often use a time frame chart of 15 or 30 seconds to time their open and closing points.

Conservative Investing and T-Bills

Most conservative investors have part of their overall portfolios invested in cash, bonds, CDs, or even bond mutual funds. One way to gain the stability of bonds with the returns of the stock market is to create a mix of one-tenth in currencies and nine-tenths in Treasury bills (T-bills).

Many financial advisors of high-net-worth clients suggest using this mix for their big investors. The theory behind it is to have low-risk AA rated T-bills systematically spread in a laddered manner. As your portfolio will be mainly in low-risk bills, nearly 90% of the portfolio is never at risk. This 90% investment in T-bills will earn 0.01–1.0%, depending on the market.

While the United States' credit rating has taken a hit recently from AAA status to AA, T-bills still rank high for safe investments. Other government bonds might be rated higher, however, they often are issued in the foreign nation's currency and are not as lucrative as the United States government debt's dollar denomination.

The remaining 10% of your conservative portfolio will be shunted over to your FX account. Using the strategies outlined previously, you can handle this portion of your investment to capture capital gains and interest for carry trades to enhance your bond portfolio. This strategy allows you to remain conservative, while still trading to capture part of the risk sentiment of the worldwide market, therefore realizing gains from risk trades or by proxy.

The 90/10 strategy can earn gains similar to having the FX portion invested in the S&P 500 index. In other words, you will try to replicate the effect on your account with 10% invested in index options. By using the FX in place of using index options, to options, you can skip the massive fund requirements and intricate trading that accompanies trading options. Plus, Forex trades have no expiration date—unlike options, which expire in a few months at most—and so may be carried for weeks, months, or years. In addition, FX trades enjoy the benefit of netting worldwide gains in the market. Lastly, FX offers diversification by allowing you to trade four, five, or more currency pairs simultaneously.

Changing up your Forex currency pairs can makes it simple to go long on AUD/USD or short on others. Developing economies, such as Poland, may catch your eye. Try a pair like EUR/PLN for moderate risk and a bit more growth potential. Countries like Poland are working to run a conservative national currency, with some nations successfully paying down debt and others running cash surpluses. Some countries may have stronger economies than their counter-currencies. For these reasons and more, currency pairs can make a lot of sense and keep you diversified.

Keep in mind that putting 10% of your funds into an FX account can capture gains and quickly add to the lower returns of the T-bill nest egg. You can further reduce your risk by limiting the amount to only 25% of available margin versus the previously suggested 33%. Check your risk even more by taking that 25% and sectioning it into fourths. This type of trading will also help you get a feel for the market and how it works. The broader you cast the net of currencies, the wider your diversification will be and more likely to stand strong in the shifting market. For example, see Figure 7-1 showing the volatility and returns of the CurrencyShares ETF (FXS) Swedish Krona Trust against the steady returns of the 3-month U.S. T-bill ETF (BIL).

Currency Exchange-Traded Funds (ETFs): Watching, Dealing, and Trading

Here is another safe way to invest in the currency market, the currency ETFs. Although they are inwardly structured like mutual funds , outwardly they trade just like stocks. Gaining in popularity over the past five years, ETFs have become more common. A few of the highly prosperous ETFs rank high up on stock traders' day trading favorites. Some are even utilized by large fund managers to establish positions in otherwise hard-to-access markets.

Currency ETFs are often invested in money markets, made up of bank CD's and cash denominated in the home nation's currency. ETFs follow the ebb and

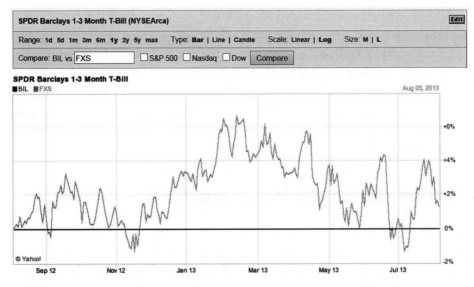

FIGURE 7-1 · ETF (FXS) Swedish Krona Trust vs. US T-Bill ETF (BIL)

flow of the currency price as their value, and can pay out a plump dividend as interest rates change. However, the interest is paid just monthly and it is not reinvested into the ETF.

Traders can find a list of the best currency ETFs on the CurrencyShares website at http://www.currencyshares.com/home/CurrencyShares. Currency-Shares also has different FX substitutions, including ETFs for the Euro, Swiss franc, Australian dollar, and others.

For investors seeking to work on currency trading for diversification and who want an ideal way to capture gains versus the USD but avoid highly lever-aged accounts, ETFs may be a suitable match. Normal full-service brokerages, as well as some discount brokers, offer ETFs for purchase just like stocks. A trader inputs limit orders, stop losses, and take-profit orders, just as you would on stocks, and very much in the same way as a typical FX account is handled.

Other ways to use currency ETFs are to build a hedge with the ETFs. This is a great way to spread out your risk. Consider creating a hedge against your long AUD, SEK, and CZK positions by purchasing an index-future EFT like VXX. This ETF allows you to gain upside returns when the markets are tumultuous and your FX trades fall. This works because this ETF gains in value when the market enters into turmoil. VXX follows the Options Exchange Market Volatility Index, also known as the VIX.

Additionally, you can use leverage to buy ETFs but your leverage amounts are limited just as if you were buying stocks.

Currency ETFs are an excellent solution for new investors who are still wearing training wheels and learning about the Forex currency pairs market. Check with your broker for ETF reports and be sure to visit the central banking sites, as well as delve deeper in the specific ETF of choice. FX investing with currency ETFs may be an ideal solution and can be worked into your overall investment strategy.

Taking the Demo Account Out for a FX Test Drive

It is always a lot more exciting to take out a demo account full of fake money to test out the real markets. Signing up for a free demo account won't cost you a penny and you can gain a lot of knowledge painlessly by using it for practice. First, research which Forex broker you prefer and then sign up to use their free proprietary demo account. Many of them will allow access to their free trading platforms as well.

After you've signed up, go ahead and login and select your starting balance, usually $100,000 to $1,000,000. As fun as it might be to click on the $1M box, try to remember that unless you're really putting in a million dollars, the demo won't run very realistically for you when the time comes to put in your actual cash of $3,000. Head down to the lowest setting to practice on and it will feel a little easier when you fund your real account later on, and your overall experiences will be closer to reality. Once you get used to buying outrageously high amounts of currency in a practice account, returning to a base level of $3,000, $5,000, or even $500 may tarnish your viewpoint tremendously.

Secondly, set your margin. Again, keep it close to reality. If you plan on using it outside the demo at 50:1, set it to 50:1 now. Otherwise, changing it after the demo will dramatically shift the speed at which you collect profits or losses. If you get used to using a lower margin ratio at the start, and switch it later on, the odds are high that your account will dry out swiftly and you will struggle to figure out what went wrong. A typical novice mistake, changing your leverage ratios can blow up an account very quickly. New investors may place too big of an order and forget that the FX pair moves five times faster in a 50:1 account versus a 10:1 leveraged account. The best way to prevent this is to set your margin and leave it untouched for the rest of your FX trading investment business.

A key point about this book is the underlying assumption that the margin for a trading account will be set at 50:1. Although the 50:1 ratio is five times higher than the 10:1, even conservative investors can still maintain control by limiting the size of their overall amount of margin used.

Smaller ratios means smaller gains, but it is still best to park your margin and leave it alone. It will be one less thing you will need to worry about when the markets are in full swing. Training yourself to be an expert on a single ratio will go a lot farther for improving your investing skills than acclimating too slowly to a different ratio.

Living the FX Trading Lifestyle

Many folks believe the daily life of the FX trader affords an admirable lifestyle. It is really all up to you and your own choices of what is most important. Parents with kids might get in snatches of market news during the evenings or weekends. Single adults may work swing shifts that allow them to trade during select times only. Still others may aggressively trade night and day. The idea is still the same for all these traders, which is to make the FX trading lifestyle a part of your natural rhythm instead of forcing it on you.

Forex trading will just not work if it becomes a hassle, or is too difficult or stressful to find a smooth flow to your trading commitments. Perhaps it is a time issue or a scheduling conflict that forces you to halt your preferred routine of trading. Some folks can't find the right budget and lose interest in funding their accounts after a while. Others decide to remain conservative and only trade once in a while when the setups are too good to pass up. Any way you slice it, the markets won't mind if you take off a week, a month, or even return to the demo account for a while. Trading is a skill that only gets better with time and practice and even the best traders still take a vacation from it once in a while.

Redefining your life for the sake of a trading account is not the path this investment guide seeks to put you on. Whatever your current state of employment, marital status, economic class, geographic location, that needs to be taken into account as part of your trading lifestyle. Some investors get ramped up with $50.00 in their accounts. Others start with $10,000. Some may start wading into the markets and then find out they need fresh ideas for setups. Others may never have heard the word Forex before in their lives and had to look it up on Investopedia just to understand the title.

No matter where you start from, you have the ability to take it further on from here. New traders and expert traders can use low-risk, high-risk, or middle-of-the-road plans, but all the time put towards reading, learning, and looking for good trades will solidify your own personal FX trading system and make it work for you. It also makes you stop and think about how much time and effort you really want to put into your trading efforts. Finally, the amount of money you would like to earn from your efforts can go a long way to defining what your lifestyle will be like.

Building Up Your Winnings

Losses hurt and winning feels great, so naturally, you'll want to go for more winning trades. But if you're new to currency trading, the cold splash of reality and losing your money can be a strong wake-up call. Let's get you to the winning side by using knowledge, planning, loads of skill, and a bit of luck and your FX account will become a cash cow. The best part is, once you've earned some dough, you'll be able to take some out and enjoy it!

Compounding your money to make more money and never taking time to enjoy it will set you up for a major fallout in the markets. Accumulating bigger and bigger piles of money for its own sake is not the end game. Many investors fall victim to the winner's curse when they win too often. They feel invincible, usually right before a massive loss that wipes them out. Be extra careful when you seem to suddenly be on a "winning streak."

Here is the best way to prevent the winner's curse: give yourself permission to take out some of the money in your account; let's say any amount over 20% or 25% gains on a weekly basis. Many traders will disagree, saying this is illogical to pull out funds when you should ideally let them grow larger. However, the fact remains if you don't enjoy your winnings, who will? Large amounts of money are not bad by themselves. Piling up cash in order to skim off a bit to pay bills or enjoy a special vacation is not a losing strategy. In fact, consider this: you are simply paying yourself for your patience, skills, expertise, and hard work when you take a bit off the top to put it back in your pocket.

Reward yourself with a personal paycheck, paid by you, for you, straight out of your FX trading account. This is for when your account is profitable and you are making enough winning trades to cover losses and make gains regularly. Put a preselected amount to the side for reinvestment and take out the rest over and above that amount. Perhaps you've got a goal in mind, such as a vacation, a down payment on a new car or home, or eliminating a nagging credit card debt.

If you run your FX account as if it were a business, you'd expect a paycheck after the first two weeks. It may take a bit longer to get your account established and profitable, but the idea should persist. Pay yourself! When you have a preset amount of money coming out of your account every two weeks, you are setting yourself up for an automatic reward. You will begin to see your trading account as a valid business, which in turn will help keep you on track and stay motivated to do more than rack up piles of cash.

Sadly, too many traders fall victim to the winner's curse and lose interest in currency trading. Perhaps the challenge they thought was there, the attitude of beating the market, is no longer appealing after creating such large profits. Some traders may feel it is too easy, too simple, and are bored. Others may up their risk levels, change their margins, and try to whip things into a higher gear to see what risks they can take. This is exactly how many fruitful accounts get eliminated. Becoming overconfident, feeling flush with winning, can all lead to risky decisions and less reliable setups for trades. When this attitude arrives, it is best to remove some money from your accounts. If nothing else, use the excess to diversify some of your holdings such as by buying a mutual fund.

One type of mutual fund that may work well in this situation is a multi-strategy fund, such as a Barclay Multi Strategy Index fund or UBS's Dynamic Alpha. Funds such as these step outside traditional definitions for hedge funds and use a variety of strategies to allocate capital. They are essentially a mutual fund that is managed like a hedge fund, with long/short and leveraged stock/bond/derivative investments. Although their performance can add stability to your larger investment goal, they can also reduce risk out of your portfolio by further diversification. Keep in mind, however, that multi-strategy funds never follow a standard so their performance lies outside of the stock and bond market.

The above suggestions are just a random selection of ideas of what to do with excessive amounts of winnings. The first step is to always build up your account first. Then, later on, you can remove some funds every so often to reduce the risks. Forex portfolios can accumulate funds quite fast. Learning how to deal with a much larger balance is also something that takes time and practice. A $50.00 trade runs differently than a $5,000 trade. Again, allow for a learning curve when the money levels change. This is a great place to be in and be sure to enjoy your profits!

Paying the IRS

Enjoying profits does come with responsibilities to the tax man. Keeping excellent records of every single transaction on your account is vital at tax time. It is also important to have a very good tax accountant. Consider opening a separate checking account (for your FX business only) that you can take profits from and record losses through, as well as indicate cash flow for deposits and withdrawals. Keep copies of all your expenses, including broker fees, newspaper subscriptions, periodicals, books related to trading, CPA fees, and training materials.

Running your currency account like a business will help you to consolidate your bills and expenses for recordkeeping purposes. The IRS likes to see a clear paper trail of deposits, withdrawals, receipts, and bills for reasonable work-related expenses. In addition, all the income and interest your account gains will be recorded and forwarded to the IRS from your brokerage account.

Plan ahead with your accountant to get the most out your dollars spent on building your Forex business accounts by maximizing deductions for your home office (if applicable). These may include your laptop, other computer hardware, Smartphone, iPad, Internet connection services, and other services related to your business. Talk with a certified accountant to find out what type of deductions you qualify for. In some cases, you can also write off expenses such as coffee and meals out that you paid for while trading outside your home office. If you are interested in taking a self-study course in trading or similar training education, these may deductible as well.

Finally, running your Forex account like a business is a major responsibility. Then again, handling your finances is not to be taken lightly. Remember to track your income by printing out a monthly screenshot of your profit-and-loss statements, and resetting them to zero at the first of the year. Aligning your account with a business plan or model can help you to stay organized and efficient in your business (and less emotional), while creating motivation to reap more profits from your hard work and training. By creating a high standard of professionalism in your currency trading account business, you will also reinforce why you're doing this. Businesses only exist to make profits!

Working Solution for Your Currency Trading Program

This is the part where everything we've talked about in the past few chapters aligns to make a working solution for your currency trading program. First, we'll discuss selecting an appropriate FX brokerage, then this section moves on to some key elements for growing a sizable trading account. Learning how to develop skills such as these takes time and emotional maturity as well. Finally, putting currency trading together to make it work for you and help you become financially independent is the last piece of the Forex currency account puzzle.

Everyone has a great broker they'll tell you all about. The one they wish they had! You can always close your eyes on the Google search page and wave your finger or your cursor over a broker's website if choosing one gets hard. However, FX brokerages essentially offer the same basic packages with low account minimums and access to high margins. Comparing them side by side can reveal a lot more details.

Getting your money loaded into an FX account is fairly simple across the board for brokers. Here's the key: The way it gets loaded in is the same way you'll get it out, in most cases. This comes by way of the anti-money laundering laws from a few years back. So if you do not require the funds immediately, a simple check can work just fine. Some traders prefer instant transfers and that can cost a lot more. Decide beforehand how you want the account to reside, with fast payouts or slow payouts. Be sure you can live with it.

In addition to following anti-money laundering laws, many brokerages follow U.S. law even if they are based elsewhere. Still others follow the trading laws of the country they are residing in. Some FX brokers allow gold and silver margin trading in addition to currency pairs. Regulated by European Union authorities, they have margins up to 500:1. On the opposite end is OANDA, which uses U.S. regulations, with only a 50:1 margin for FX trades, and allows gold and silver trading, but at the spot price without leverage.

Keep in mind too, that brokerages must remain competitive to gain your business and cash. They hold similar pricing arrangements and usually only differ on the number of currency pairs offered in trading. All brokers will offer the Big Four pairs JPY, USD, EUR, and GBP (the "big four" pairs are the currencies that are of the largest trading volume as recorded by the Bank of International Settlements) and the basic favorite trading pairs, but only a few brokers will offer the proxies on European currencies like NOK, SEK, and various exotics like the Icelandic krona (ISK), Hungarian forint (HUF), Polish zloty (PLN), and Russian ruble (RUB). As discussed in previous chapters, those types of pairs are key to trading currencies as has been described. Figure 7-2 compares these exotic currencies.

Interested in futures and options? Some currency brokers are set up for these as well as international currency exchanges. Look into brokers that offer a wider range of services to find one-stop shopping for your portfolio needs. One of these brokerages is Interactive Brokers, which allows trading with many different investment vehicles in one centralized account.

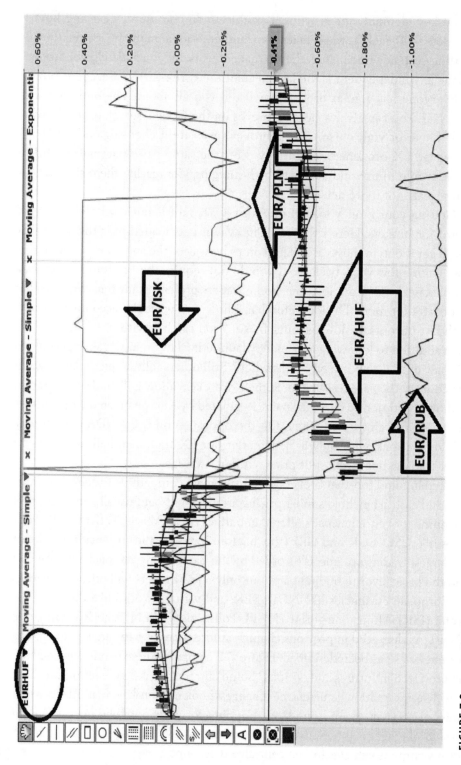

FIGURE 7-2 • Exotic Currencies

The tools of the Forex trade, the trading software, is the one element all brokerages maintain bragging rights about. "Easy to use" is the description of choice used by many of the brokerages to talk up their proprietary systems, but all the software runs on the same data. In reality, each trader works in their own way and what works great for one person may or may not be ideal for the next trader. As a new trader, simple and easy will work for you; however, a seasoned trader may feel restricted if they are running on a bare-bones system. A more complex system often means more automation for trading program platforms using C++ or similar computer languages. Check with your selected broker to see if they will accommodate your needs down the line should you decide to dive into more complicated trading waters. One of the more common advanced trading platforms is Call MT4 or Meta Trader 4. Many Forex companies allow trading in two formats, the more intuitive, basic style and the MT4 platforms.

Finally, many of the introductory-level brokers do not offer a basic report of your trades. Much like a checking account ledger, FX accounts need to have records of each transaction as well as each gain or loss and the fees paid. Some brokers will offer a simplified profit and loss statement or they may have something more sophisticated linked to your account. Regardless, this trading history must be documented over the weeks, months, and years. A detailed report generated from your broker will be of great value when it comes time to pay your taxes.

Not everyone wants to go at a snail's pace when trading FX, yet each trader must fund their first account, be it with $250 or $50,000. Whether choosing to be aggressive or conservative in your trading habits, over time you will grow the account and have fun doing it. In fact, smaller sized accounts are great to start with, as losing $0.50 is far easier to handle than losing $5,000 on a single bad trade. Everyone has trades that fail (or lose money). Some traders lose 60% of their trades and rely on winning trades 40% of the time and they are still highly profitable. It takes time, patience, and effort to learn how to build smart trades and then work them into profits.

For many people, working with money is a different sort of skill. Always start with smaller amounts when beginning to trade currency, as this is the time to take off the training wheels, but not hit the hills yet. Just like riding a bike, finding your natural balance in the ebb and flow of winning and losing trades is something that each investor works on at their own pace. Falling off a bike or losing a trade can hurt, but getting mad at the bike or the market won't help. Fear, greed, and guilt also play into a trader's mindset and oftentimes run wild through the markets. Learning how to deal with such feelings while running a trade is best done with smaller, less risky amounts of money.

For some people, it is easier to simply add more money into their account on a regular basis, such as $50 every Monday or $100 the first of the month. This helps you level out the amount of money you are working with in your active trading account, as well as helping you to gain increased knowledge of trading by the time the increases affect your account's balance. This is the easiest way to ramp up your skill with using money, as well as offsetting the emotions of bigger wins and (eventually) occasional bigger losses.

Handling money is a skill key to FX trading and not one to ignore. Finding success in your trading will encourage you to add funds. Having a regular weekly or automatic monthly deposit to rely on will help you grow your account faster as you continue to grow your skill set.

The easy part is adding money to your account and trading bigger and bigger amounts. The next challenge will be finding the money to continue to fund your account over the long run. A trader needs to have access to increasingly more amounts of cash. After getting fully invested, the next thing you can do is arrange a personal budget to find "extra cash" that can be diverted into your Forex account, from your everyday expenses to larger savings, getting more money into your trading account can be key to getting the account big enough to win profits that affect your lifestyle. Find low stress ways to free up more cash, such as that unused $30 monthly gym membership, or brown bag your lunch twice a week at work. Investing in your future can be painless and fun at the same time.

Building up your account should not be a source of anxiety and it does not need to consume large sums. It does need to be set up with a minimum amount each month, determined by your balanced budget at home. If you don't have a balanced budget yet, even better! You can set it up to pay yourself first before your other bills are taken out of your monthly take-home pay. If you take $100 off the top, and act like it doesn't even exist, then you won't miss it when it comes to paying bills and you'll automatically adjust your cash flow to accommodate it. Even better, how about that next raise that is coming your way? You've already been living without it for the past 12 months, why not put it all into your FX account as an investment. A person making a wage of $35,000 a year with a 2.5% raise can put $875 right into their account. That's already $72 a month (before taxes), so why not skip the $5 latte and go for the $1 McDonald's coffee twice a week and you're in the black for funding your FX account over $100 a month, every single month! Now put that $100 to a 50:1 margin and that's $5,000 worth of currency. Invest that in a carry trade at 4.5% net interest for 12 months and you'll be a lot farther ahead than a mere 2.5% raise.

Gaining Trading Skills

Not all traders are born with their best trades winning straight out of the gate. It can be very frustrating to new traders who are riding the learning curve to have their trades lose frequently, especially in the beginning. Dedicate the time and effort to reading the central bank websites, financial news feeds, brokers' reports, and articles. It will become second nature soon enough to read the technical charts and know before you pull the trigger why the trading pair you are about to use makes sense. Read and absorb as much information related to your favorite pairs as you can. Gaining more information, finding additional resources, and reading new books and periodicals will only help expand your knowledge base and improve your trades exponentially.

Getting into currency trading is an ideal way for those long-term investors who seek to ride a new endeavor with a hands-on approach to expand their portfolio. As with any new job, hobby, or skill, it takes time to learn about the FX market and even more time to get really good at it. Keeping the losses at arm's length and remaining objective is also a learned habit that experienced traders appreciate. When you're good enough to draw a part-time paycheck from your FX account, that's when you'll know you have expertise and skill.

Worldwide events have a ripple effect on the international economy. Some of the best lessons can be gained from watching stories unfold over time. A specific condition that results in an effect on the FX market could take months to finally fully develop, and even longer for traders to recognize a trend. But eventually, you'll see enough patterns that you'll be able to see the likely outcome before it finally occurs.

Without a doubt, the best learning is done over a long period of time. Patterns and trends will come later, as you work through the mountains of information on a daily basis. Regularly checking the news feeds and taking a step back to digest the data will put you on top of the next trend. With this being said, trading over time is the best way to trade. A scalper only wants to be in a trade for less than 60 minutes. Perhaps you're mostly a carry trader and decide to be in a trade for several months or even a year or two. Both traders need to learn about the system they want to follow and devote the time necessary to learning it inside and out. A demo account should whet your appetite for the real thing and inspire you to learn even more before jumping into the real deal. Continuing to practice along on the demo account as you watch real-time events unfold to better understand how the economies of the world interact and why. This will put you in the driver's seat of the dynamics underlying the FX market, allowing you to find the threads of a trend that will drive the direction of currency pairs.

Building up your confidence levels while you're in training mode will help your portfolio's accuracy tremendously. Getting past those early rough spots and onto greater trades will help acknowledge your losses while continuing to gain in your profits. Sooner than you think, you'll be catching trends and patterns in the marketplace and be ready to call a setup based on it. The experience will build on your knowledge base and you will see the best time to get into a trade and how to anticipate its movements to net major profits in a short amount of time. You will know how you work with your fund and how to handle the big losses without being crushed out of the market completely, while feeling the exhilaration of a great win. You will quickly learn how to stay out of the market when the volatility is too much and especially how to walk away from your computer after a winning streak when you're on top of the world.

Emotional Turmoil in Trading

As many traders have realized, the thrilling rush of a huge influx of cash from a winning trade can make many people feel like they've just won the lottery. You feel like you've beaten the market, won the day, and outwitted the system to make a big gain in your account balance. The professional traders know this feeling all too well and how fleeting it is.

Emotions can easily be generated whenever money is involved. Add in a vast amount of money and risking it on a trading pair and the turmoil increases tenfold. Now do it all at 2 a.m., and you'll soon find that the anxiety a trader faces is not for the faint of heart. New traders should not despair and should find trades that will maintain their interest even outside the marketplace to enhance their motivation to continue trading.

All traders face losses and how you control your emotional low after a bad trade is vital to continuing your training in the world of FX trading. Guilt, doubt, and worry can nag even a seasoned pro but trusting your expanding knowledge base, growing your resources and information sources, and running through more trades (even on a demo) can boost your confidence and emotional levels. Starting out slowly and using some of the risk management ideas noted in this book will help as well. Understanding that you have access to giant sources of margin but not using them and avoiding a margin call situation will cushion a loss. Having enough extra margin to "double down" and dollar cost average into the trade that failed will also reduce the negative impact. Of course, another way to look at it is to switch it over to a longer term perspective and wait for the trade to turn around.

The reality could be that the market is suffering. Perhaps trades that were unheard of at the beginning of the month are now possible and within reach. If the interest differential is the same, try a trade that is a long-term carry while you wait for a recovery within the market. It may be several months or years.

On the other hand, your FX account should be set up to maintain a holding pattern if you suddenly need to leave off from trading for any reason, such as an accident, illness, or a poor marketplace. If the markets are not good, and you are simply not comfortable risking your assets and margin on trading, remove the money from the account. We suggest that you put the money towards something of value. Forex markets and currency trading should never add to one's level of stress and anxiety. If you feel that trading is not adding to your life and bringing you satisfaction for your time and money, then take a break and use the money for something that will benefit you.

A good way to eliminate some of the stress of trading Forex is to set up your FX account like a business. This way, you can be sure to set a regular schedule, with work hours, lunch breaks, and days off. One of the joys of being a business owner means controlling how your business operates. Your FX business works for you, you don't work for it.

"I got killed today in the market. I've got to slow it down a bit." Never fear if this situation describes you. The currency markets and international community will continue on while you take a break. Your FX broker will gladly accept your funds when you decide to jump back in later. All traders know that life happens in the middle of a trading session. Cars need to be fixed, kids need braces/shoes/iPads, and other expenses can rack up, so dip in to your FX account as necessary. You'll soon be back and gaining profits on top of your automatic deposits.

Forex and Financial Independence

The markets can be unpredictable and react in the most illogical ways. For example, you've prepared some long gold and silver trades on your accounts as you see some major inflation flaring up soon. However, the market explodes and causes gold and silver to free fall into losses. It could be that this is an upset in the market so that traders and big funds sell their position in (usually secure) gold and silver to raise cash for margin calls in their various portfolios elsewhere. It is likely that the emotions of the market have reacted negatively and rapidly made a poor situation even worse in a short span of time. Now there is a rush of sellers and the market cannot level out fast enough to handle it. The whole world market may be caught up in a huge fray and your trades simply got wedged in the maelstrom. When traders talk of "it's bad out there," or the news media reports massive percent drops in the market, then you realize it is time to make a decision on how to handle it.

The choice is this: be a victim or be an independent decision maker. The former stumbles around the markets and gets blown easily off course by volatile markets and bumps in the road. The independent decision maker operates a business with their FX account, has a plan, has not overmarginalized their account, has proactively created a double down buffer, and knows when to sit tight and wait for it to blow over. If you've followed any of the advice in this book, you'll have liquid assets outside the markets in a sizable amount, you've used a limited amount of your FX account capital, and you've kept your margins to a reasonable amount of actual cash used.

At this point, you are your only customer and manager of your FX fund. Maintaining a level of sanity in an uncertain market can strain the most professional traders. This is why they behave in a manner that exudes a strong level of independence and financial self-reliance. You cannot eliminate all risk and live on an island, but you can soften the impact the market has on your accounts.

You're probably doing it right when others laugh at your emergency plan. Independent decision makers are insulated and are prepared for sharp market downturns. Let them laugh now, because the markets catch the unprepared, leaving you to profit while they scramble to make the margin call.

Let's rewind to the devastating fallout from the 2008–2009 banking crisis. Bad news travels fast. Catastrophic news moves at light speed. Gold, stocks, house values, and even central banks can face enormous pressure. Yet in the middle of this disaster, market emotions do not need to force your hand or overcome your emotions. Envisioning yourself as a fully-fledged currency fund manager can help you insulate your portfolio when it comes to your investments and strategies. It can help to keep your positions liquid and low risk during rough markets.

Surviving a downturn is not impossible. Flexibility can go a long way to bringing your bank accounts back to life. Taking a second job is another way to gain additional income while your accounts hibernate. Perhaps taking time off from piling money into the market, taking a break, can help you reallocate and streamline your financial outlook. Still, others may leap further into the market seeing opportunities where no one else dares to go and add to their portfolios regardless.

Ultimately, the key to financial independence is different for everyone. There is simply no one right path that fits everyone. Take the time to design a specific plan that works best for your own individual situation. Creating a financially independent life is not as hard as it may seem. Just because the markets tank does not mean it should dictate the quality of rest of your life and personal economy. Removing the invisible attachment to the concept of happiness equaling the "good market" is one way to take back control. Limiting your emotional connections to the unpredictable market is another.

QUIZ

1. **A 90/10 bond/FX portfolio is a very conservative way of boosting the returns of an otherwise conservative portfolio.**
    A. True
    B. False

2. **One simple, conservative way to invest in foreign currency is to:**
    A. Keep the cash and coins when you go to Europe
    B. Invest in currency ETFs
    C. Trade with a low amount of margin
    D. Trade with a large amount of margin, but with a small balance

3. **Forex demo accounts are the best way to learn how to trade Forex with no risk.**
    A. True
    B. False

4. **It is best to keep in mind that Forex trading should:**
    A. Fit with your lifestyle
    B. Not involve more risk than you can handle
    C. Be fun
    D. Not cause too much stress
    E. All of the above

5. **A popular way to keep Forex trading paying is to take profits out of the account periodically.**
    A. True
    B. False

6. **It is best to keep track of all of your:**
    A. FX interest income
    B. FX capital gains
    C. Expenses related to your FX trading
    D. All of the above

7. **One of the best ways to gain skills with Forex trading is to:**
    A. Watch the markets develop over time
    B. Trade often
    C. Trade over the weeks, months, and years
    D. Trade in a Forex demo account often
    E. All of the above

8. **It is best to learn how to manage the stress and anxiety of Forex trading.**
   A. True
   B. False

9. **Forex trading, watching the markets, and running your FX business can lead to:**
   A. Additional income
   B. Added stress if you're not careful
   C. Knowledge of the economy
   D. Financial independence
   E. All of the above

10. **It is best to keep a financial emergency plan because:**
    A. It will keep your stress low
    B. It will help when the market goes bad
    C. It makes good financial sense
    D. It is part of beginning to be financially independent
    E. All of the above

Chapter **8**

How to Look for Good Forex Setups

In this chapter, you will learn the following:

- How to read the news for good trades
- How different short-term trends affect trades
- How different long-term trends affect trades
- The importance of using a trading notebook/calendar
- How to make a good trade with bad market news

You will find that currency trading can be profitable for you if spend time looking for good setups. This refers to the times that either the technical indicators, fundamentals, or both of them are saying to enter a trade as an FX pair is ready to move. Finding setups will take time to plot and plan but trading news can quickly happen, and when this does occur, a fast situational analysis can put you in position to gain fast profits.

Diverse News Determines Different FX Pairs

During relevant news, you should be trading the FX pair that is part of the story. Market movements will provide you with opportunities to make money off the trade. A stationary currency pair will just hold up cash without any gains as the amount will remain at risk.

You can do well trading under a short- and long-term trading on the news, and it is something you need to consider to increase your FX returns. By doing so, this sets up a scouting process and it provides opportunities for you to make money in the marketplace.

This scouting the market process will be done when you're not actually involved in a trade.

Finding potential setups can be done days before the news, and this includes determining the appropriate risk tolerance for you and the right potential return. Scouting for setups involves a process that will allow your money to stay safe while it is not part of a trade; by using your time wisely, you can preset your risk limits, determine your entry and exit points, and otherwise build a trade that will give you the best chance for you to get back your money with profit when the trade is over.

At some point, you might prefer that your cash not be in a trade. You should only be in one when it offers you a rational chance to profit.

In the short term, you can create a trading system for extreme safety by having cash more than 90% of the time during the week and actually in a trade (and technically "at risk") only 10% of the time. This equals around 24 very short-term trades each week. With less cash exposed to the market, you'll find your account will stay safe and secure.

When you are entering a trading week, you should look out for points that evolve into a potential trading opportunity. You may even find them before the new week kicks off by reading charts and fundamentals on Saturdays. By the time the new trading week starts, things may have changed—sometimes in your favor—and an improved directional trade may come your way. You may change course, and now that money is available to go to the FX pair that had been discussed in the news cycle. You may also discover during the week that information about currencies and their economies could be topics in the news, while stories that you began following over the previous weekend could exit the news cycle early in the new trading week as something more urgent develops. This may have first appeared in either a broker's report or on the news wire. As you watch it grow, it may be time to get ready for a trade and enter it on the win side.

Here's one scenario: The Hungarian forint (HUF) is attaining too much value versus the Swiss franc (CHF). A developing story could be that the HUF may be changing direction versus the CHF. After reviewing the story more, you decide that the CHF/HUF is setting at the peak of its 200-day moving average. You have also discovered that a resistance point is at the present trading level with increasing volume.

In this type of scenario, a small but very leveraged long-term trade should be your preferred one and you should begin considering a trade like this for later in the trading week.

A Scenario for Evolving News

Let's look at another scenario. This time there's more going on for a trade. As you are looking around for a CHF/HUF entry point, a second news story could develop such as one centering on U.S. economic and employment numbers. The numbers have been announced, and they're worse than anticipated.

This information makes risky assets worldwide withdraw. The U.S. stock market takes the news badly and investors respond by changing their risk to meet this emerging news.

Things can move quickly in the market, with risky investments losing their appeal. Currencies such as the AUD, NZD, and SEK will fall as compared to the safer USD. Figure 8-1 shows the correlation between the AUD/USD and the NZD/USD Forex pairs. It can be seen that overall, they move in the same direction as each other as the market develops.

If you haven't already done so, you should have positions in these pairs for the risky side as they will now be inexpensive to pick up. A good way to set yourself up for gains in the future will be to go long the risk-oriented currencies and short the less risky currencies. In other words you will be long the AUD, NZD, and the SEK, while shorting the JPY or the USD. Keep in mind that the trade should be entered into after the bad news is absorbed into the market,

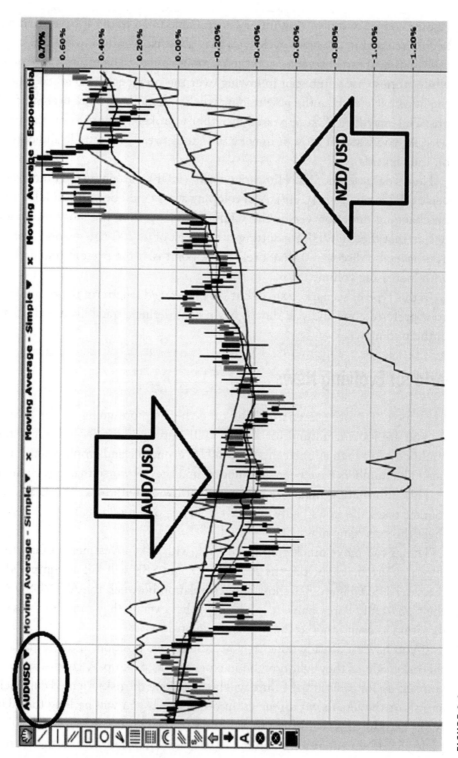

FIGURE 8-1 • AUD/USD and NZD/USD Forex Pairs

and the prices for risky assets have fallen. This way you are buying in at the bottom of the market (if in only the most recent term).

One way to approach this new story and your currency pair is to alter your focus from the initial long-term CHF/HUF trade to a shorter-term one that is high-yielding and risky. These trades will have a positive reaction to global gain in the stock market. It is commonly known that market knowledge following a large news announcement will include big stock market reaction, but in the following days the market can change its direction for a few days.

This comes as stock market traders worldwide are either acting as bargain hunters or profit takers. Regardless, stock markets will move in the opposing direction at some point. At this time, it is a good opportunity to grab the gains through owning a position in a high-risk, high-yield trade.

For times of bad news, you could diversify your portfolio three ways, representing 18%–21% of the total for your portfolio. This could include combining positions of EUR/CHF, USD/AUD, USD/NZD, and USD/SEK, and having 6%–7% of the total cash value in your currency portfolio.

Say the market reacts negatively to the news; your FX pairs will quickly fall. With a decline greater than 1.25% since the news was announced, now is a good entry point for the pairs. You don't have to be as exact with the entry points but place your trades prior to the market changing directions, which could happen quickly.

After the orders have been entered, now return to the "modify order" screen and enter the exit profit points automatically between 0.65%–0.75%. This will give a quick profit and enable you to exit the trade and move on with your day. Do a different activity other than trading to take your mind off of it.

Your hands-on work has been completed and now all that's left to be done is to let the computer complete your trade though an automated take-profit to ensure the closing position is executed at the correct time.

This scenario represents a good example for finding setups, keeping on top of news, and learning to be flexible to jump on news when there's an opportunity to grab a profit on an evolving news story with an FX pair.

The Market Always Reacts

You'll find that the market is always responding to news that develops during the trading day. With global markets now open for 24 hours each day, six days per week, there is something always brewing somewhere across the world and it has a good chance of affecting the currency in the country the news is about.

Take a look at this example.

News may have come out from a top Asian money area such as Tokyo or China at the time that the U.S. and European markets are closed. This could include a potential story regarding China's growth numbers coming out higher than estimated. This would affect China's currency markets and the price of different commodity currencies, as well as impacting China's trading partners.

But positive news coming from China also is good news for nearby emerging economies, including Southeast Asia's Malaysian ringgit, the Thai baht and the Singapore dollar.

Why is this so? China has started outsourcing some light manufacturing to the above economies across Southeast Asia. Now when capital comes from Europe and the United States into China as a means to pay for rising Chinese goods, some of this capital will then be exported to the developing markets used by China for labor outsourcing.

In addition, China's growth is also tied to the upcoming consumption of commodity inputs including copper and steel, and soft commodities such as wool and cotton. These commodities currencies will also be impacted. In this way, the economy in China has an effect on the economies of the regional commodity-producing countries. These include New Zealand and Australia as discussed before, but also the smaller countries such as Indonesia, which is a source of copper, and Singapore, an oceangoing shipping center.

On occasion, some news is purposely set to be distributed after the top trading hours, such as between 5 and 7 p.m. ET. This enables currency traders enough time to review the new information during a quieter market after the trading session has cooled off. The timing exemplifies that information can be released throughout the trading day as a means to regulate reactions by currency traders.

Other times, news will develop at specific times throughout the week and during the month as central banks around the world issue different reports or hold conferences that occur at pre-established times. Almost every currency that trades regularly has an English website and the body that governs the currency will update it. Examples include the Magyar Nemzeti Bank (Hungary's central bank), the Reserve Bank of New Zealand, or the Riksbank of Sweden—to name a few—that will have their websites publish times and dates for economic numbers, rate adjustments, and additional guidance information as to the state of the economy and the potential direction of future official announcements.

Should you be trading a specific currency pair such as the CHF/HUF, the EUR/SEK, or the USD/NZD, it is a good idea to have these central bank websites marked and a familiarity with them as ones that are managing the currencies you are currently trading.

Use a Trading Calendar

Markets will react to developing news at any time of day, so it is important for you to keep a desk/trading calendar to allow you to track the times and dates of certain news and the information that comes from it as it applies to your often-traded FX pairs. This will enable you to track developments and to know when things will be scheduled to occur.

One piece of information to include in a trading calendar is a future announcement about an interest rate from a currency's underlying central bank. You may watch the FX market and, on your calendar, have a reminder that the Federal Reserve will be making an upcoming announcement, such as a jobs report, or something else that is relevant to your current or upcoming currency trades that include the USD.

In addition to upcoming data releases, a trading calendar can track a currency pairs' market sentiment as it evolves through time. If you have a pair that you consistently trade and it encompasses currencies that are volatile, then a calendar can assist you to remain focused on market commentary for this traded pair.

Another entry for the calendar is to keep track of the recommendations from your broker as they evolve in the short and long term and as they approach a potential change in the country's economic numbers. Additions to the calendar may also include records of market chatter that you have overheard regarding the countries' stock markets and their leading indicators.

If you have either already opened a trade or have considered entering one, you can take a look at the calendar and utilize it as a record that includes your personal market sentiment toward the desired Forex pair.

Just as markets will react to different news, as a FX trader you too will also respond to the news—even more so when you are involved in a trade. It can become common as a trader to really like your currency pair, causing you to wait before entering a trade only to then feel buyer's remorse after you have spent the money on the transaction.

Don't worry, this is very normal.

Many will suggest exiting a losing trade before you get stuck with with a trade before it turns into an an investment. But before you quickly bail out of the position, review your trading calendar and take a look at the trade's developments.

It may be too early to exit. Feeling regret a few minutes after exiting the trade can be overwhelming.

Which leads to another word of advice: Do not act on your emotions to get out of a trade on short notice. It is better to implement stops into your program within your trading software and determine the right time to leave the trade. You'll become more comfortable doing this through practice and soon you can look to conduct your currency trading through fundamental analysis, technical analysis, and some math, rather than relying on emotions.

Any time you want to trade, you'll always have to deal with the market moving thanks to news. This is a doubled-edge sword: It's a good thing that the currency market moves nonstop, but it does so by moving in two directions: down and up. By remembering this, you will trade when you have a solid reason to do so, including exiting a position using the same solid reasoning.

After a time, you'll become comfortable with keeping a trading calendar and then you can take it to the next level by utilizing it as a news journal. Doing this will enable you to see and then understand how the news on your pairs develops over time, whether it is months or something shorter like weeks. This will assist you in seeing how an FX pair has most likely moved up and down as the market reacted to developing news. Then, after taking a fresh look, you may see that market sentiment has been swayed from one way to the next. By seeing this and then taking note of it, you are building a history for it and you can then ask yourself a few questions.

One is, "Do I react to news similarly to the market or am I just following along like a sheep?"

You may also want to ask, "How has the currency done before in a similar situation?"

Another question you may want to ask yourself is, "My trade is not in a good position, as I am losing money. Do I think the market will bounce back or will it move to a point where the trade can be closed at a break-even point without a loss?"

These are all important questions that you need to ask yourself and one way to answer them is by utilizing your news journal to assist you with staying abreast of some vital developments, prior to them happening, that will ultimately affect your trades.

Journals can also help you in determining the correct time to exit a trade for a current FX pair that you own.

Trade with the News

There are numerous sources of information that you can read during the trading day to access current news. Some of the top outlets, including *The Economist*, *MarketWatch*, and the *Wall Street Journal*, will have up-to-date news relative to economies across the globe. This news flow will affect global traders' ideas regarding future capital inflow to a region, upcoming growth rates for the area, or the central banks of the region's upcoming interest rates.

Studying and reading about the economy and the world's markets is an ongoing process. It does, however, get easier. As time goes on, the stories and developments will intertwine. You will quickly see that what happens in one part of the world will change what happens in another part of the world—this is true especially in economic news. Also, if the terms and ideas seem too much to grasp all at once, don't fret: the skill is best acquired over time. You will naturally get better as you stick with the program of daily study and keeping on top of the markets.

Economic news can result in a certain FX marketplace reaction, while the FX markets can cause their own reaction to the home economies and a trading partners' home economy. Remembering this may help you to stay ahead of the news and then plan around it for trades to go with it.

One helpful way to do this is through FX news feeds. You will find currency brokers may let you routinely subscribe to a few different ones. They could also enable you to employ an open news feed window right on the trading platform so you will have immediate access to the news information.

You'll see over time that news really can be a good friend to a currency trader. It is also as helpful as a technical analysis and fundamentals when you select and time solid FX trades.

In the end, it is the combination of news as well as a solid understanding of technical indicators and conducting strong fundamental analysis that will really make your trading system a lock. Statistically, news can make your trades more profitable, whether it is in the short-, medium-, or long-term.

Remember, numerous factors can result in a currency pair moving up or down. This includes diverse factors such as a macro event like a crisis to the banking industry or possibly events that only affect one country. Whether it is especially good or shockingly bad, economic news can affect one or both ends of your currency pair.

During these types of events, there would be lots of different news developing, whether it is the leader of the country making a speech, tsunamis, or even fights in the street. Regardless of what transpires, with today's digital world, the news will be communicated immediately.

Whether you are okay with it or not, people do respond to evolving news. You may have heard the saying, "news rules," and it really does.

One way that you can review and see all of the factors and news affecting your AUD/USD pair is to go to the website of the Reserve Bank of Australia. You can also read broker reports for the pair and keep an eye on the global markets. You should probably also monitor the VIX.

Here's an example of some observations you may have made prior to executing a long AUD/USD position:

- In the two previous terms, the Reserve Bank of Australia (RBA) hasn't increased rates.

- RBA has scheduled a meeting to take place in two weeks.

- The broker's reports advocate the RBA will increase rates by 0.25% at its upcoming meeting.

- The currency NZD underwent a rate increase by it central bank at its previous meeting.

- Global stock markets, as well as the SEK versus the EUR have been gradually increasing; this suggests risk appetite is increasing.

- The VIX has been declining lately which means the market is quiet and comfortable with risk appetite increasing.

After reviewing your trading notes and seeing this rising risk appetite as well as the likelihood of a rise in interest rates by the RBA, you may determine its time to open a long AUD/USD position that will make you money if the AUD rises versus the USD. You are also aware that money can be made if stock markets remain on the rise, the market sentiments appears to feel great about assets with risk, and the RBA increases rates.

A Positive Trade with Bad News

Let's take a look at another trade you may have open: a small, long-term one. It could represent 7% of your portfolio and you may have opened it as a carry trade over the next couple of weeks before the RBA has a scheduled meeting and is expected to increase rates. From this, you grab a capital gain.

This carry trade has a 50:1 margin and you hold on to it for two weeks before selling. Because you own a currency that will pay a greater interest rate as compared to the short currency that you have, you can accumulate interest on this trade of AUD/USD.

The interest that you accrue will be deposited each night to your account. It can add up quickly as it is continuously compounded. It can be measured in not only minutes but seconds within the trade; this is different from the usual time accounts that compound either each month or quarter. The trade in question, the AUD/USD trade, is a risky one and the greater the market is attracted to risk, the better performance it will have.

While the aforementioned trade is logical, it doesn't mean the market is. As you have repeatedly learned, news can quickly take place and a number of factors can make the market rapidly switch course. The world could panic and quickly leave their assets with lots of risk.

An event such as a blizzard on the East Coast of the United States could result in local traders from New York staying at their homes and away from their trading desks. There could also be a negative event in a European country. Regardless, the chance exists that news may happen and your long AUD/USD trade could spin out of control as the USD would increase since it is a safe-haven currency.

On the other hand, from the market's response you could expand the long position of the AUD/USD at a less expense rate than you could before the event.

When you regularly read the news, you can keep abreast of your present trades. It will also keep you aware of your opportunities, which may include a short-term step back from the world's appetite for risk. In the above situation, the RBA will likely still increase rates 0.25%, as the bankers will take a long-term view where news usually looks at a very short-term time frame.

And from this comes another lesson for you: As an FX trader, you will learn it is often a good thing to just walk away from one's trading desk. If you employ a thought-out trading strategy and utilize automated profit points as well as stops in your trading software, take a step back and let the marketplace and computer do their work. It is important to not be either impatient or concerned. Let the trading system do the work for you.

Always remember to keep your initial observations in your trading journal. Keeping an eye on the news may make you aware of a possible chance to tag on an additional position to your trade.

You may also utilize a risk-management strategy to change your position to a few entry points over the upcoming days. This could include setting exit points to a 1% average price movement for the upside. Now could be a good time for you to again leave your trading platform for a few days. Continuing with the previous scenario, you can still keep an eye on the AUD/USD price, reviewing the currency ETF FXA on your smartphone or tablet over the upcoming days to stay on top of the price. Allow your computer to automatically get out of the long AUD/USD positions trades when the time is right.

Be patient, as it will happen. Don't worry about the AUD. Its value will return as it historically does. Just be patient and trust that all of your hard work has paid off. Now it's time for market forces to take over and allow you to make profits.

Fast and Slow News Developments

One secret to executing good currency trades is to undergo the arrangement of FX trades along with news development and its direction. In other words, if the news of the day is generally good for the markets, then risk-on trades will have the chance to do well. The opposite is true for bad news days: the world's markets will fall, and the risk-off trade will then do well. In this case any carry trades or high-yielding, growth-related currencies will lose in value against more solid, lower yielding, less growth-orientated currencies. On occasion, news will quickly occur, while on other occasions it will evolve over time. Regardless, if you can recognize the market's directional move whether it's before the news, during, or post-development, then you'll be undertaking a solid effort to move your FX account towards a position for profitable trades.

Changes in Interest Rates

By this point, you know that news will move currency markets. And you are also aware that the news can be described as quickly happening and also at measured rate or slow happening, giving you plenty of time to plan your trades. An example of fast news includes an announcement about a change in an interest rate, which could be a source for quick movements of your currency pair. With a pair, one of its ends in the trade will change with the interest rate move and then you are prepared that a big move is on the way. Figure 8-2 is a one-month chart showing the correlation of the returns of the SEK and the S&P 500 Index.

You'll have time to get ready for announcements such as these, as central banks give plenty of heads-up to the markets before they announce a change to interest rates. You can learn about these announcements and their individual timetables by reviewing the websites for central banks that are linked to your currency trades.

If you believe the stock market will decline and you have a long position in EUR/SEK, take a look at the Riksbank website (http://www.riksbank.com)

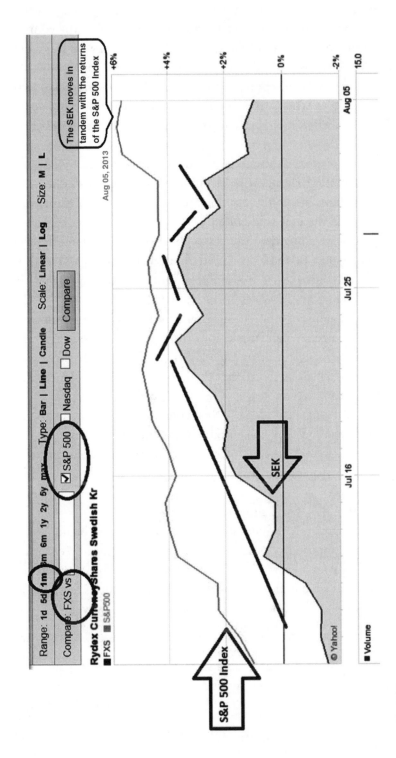

FIGURE 8-2 • Returns of SEK and S&P 500 Index

and see if an upcoming announcement is set regarding any changes to their interest rate at week's end. This can help you set the timing of your trades and keep you organized. Should an upcoming rate change be the case, you will need to be cautious and take it down a notch with your trades. At the minimum, be sure to have enough margin to take on a market downturn should the Swedish central bank increase the repo rate. If the bank does raise its figure, then this will affect your currency pair prices as well as your potential profit.

Another way to prevent a substandard trade is to have a large enough amount of spare margin to purchase a new price into the currency pair should it not go your way. This will enable you to cut down the average cost for your currency pair and to factor in the new trade price.

Building your FX trading this way can help a lot by containing the trade at a level that money can be made as the stock market declines and as the SEK does so as well. Of course this is an example, as the system of averaging out the entry points of a Forex trade works on all FX pairs.

For Forex trading, interest rate changes are an important element to define a fair price for a currency pair; this comes from predicting countries' growth rates. One country may appear to have a growth rate greater than a second country. There may be a possibility that the home country could increase rates as a means to control its economy.

Then there's the opposite scenario. If a country's economy starts to slow, there's a good likelihood that its central bank will either cut interest rates or take another means to make it easy to borrow money. By doing so, central bankers hope that spending and borrowing will jump-start the economy and assist in pushing it ahead.

Here's an example that will show this.

Many believe that with the quantitative easing after the banking crisis of 2008, there was supposedly four times the volume of money entering the system than in previous years. This spurred worries for broad inflation and resulted in rampant speculation throughout the commodities markets. This is an extreme example and it doesn't commonly occur; however, it is good to review to understand how different scenarios can affect the markets and your trading.

But let's return to the task at hand and that's your currency pairs. If one is priced at an interest rate and an announcement for change affects one end of the pair's interest rates, the pricing of it will then change. What typically happens is a lower interest rate will fall even further while the higher interest rate will go higher. A net effect from this will result in a currency pair's altered price.

The Effect of Economic Announcements

Public announcements regarding interest rate changes may include quantitative easing as you have previously seen. But here's an expanded explanation and its effect on trading.

Quantitative easing has been in the news a lot lately—really, for the last year or two—and what it means is a way to change the money supply of a country by buying, via the open market, big quantities of that government's treasury bills, treasury notes, and treasury bonds.

When either a central bank or treasury buys large quantities of its own debt on the open market, it results in pushing huge sums of new money into the system.

It's really pretty simple: Let's say a $1,000 bond is outstanding; a bank is currently holding it when a central bank or treasury steps in and purchases it. Then, the bond will be on the treasury's balance sheet while the bank receives $1,000 of cash. As a business, the bank will need to make money from the transaction so this recently received $1,000 will now be lent to customers seeking out loans. Consumers will spend this loaned money, while the merchant will deposit $1,000 in the bank. Because of a fractional reserve banking system, just some of this money will need to remain at this bank while the remainder can once again be lent to customers.

In this second go-around, money will be spent and then deposited to a bank account. Again, because of the reserve system, only a portion of the money is necessary to stay in the bank and the remainder will again be lent. You see a pattern here: the system will repeat itself again and again.

It can be interesting to see the workings of quantitative easing, and after the banking crisis from 2008 to 2009, it was a full-on campaign. Most major economies around the world have used some sort of quantitative easing. As expected, the biggest players across the globe have purchased the greatest amount of debt and this includes Europe, Japan, Great Britain, and the United States. They then place the biggest amount of trades, which go back into the system.

But the question does remain on whether or not quantitative easing has been a good thing for the countries. That's an interesting question and the answer may vary. From Round Three of easing for the United States, commonly called

QE3, the economy stayed lethargic and the U.S. dollar's alleged value fell a lot compared to other currencies.

This generated concern about additional money supply and greater problems of debt. In summer 2011, the United States saw its credit rating receive a down-grade from AAA to a status of AA. The aftermath of this remains to be seen, but at the time, the currency markets trashed the U.S. dollar before, during, and then after this news.

Let's review an example of profiting from a country's debt by looking at the timing of news announcements that can affect your currency trading. Economic news will often be previously scheduled announcements. It is important to stay on top of this type of news and to have a plan for a worst-case scenario when you see this type of activity pop-up. On the other hand, when the negative news moves on and leaves the market cycle, then there is a high likelihood the currency in question will bounce back. Remember this and then ask yourself if you should purchase this currency that took a hit, sell it at a future time, and then reap a large profit.

Geopolitical News

Along with sudden and slowly-evolving news, another factor that affects cur-rency pair prices is geopolitical news. This can be defined as news that is more than just about money and different currencies; it can include natural disasters such as earthquakes, hurricanes, storms, and floods—just to name a few. This news can come quickly and suddenly with all-encompassing tragic results.

Additional geopolitical factors could include hostage situations, invasions, and wars. These events will develop over time and they could occur either in a foreign country, a country with close dealings with the U.S.—or possibly in your own home country.

When these situations occur, currency markets around the world will be in disarray and it may remain this way until the crisis comes to an end. During this time, it is suggested that you not take part in trading as the directions of your currency pair will be volatile and there is a possibility that your previous valu-ation model will need to be discarded.

Don't worry about it as there is nothing you could have done to prepare for this. You will need to just move on from it.

Sometimes you may have woken up to bad news and had an open overnight trade when the news broke. Maybe you had a lot of success or maybe you incurred a big loss. If you were on the winning side, close the position and take a break from your trading. You were lucky, as these situations cannot be predicted by anyone. And you know how the saying goes: for each loser, there is also a winner. If you were on the losing side, be patient and let the negative situation work itself out. Then review the currency prices. They could be forever altered.

Remember, a part of learning about trading currencies is also knowing when to close your losing positions. Should you find yourself in a trade gone wrong, you will need to determine if you should wait for the trade to reverse course or just cut your losses. You will need to walk away and wait for a new day to trade.

Maybe you had long-term positions and now you find yourself on the losing side. Before you do anything rash, review some brokers' reports before exiting the trades and taking a loss. If you have a good broker, seek out her advice as she's likely to have some good things to say as to what you should do with your open positions. She could suggest buying more as the price has changed in the short-term.

Regardless, make your next move with caution.

Actions to Take in a Market Crash

You will see that the market's appetite for risk will constantly change for numerous reasons and the FX markets will react accordingly. The first and best way to approach this is to know ahead of time which currency pairs will strongly react to the rise. Then you will need to be aware of when the risk appetite has either changed, or is just about to see a change.

Regardless of the reason, this is the time to review your trading positions.

You could be long with AUD/USD while short EUR/SEK when the markets take a sudden turn south, which will likely be a losing situation. (Keep in mind that we use the same types of Forex trading pairs throughout most of this book. This is because these pairs are relatively easy to trade, and are the most commonly traded and covered with market news—good for predicting the direction of the FX pair in the future.) If through time, you have grown your trading through using a small amount from the margin that you have, then a down market should not clean out your positions. Through some care and time spent managing risk, your account should have enough liquidity even during extreme market downturns.

You may be involved in risky trades, including EUR/SEK and AUD/USD, when the market dramatically does not go your way. One option to deal with this is to place additional funds into your account to purchase more of these currency pairs as they endure huge losses. From any situation, some pairs may be of great interest.

During a time of negative news, after an initial average AUD/USA cost of 102, the pair has now dropped to 97.75. You may, however, find yourself in an opportunity to purchase a greater interest-paying currency pair at a lower price. Depending on how much you want to augment your trading account, you can see either two or three times of the exposure to your long AUD/USD or the short EUR/SEK position, which will enhance the bottom line of your portfolio once the market determines it is time to reverse course after there has been enough bargain hunting by the market.

But don't forget, markets bounce back. It could be beaten down badly and an interest-bearing currency pair including the AUD/USD, the CAD/USD, or the NZD/USD, may drop to an undervalued point. In this case, go ahead and buy a lot of the currency pair.

For this type of situation, do as much as possible to get a lot of the beaten up currency, as this is a good opportunity to enter a currency pair and see it evolve into large profits. Meanwhile, as you wait for a market change, you will still be earning interest on your account. When you have a 50:1 margin and you can add one-third or two-fifths from your trading accounts to your trade, then you will see 70% to 90% of interest earned on your account annually, independent of any currency pair gains.

The aforementioned exemplify an example of what to do if the market and your account's fortune changes for the worse. If you have properly created it, then your positions can weather the storm during these tough times. Should this occur, ride it out, add to your position, and then switch direction for a bit when you enter a carry trade method.

During tough times, keep your head up and add what you can to the bottom line. Many FX traders understand that bad times have an advantage. You'll see this as true and you can use it to your advantage. This can include expanding your positions, carrying trades, or being a trader who likes to be a contrarian by owning risky currency pairs.

You may have trades in your books that are losers and it may be time to close them out and put the cash into more appealing trades. For example, you could be long GBP/USD and AUD/USD while short EUR/SEK. All of them most likely have declined thanks to the overall market being risk averse, and you may want to exit out of some "better-losers" including your EUR/SEK and GBP/USD positions to then go long AUD/USD.

You may also be able to give up some margin if you are near a margin call. If you lose a few dollars it may be okay, as you can utilize the margin that will quickly accumulate returns when the market comes back.

In addition, the market could be skewed for its analysis of conditions at the present time. When this occurs, money will first go back to the classics such as trades that don't take a lot of speculation to decide whether they'll recover. AUD/USD positions have had a good performance for years, and should continue performing well.

You should think of classic trades during challenging times. Most traders will do this and then you'll be able to grab profits from them.

FX and the Herd Instinct

For those times when market participants are moving the market higher for numerous days, maybe weeks, there is a good chance that a slowdown or market reversal could occur. Remember, currency markets are connected to economic growth ideas. One economic region may be undergoing very fast growth, while another experiences slow or maybe slowing growth; this sounds like a good recipe for a currency pair for you to invest your money into.

Why? Economies that slow down are probably keeping interest rates on pause, while those that are rising will probably increase rates as a means to maintain your home economy from getting too hot, which is vital to discovering positive FX currency pairs.

Then there's the other side of the story. An economy may grow while the global stock markets rise. The erratic movements from stock indexes around the world, including the CAC40, DAX, DOW 30, and FTSE 100, serve as a representation of how traders and investors believe economies around the world are currently doing.

The majority of these people will review identical charts and information and then react similarly. Don't forget, it takes a lot for global stock markets to rise and fall by large amounts. It also takes a lot for options sellers for stocks and indexes to sell everything off and have price levels decline between 2% and 4%, and possibly more.

You may review your readings, charts, and then news and perceive a slowing economy is about to take place. You will need to plan for this by putting some of your long-term trades as feelers for the current market. You could arrange a long EUR/SEK, a short AUD/USD trade, or a long USD/EUR, all of which would take advantage of a smaller price level in the global stock markets.

Maybe the global markets have taken a beating for a long time and you're feeling they may be set for a comeback. If this happens, you will act as a contrarian investor and put on trades that will respond well to good news. You know the best trade for this environment is long-risk currencies.

To learn how to pick your currency pairs, you will need to choose a greater than average growth economy and buy its currency. On the short side, select a slower than average growth economy and its currency. This is the basic tenet for currency trading: it is all about interest rates and growth rates as they relate to them.

For those involved in FX trading, they are keeping their eyes on the ticker to see what will happen next to interest rates and the respective economies of their currencies trades. The difference between currency pairs could be popularity, which may spur short-term trades or carry trades.

Let's look at two trades. They could have both good and slow growth aspects but the more popular one will have the greatest performance and more reliability.

You can accomplish this type of trade though a short USD and long South African rand (ZAR), as well as short USD and long AUD trades. The AUD/USD trade will be better to enter, as there are more traders entering this at identical levels.

Small Positions with Long Time Frames and Long Haul Strategies

You may have a feeling the market has been going in one direction, whether it is up or down, for a while. You could also be interested in placing long-term trades to seize movements in market price for the downside but not with additional upside movement.

For these types of times, going longer-term may be a good idea. The way to do so is to own small positions with a lot of margin should they move against you quickly. This will also enable you to add positions when you believe a correction is on its way.

When the market has moved in one direction whether it was up or down for days at a time and it seems like it's been going on too long, then get out of your trades with selling risk short. You already discovered the currency pairs to do this, and you also know the one-third margin rule. To grab a down movement upon arrival, further split your margins by more than one-third—something usually done for a short-term trade.

Here's a question to ponder: How do you see when it is time for markets to take that turn after a large run?

The ideal way to tell if a currency pair is approaching a reversal is to review technical and fundamental indicators. You may also want to turn on financial news such as CNBC, which will go crazy when the market has been over-bought and set to crash.

Keep in mind, the less margin amount you utilize to add to a position, the safer your account will find itself. Should you use just 1/20 from the account for a portion of a currency pair, you will be safe. Be steady about purchasing into a currency pair to make sure your account's liquidity is okay should there be any position movements.

This is something good for your currency account: Make sure you have enough margin to endure a blow. Remember, when your account increases from profits, this expands your margin and when you suffer losses, it will take away from the margin.

When a specific level has been hit, you will receive a margin call and you will be required to liquidate your positions right away at that losing price. Your account will now be blown up, which is something that can easily happen. In an effort to avoid this, do not keep too many products in your account and keep sufficient margin to deal with a market downturn.

On the other end, if you slowly move into this situation, you will then be protected. The best scenario is to have downside protection. A not quite as good scenario is to limit gains to the amount of the currency pair you own when the market changes course and plummets.

Either way you will find yourself protected and go on to have winning trades.

It is vital to defend your account against these conditions while increasing positions at a slow rate. This will enable you to create the position and protect yourself from movements in the market that don't go your way. This can be accomplished through dollar cost averaging.

One is example would be to start with 100 units at the day's start. You should also keep track of your trade's status throughout the day. If it is down, you may add units proportionate to its fall, or if it is down a lot, you could purchase 100 additional units. But if it doesn't go down too much, just tag on 25 units.

This idea of adding is called buying on the dips and it can keep your trading lucrative when the market turns around.

Keep in mind, if you transacted 10 or 15 buy-ins over just a few days and the market declines, you have avoided the blowing up of your account once the trade did not move your way. You'll also be simultaneously adding to the trade if you think it will work out for you, but be careful to stay away from overexposure as a maximum trade exposure should represent no more than two-fifths of your available margin total.

If it is three days later and the market has slowed, take a deep breath and a break from the market. Do something other than trading, such as a favorite hobby. You need to keep in mind, you have good trades and there's no need to worry. You should try to make the trades either medium- or long-term ones.

If you need to feel more secure, you could add some take-profit points into your trading platform's software to get rid of concerns that you could miss exiting the trade. The ideal thing is to let everything take its course. One of the key things about Forex trading is to not overtrade your account. Build up a position when it is time to, and leave the trade on your books when the trade hasn't risen in value enough for you to take your profits.

Putting Everything Together and In Order

Up until this point, your currency account has been open and you've been undertaking technical and fundamental research to determine which currency pairs to trade. You should be comfortable with this now, and the next step is to learn how to trade the product.

You will also learn how to utilize various buckets of money that will enable you to trade. This could include funds for overnight trades, very short-term trades, and long-term carry trades. It is also time to now become acquainted with hedging and making profitable FX trades during markets that are risk averse.

Currency Trading with Different Sources of Money

In your FX trading account, the margin will likely be divided into various buckets for trading. The first one will represent the core of the account for cash. You should have a rather large margin in your account for trading as compared to the one you would have if you were trading either a mutual fund or a stock (meaning 50:1 versus 1.5:1).

This FX account should always have approximately 60%–70% in cash as a safety net to protect against some position that could suddenly go wrong. But keep in mind that you can still see a good profit in your account with only 25% being routinely available in cash.

If you have an account with $2,000 available, you could still trade $500 at a time with a 50:1 margin; this comes to $25,000 in trading for currency each time. From this amount, you may earn $500 to $1,000 each week just by using a trading style that is considered conservative.

To begin, you should state a goal regarding the amount of money you would like to earn from currency trading for a basis of one week. Maybe if this goal is too easy to attain, it could give you confidence with your trading and you will feel happy once the profits begin to roll into your account. Starting with a conservative goal will also allow you to stay away from too much trading in your account.

Your next bucket will include 25% of the account that will be used to trade very short-term trades or scalping in a 10-minute time frame. This can result in earning a lot of money but the challenge to doing this is that the majority of currency pairs don't move a lot in this short amount of time.

To make an acceptable amount through this type of trading, you'll have to pledge about 25% from your trading account for every single trade.

A third money bucket needs to go to overnight trades. These will require only 10% of the available margin; you could even go down to 7.5%. The reason for this small amount is because these trades will take a bigger stop for profits and your trading software needs to be programmed this way. This means that you should program into your software more room before the take-profit point and the stop-loss points are reached. This is OK because of the smaller amount of your capital that is at risk. Knowing how much to program into take-profit points can be easy: It is usually built into the software at the time when you place the trade. The take-profit point will be measured in dollars and cents, allowing for a quick view of how much you can expect to make from that trade. The same goes for stop-loss points, where the amount of the maximum trade loss will be listed. Keep in mind, an overnight time frame will enable you to seek a greater percentage move from your currency pair. The majority of currencies will go down and up throughout the night and so you may enter a stop to give you a nice profit from this small capital amount.

A fourth and last capital bucket is your carry trade, which will stay around for weeks, or maybe months, as profits will come slowly over time. Because this is a longer commitment, a small portion will need to be put up for it, with approximately 3% to 5% to get it done. With the 50:1 margin, large gains can be accrued as currency pairs see movements during longer time frames.

Quick Trades Come with Quick Profits

You can take risks in your trading account that will equate to the time you sit on a trade. For the trade that only takes a minute or two, you will be cutting your risk exposure and your likelihood that the trade will go wrong. Remember currency pairs typically don't move as much during shorter-term trades. To overcome this, you will need to put up a larger capital amount for this type of trading. In addition, because these are short-term trades, stick with just doing one or two trades at a time.

If you are concerned about your money being at risk, that concern can be alleviated if you don't enter the market. Even if you enter the currency market-place for maybe 5 or 10 minutes, you are restricting the amount of down risk since a currency pair typically needs hours before it moves a lot.

This type of trading can result in quickly gaining profits in a pretty risk-free way. You should just focus on a few currency pairs, which could include EUR/CHF, AUD/USD, and NZD/USD. This trading will be best to do during a trading day's slow times, such as late in the evening. At this time, you can enter and sell trades from your home computer.

You may find that trading in this very short time frame can be a form of relaxation or a new evening activity, as the markets are good for this type of trading in the mid to late part of the day.

If this piques your interest, then you should definitely add it into your FX trading activities. But remember, only utilize 25% to 33% of your margin for a trade and just keep a single trade in your book at a time. You should also disregard currency pair's long-term directions for this trading.

Another way to assist with this time frame of trading is to have either a one- or five-minute trading chart. This will enable you to view the trade as it begins the trading session. You will be able to watch the bar chart go down and up.

Scalping

A good way to become more comfortable with trading is to go to your trading window to enter orders and then put in a trade's size. Then put the mouse's cursor on top of the button that sets up the placing of the trade. You may incur results just by waiting for a quick move in either direction.

Many times you'll be able to grab this quick movement in price, seize the trade, and then get out of it as the market has stopped moving and has gone to the next level.

Again, one way to do this is to settle down after a busy evening, flip on your computer, grab a cold drink, and sit down to watch your computer and your currency pair. This can be a long process but over time you will see the benefits.

Let's use the AUD/USD pair again as an example. Don't forget to also have your one-minute and five-minute charts readily available to go back and forth between on your trading platform. By doing so, you can see what the Asian markets, such as Sydney and Tokyo, are up to, since it is already their trading morning.

Remember don't get stuck on a specific length of time for your trading charts. It will be better to review a variety of charts for times such as short-, medium-, and longer-term. This will enable you to get a good picture of where the currency pair is moving.

You may find your chart will not have a lot of movement and you may think the FX market is not open but don't worry, soon the chart will move in both directions as each minute ticks by during the trading hour. Overall, there won't be tons of activity; however, you will be able to see what's up on your trading platform with your AUD/USD pairing.

Now it will soon be time to trade. Again open up your window to enter one but first make sure you calculate around 25% from your account to commit to this trade. Then enter the desired size of the trade, and again, place your cursor over the "place trade" button and wait.

Why wait? You want to hit the ideal time to enter the trade. Trading can be a waiting game even with these very short transactions. Don't worry, the right time will come. This is when there's been a move in your chart whether it is down or up.

Since this time of trading will result in little movement, you could see minutes where there's no trading at all but this will change. The right time will come when your chart has an up movement or a down one. The chart could be horizontal, meaning zero movement, for maybe two or three time periods (when you use a 5- or 15-second chart). The longer charts (1- and 5-minute charts) take longer to change, but when they do you will see a greater movement.

At this time, FX traders worldwide will begin thinking it is time to make that trade. Nobody wants to be the first to make that move; it is one big waiting game and you are involved in it. You are all set to go, as your trade has already been entered; you are just seeing when the right time is and then you'll join everyone else on this trading ride.

FX traders will begin to see movement in the chart but you should wait to enter a trade until the chart moves quicker and more emphatically in a particular direction. Once this happens, then you should enter your trade. When it continues in that direction with a quick price move, you should be queuing up your exit trade.

Be quick about this and get ready.

This should come when the current movement has either stopped or drastically slowed. Or maybe you can see your profit in front of you and you are happy with it. When a movement has stopped, then it is really time to close the trade.

You will also know it's time to exit the trade and take your profit when your indicator suggests a profit has been hit. Take it and enjoy your newly-made money. Only you will know if this is the right profit for you and whether it is time to now exit the trade.

Always remember one thing: You should be having fun doing this while you're also making money! If you're not having fun, then take a step back and think what you can do to make it fun.

Do you want to discuss your findings with a loved one? Do you want to bring in a trading partner just to bounce ideas off of? There's a lot you can do to make this a good evening activity instead of feeling like it's a chore just to make money.

Participating in Overnight Trades

Typically in your trading hours, you will have your money in cash as well as those aforementioned buckets that will also include additional cash for you to invest through a few different options. One way to use this type of cash is to participate in overnight trading.

This can be defined as looking at the Asian markets for developments during the late evening and seeing an idea of the direction for your trading bets. When you have determined this, whether it is short or long, you should make an entry point within your at-home trading platform.

While you are sleeping during the night, the Asian markets are busy trading away for their usual trading hours. This activity should initiate your trades and enable you to close them out at a predetermined and already programmed profit point.

To find success in overnight trading, it is key for you to have productive placing and profiting of your trades. You will need to first ask yourself if it is even a good time to enter a trade. Start with that question. If you have answered yes, then you should next ask if your currency pair will be a short or long position that will get the profits into your account.

This is a lot of questions and now you may want to ask yourself at this time, why do global markets move up and down every couple of days?

Whether it is the stock market, currency market, or even the precious metals markets, they can only rise for so long before they will all change course. This will come as traders around the world have participated in taking their profits, while exiting positions after just a day or two since incurring their gains in the marketplace.

This may now pose the question of when the ideal time is to enter into an overnight trade if global markets have been on the rise for the last few trading sessions and the Asian markets have started to decline for a second or maybe third trading day.

One trading idea is to short EUR/CHF and AUD/USD, and then go long EUR/SEK.

If you use 9%–11% of your trading portfolio for each position you will be ready to seize risk-averse price movements. FX markets will typically be risky for a small number of days but then switch course and become risk averse. To work with this pattern, you should put up a few overnight trades to grab when global traders are planning to establish their own trades at less risk.

Your trade of short EUR/CHF and AUD/USD and long EUR/SEK will be a decent hedge for when global risk declines in value.

In your current hedge you only have a single USD long position, as this trade is challenging to forecast alongside the EUR as well as additional currencies. This is due to the fact that the USD is the most extensively-traded currency across the world, and therefore, believe it or not, it can be hard to predict. When trading overnight it is the euro and carry trades that can easily be estimated.

Why? There are a few reasons. One is because a carry trade is regarded as a risky situation and the European and U.S. markets are starting to fall, following Asian markets such as Tokyo and Hong Kong already having done so. The majority of global currency traders will then exit their long AUD positions with their other carry trades, such as the Mexican peso (MXN), the NZD, and the South African rand (ZAR)—to name a few—as they're typically riskier, and then go long a safe currency like the USD.

Another trade you could do in this market scenario is to go long the Swiss franc versus the euro, and go short the Swedish krona versus the euro. Here, the

Swiss franc will rise as compared to the euro because its currency is seen as a safe haven. On the other hand, the Swedish krona is viewed as risky when you compare it to the euro, since the Swedish krona is regarded as a "high-beta" currency. This means that its value moves up and down in sync with the U.S. and European stock markets.

More about Overnight Trades

You can get an idea of the direction that global markets are taking just a few hours ahead of midnight on Sundays to Thursdays. You can evaluate if the timing is right to enter an overnight trade, but you will also need to determine if the trade will be a risky one or risk averse. When you make this decision, you can decide to be an investor who is a contrarian—or one who will go against the crowd.

You have probably been keeping on top of the global markets and your FX trades, which you can continue to do by using your various sources of information throughout your evening trading hours. At some point, you will you see in the last day or two a rough direction has taken place, maybe down or up moves, and it will make you aware that a reversal could be on its way for the Asian markets.

Should the Hang Sang or the Tokyo markets sit at the top of another position, such has 0.65%–1.0%, this is an ideal time to prepare your overnight trade.

If everything looks good to go for the trade, bring out the calculator and figure out the size of the trades. You may utilize ratios to assist you with gaining a feel for the 9%–11% within the trade. Keep in mind that the largest that you would want to trade at any one time is 1/3 of your entire available margin. In this case you will keep each part of the three positions within 9% to 11% (or 27% to 33%) of your entire available trading margin. When you stick within this limit usable margin you are adding in a level of a cushion against any bad trades that might go against you. Then with 66% of your available margin unused, you have much room for error, and have greatly reduced the chance for margin calls. The markets may have had a large increase in the last two or three days and it appears that Asian markets could decline by 0.75%–1.0%. This would be a good time to accept that the AUD/USD will decline more percentagewise versus the CHF/EUR trading pair.

The SEK will plummet a lot as compared to the EUR as it moves similarly with the U.S. and European stock markets. When the U.S. stock market falls, there is a strong likelihood a short SEK position can give you profits from your trades. You can short the SEK against either the USD or the EUR for good results.

When you are aware of this scenario, you should place 4% in a long EUR/SEK and, for your short positions, 4% in AUD/USD and 2% in the short EUR/CHF as a good means to see gains when the USD increases. In addition, you will have 200% coverage should the EUR rise.

To determine the hedge, look at it as making two dollars for each EUR that rises (remember that the long EUR/SEK is 4%) and you may lose a dollar for each EUR that falls (on a short 2% EUR/CHF). Should traders around the world be unable to determine what they should do for the EUR/USD, at least you'll have an effective hedge for directions on both sides for the U.S. dollar and the euro.

This shows a good limited hedge for the erratic currency pair of EUR/USD.

Remember, trading in the currency markets should be fun and one part of it is computing and planning your trades and hedges. Take your time with it to select the best alternative for you. It will take time to feel comfortable with this, but it is well worth it.

Keep in mind, mapping out an actual and dynamic hedge can also be challenging, but a three-sided trade can be an effective way of managing a hedged currency trading system.

Now it is time to determine before your trade where your profit points will be. In each currency pair, consider a 0.50% gain and then, for the stop-loss order, triple it to 1.5%. For this scenario you will close your trade with triple profit then you would lose if you had to exit the trade with a loss.

Don't forget, currency trading is about winning. The greater number of wins that you have, the stronger your account will be and you'll have more confidence as a trader. This will result in greater amounts of money to be made.

And at the end of the day, this is your ultimate goal.

Looking at Carry Trades

Another bucket of money that can be allocated for trading will go to carry trades. This is a longer-term trade and it will continuously gather compounding interest for weeks and months while you are in the trade. Carry trades are entered through the sale of a currency with less yield, while buying one with a higher currency yield. Recent low-yielding currencies include the JPY, the USD, and the CHF.

Carry trades make profit from the fact that the trader pays interest at a low rate while earning interest at a much higher rate. If a trader entered into an FX carry trade with the CHF and the NZD, he would pay the interest that the CHF charged and earn what the NZD paid. If the CHF charged 0.5% yearly and the NZD earned 3.5% yearly, the trade would earn 3.0% per year (the difference between the high/low interest rates). While 3% may sound fine, multiply this times the high leverage in your Forex account to get the true annual interest. For example, if you are trading one-third of your margin at 50:1, you will earn 50% interest yearly ($100 × 50 = 5000 × 33% =1,665 × 3% = $50 interest on a $100 FX account balance).

You'll see that some of these trades could last for years at a time on certain occasions. One example that illustrates this is a carry trade that occurred in 2005 and ran until late in 2008. This included the currencies of AUD, NZD, and JPY. What transpired is that worldwide carry traders suddenly changed course for their positions for the time period of 2008–2009 during the banking crisis; this resulted in carry trades quickly collapsing.

When you are in a carry trade, remember to not place a profit point in order to close the trade. What you should really do is just mentally check out from it. Tuck the trade away and only review it every other week or so. Over time, it will accrue interest and rise in price as the trade returns to its pre-correction level. Carry trades occasionally will linger for some time.

From a conservative standpoint, with the AUD/USD currency pair, when it returns to the price prior to the 3% to 4% correction, then you will have a safe opportunity to exit the position and grab your profit. Don't forget that you are trading at a 50:1 level and a 4% rise would equate to a 200% increase.

Let's look at an example with a portfolio of $10,000. You put in 5% for the trade and now you would have seen a $1,000 profit from it by using this calculation:

$$\$10,000 \times 0.05 \times 50 \times 0.04 = \$1,000$$

Again, a carry trade really can endure for numerous months, possibly a year. You really need to have the right frame of mind that this will be a longer-term transaction that won't need maintenance throughout the day by you. If you properly set up a carry trade and the market does go your way, you could potentially earn 8% to 10% based on a six-month time period. This is the potential capital gains of the trade, over and above the interest earned in the account from the trade. You can do you the math and you will see this will equal a return of $2,500 from a $500 investment that occurred just six months ago.

This is not a bad return and it didn't involve too much work from you other than possibly challenging your patience. Remember, trading can really be a waiting game with patience as a payoff.

Now you can see why keeping unique mental buckets within your account for various trades is a good thing. Whether it is a very short trade, a scalp trade, an overnight trade, or maybe a longer-term carry trade, they are all unique with their individual qualities. Each and every one will also have its distinct situation within your currency trading program.

QUIZ

1. One of the key elements to making profitable Forex trades is to wait for good:
   A. News days to trade
   B. Setups
   C. Strong risk-off days
   D. Strong risk-on days
   E. All of the above

2. A good trade for a risk-on day is a long high-yield currency/short low-yield currency.
   A. True
   B. False

3. An example of a traditionally risky currency is the:
   A. Australian dollar
   B. Swedish krona
   C. Hungarian forint
   D. Swiss franc
   E. A, B, & C

4. Markets follow trends and then seem to reverse directions after a few days.
   A. True
   B. False

5. One of the best ways to place a long-term trade is to:
   A. Use high amounts of your available margin
   B. Use small amounts of your available margin
   C. Use less than 33% of your available margin
   D. B & C

6. The shorter the time frame of the trade, the more margin is required.
   A. True
   B. False

7. It is best to look at _____ when scalping.
   A. 30-second charts
   B. 1-minute charts
   C. Short-term charts
   D. It doesn't matter because the trade time is too short
   E. A, B, & C

8. **One of the best ways to reduce risk in an overnight trade is to:**
   A. Limit the amount of margin in the trade
   B. Diversify the trade with different currencies
   C. Diversify the trade with both risk-on and risk-off trades
   D. All of the above

9. **One of the most highly traded currency pairs is the:**
   A. Euro/Swedish krona
   B. Euro/Swiss franc
   C. Euro/Hungarian forint
   D. Euro/U.S. dollar

10. **The EUR/USD is one of the most difficult FX pairs to predict.**
    A. True
    B. False

Chapter **9**

Forex in the Corporate Environment

CHAPTER OBJECTIVES

In this chapter, you will learn the following:

- How Forex is used in accounts payables and receivables
- What is Exchange Rate Risk
- The basics of Forex forward rates
- The basics of using Forex futures
- The basics of using Forex options

In addition to using Forex to increase the returns of a portfolio and to provide a leveraged method of producing interest income, there is a third application of the FX market. In this chapter you will learn the basics of using Forex outside of the spot market by using derivatives. Derivatives allow the hedging of risk of the price of an FX pair in the future. Forex derivatives (a derivative is a financial instrument that "derives" its value from another financial product and therefore has its value "linked" to another financial product) are used to limit the risk of a portfolio, or more frequently are used to limit the risk of a company's accounts payable or accounts receivable that will be paying out or receiving funds in a foreign currency sometime in the future.

To put it another way, a trader buys and sells Forex in the spot market in anticipation of gains, or for a simple hedge against an investment portfolio. In the nonretail setting, a large institutional investor such as a multi-strategy hedge fund will attempt to add to its monthly and annual capital gains by trading in the Forex spot market. While they might be shorting the EUR, USD, or other currency, they do so for the most part with the goal of acquiring more wealth.

On the other hand, Forex derivatives are usually bought and sold with the intent of risk reduction, and either bought or entered into for the purpose of managing either an expense or income sometime in the future. The risk of a currency pair moving in a direction that is against the best interest of a company is called Exchange Rate Risk.

Using Forex Futures

A better way to describe this is to use a classic example of when the financial manager of a multinational company would look to FX derivatives to manage risk. In this case, your company is a commercial aircraft engine manufacturer based in the United States. One of the engines the company makes, the "Super-Turbo" is used on both the Boeing 757 and the AirJet 5000. The company has just received an order for 10 SuperTurbo engines. The order of 10 SuperTurbos is for AirJet, a Swiss Company.

Since it takes the company six months to build the engines from start to finish, they only require a deposit of one-half down on each order, with the other half due upon delivery.

Each engine costs the company 150,000 euros in direct and indirect labor and expenses to produce start to finish. Each engine also costs $25,000 U.S. dollars in parts. The company sells the engines for 375,000 Swiss francs each, with shipping to be paid by the buyer.

As stated, your company is U.S.-based and the operations department has decided to order all parts required for manufacture from the United States. But, due to an affordable, yet highly skilled workforce, the engines will be manufactured in Ireland. This is being done to capture and utilize displaced workers from the electronics and other manufacturing industries. Ireland is in the European Union, so all of the worker's wages, benefits, and any employment expenses/taxes will be paid in euros.

The order is placed on 1/1/20*xx*:

The group of 10 engines is to be built for AirJet (a Switzerland-based company)

Labor Cost:	1,500,000 EUR
Parts Cost:	750,000 USD
Income Received:	3,750,000 CHF
Actual Exchange Rate on 1/1/20*xx*	EUR/USD 1.30
	USD/CHF 0.98
Six-Month Forward Rate on 1/1/20*xx*	EUR/USD 1.50
	USD/CHF 1.05

In this scenario, the company would have to pay $750,000 in parts costs, and $1,950,000 in U.S. dollars (1.5 million EUR × 1.30 to convert to USD) if expensed at the date the order was placed. The total cost to manufacture the 10 engines is $2,700,000.

The income received from the order would be $3,571,428 U.S. dollars (3,750,000 CHF/1.05 = USD) if the accounts receivable was paid at the time the order was placed.

In this case, the company would have a profit on the job order of $3,571, 428 − $2,700,000 = $871,428 U.S. dollars.

To review, the company has ongoing expenses in both USD and EUR to manufacture the engines. At the same time, it will be selling the engines to a Swiss company, and has negotiated the engines to be paid in CHF. Since the company is U.S.-based, it must convert all expenses and income back into USD.

What about the fact that the cost of the labor force is paid every two weeks for the entire time of manufacture (six months)?

In this case, the expense that is tied to the labor portion of the engines can be best calculated by finding the average of the spot rate and the six month estimated rate. How do you know what a good, reasonable estimate of what the EUR/USD exchange rate will be in six months? The easiest way to determine this is to look at the six-month EUR/USD forward rate.

A forward is a form of a derivative in which one party agrees to buy an underlying asset from another party on a specific date in the future. A classic simple example of a forward contract is the pepperoni pizza order. When you call up your neighborhood pizzeria and order a large cheese and pepperoni pizza, and they say "Your order is $27.50 and it will be delivered in 20 minutes," you are entering into a form of a forward contract. You are agreeing that within 20 minutes, you will "sell $27.50" and "buy one large cheese and pepperoni pizza." The pizza place will "sell one large cheese and pepperoni pizza," and "buy $27.50."

With forwards there is risk or "counterparty risk" where each holder may back out of the deal and default. In other words, you might decide on a burger instead, and leave your house to go to "BurgerShak" before the pizza is delivered. The pizza man would show up, pizza in hand, but he wouldn't be able to sell it to you, as you left for burgers. You "defaulted" on the "Pizza forward." On the other hand, the pizza man could decide that there was enough business in the dining room, and that the weather was bad, and that he just didn't want to deliver the pizza. He would then "default" and you and your friends would be left to watch the game without the hot, cheesy pizza.

Forward rates are published daily, and from this you can see the market's best estimate of the direction of the FX pair's exchange rate.

You can see from the marketplace's estimate of the future of the EUR/USD exchange rate, the EUR is expected to get stronger in the future. Since this is the case, and you will be expected to pay your workforce in euros, your labor cost will go higher and higher as the weeks go by. Luckily, you know that you can enter into a derivatives contract to limit the amount of risk that your company will face in the future.

You decide to enter into a futures contract to offset the exchange rate risk of the labor costs. A futures contract is a derivative that allows the owner of the contract to either buy or sell the underlying financial product at a set price at a set time in the future.

Forex futures contracts can be set up to make a profit when the exchange rate gets stronger or when the exchange rate gets weaker. You can see from the forward rates that the EUR will get stronger against the USD, which will cause you to be paying more in USD to convert to EUR in the future. In other words, your USD will get weaker during the manufacturing process until the six months are up and the jet engines are finished and delivered.

Because you will need to buy EUR in the future, and your USD will be getting weaker, you decide to enter into a Euro futures contact. You set up the futures trade so that your position gains in value as the EUR gets stronger against the USD.

By the way, it is important to know that in the futures market, trades are settled up daily. In other words, when you have a futures trade on the books and at your brokerage account, the daily gains will be added to your cash balance at the end of the day. Also, it is important to know that futures are traded with high degrees of leverage much like the Forex market. Just as with a Forex account, a trade will go up and down in value with the different FX pair values. But, where in an FX account your losing trades are subtracted from your margin, they are allowed to "ride" until the trade is closed out at a loss or gain, a futures account is a bit different. With the futures account, as the trade gains and loses with the change in the FX pair daily change in value, your account is settled at the end of each trading day. Losses are deducted from your margin account and gains are added to your margin account. Figure 9-1 shows the correlation of values of the Chicago Mercantile Exchange's (CME's) DEC 2013 Euro futures contract (6EU13.CME) versus the EUR/USD proxy CurrencyShares Currency ETF (FXE).

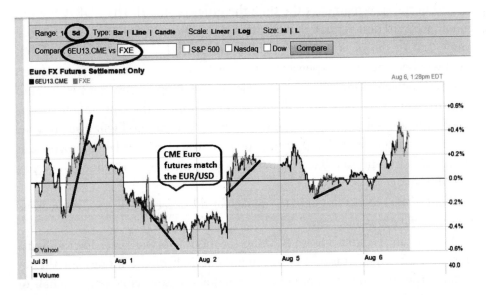

FIGURE 9-1 · 6EU13.CME vs. FXE

This feature of the daily settle actually works to the advantage of those who are using FX futures as a hedge, as we are discussing here. That is true because as the euro goes up in value against the U.S. dollar, your expense for the labor costs will get higher due to the higher exchange rate. It will in effect become more expensive to have the engines manufactured in Ireland for that pay period. While it may be more expensive in U.S. dollar terms to buy euros to pay your Irish workforce, your EUR futures contract was set up to make a profit when EUR got stronger against USD. So, for every dollar more that it costs you to convert to the same amount of euros, you make that much back with gains in your futures account. This way you are insulating your expenses by earning gains in the futures account at the same rate that you are paying at a higher rate in the FX spot market to pay for the higher expenses. In other words, as the exchange rate in the FX market moves against you (costing you more money) you will be making exactly the same amount in your futures account, insulating you from losses. In fact, it is possible to build a position in FX futures that mirrors your future foreign exchange expense exposure (called currency risk) to the point that the risk is fully insulated. In other words, you can set up an FX futures trade so that you earn dollar for dollar what you lose on FX rate movement.

To review: The company has labor expenses that span over six months. The labor expenses are paid in euros. The company must convert USD into EUR every two weeks to pay labor expenses. The exchange rate for the EUR/USD is 1.30 in the spot market at the time the order is placed. The EUR/USD six-month forward rate as quoted in the financial sections of the media is 1.50. You know that this implies that the exchange rate will be getting worse, and that EUR will become more expensive as time goes on until the end of the contract. You decide to enter into a futures contract and set it up to earn gains as the euro gets stronger. In this way you will be earning a profit at the same rate that your labor expenses get higher. You know that using this method will insulate your expenses to a set rate in USD terms. You can now plan your labor expenses, as they are "locked-in" to a fixed EUR/USD exchange rate, even though you pay the labor expenses every two weeks.

What about the fact that half the money for the order will be received in Swiss francs six months in the future?

As you can see from Figure 9-1, the six-month forward rate for the Swiss franc is 1.05. Since you will be receiving one-half of the money for the jet engine order up front, you are only worried about the remaining one-half of 3,750,000 Swiss francs, or only 1,875,000 Swiss francs.

At the time of the order, the first half of the payment in Swiss francs is valued at $1,913,265 U.S. dollars (1,875,000 CHF/0.98 =1,913,265 USD). The six-month futures quote for the Swiss franc is 1.05, so that means that when you are paid the second half of the payment, the 1,875,000 Swiss francs will be converted back into dollars at 1.05 Swiss francs per dollar: 1,875,000 CHF/1.05 = 1,785,714 USD in future income according to the six-month forward rate.

In this case, the Swiss franc is estimated to get weaker. Since you will be paid in Swiss francs, they will convert into dollars at a less favorable rate. You know that this means that the actual amount of revenue from the order of jet engines will be:

1,875,000 CHF at 0.98 on 1/1/20xx =	1,913,265 USD
1,875,000 CHF at 1.05 on 7/1/20xx =	1,785,714 USD
Total without hedging	$3,698,979

You understand that by going into the futures market, you can set up a futures trade that will earn profits when either the Swiss franc gets stronger or weaker against the U.S. dollar. Since you know that the Swiss franc is predicted to get weaker, and that you will be receiving Swiss francs to convert back into U.S. dollars in the future, you decide to buy a Swiss franc futures contract that is set up to make a profit as the Swiss franc gets weaker.

You also know that it is possible to set up the future in such a way that it earns profit at the same rate that you are set to lose money. In other words, if the forward market quote is off, and the actual USD/CHF spot rate in six months is 1.10, you will have to convert the Swiss francs at an even less favorable rate. Even though this may be true, your Swiss franc futures contract will be worth that much more in six months; in fact, it is worth more dollar for dollar for each dollar that the Swiss francs are worth less in the spot market.

With the hedges in place, it is possible to lock in future expenses and income.

Foreign Exchange Risk Hedges Made with Options

Hedges can also be made with an option. Options are the right, but not the obligation, to buy or to sell a financial product at a point in the future. In the case of the option, the buyer pays a small fee, called a premium, to own the right to buy (called a call) or the right to sell (called a put) an "underlying financial product." In the case of a PHLX Swiss franc option, the options price is based upon the value of the USD/Swiss franc exchange rate. In this case the USD/Swiss franc exchange rate is the PHLX Swiss franc's "underlying financial product." Figure 9-2 shows the PHLX Swiss franc option values over a one-week period.

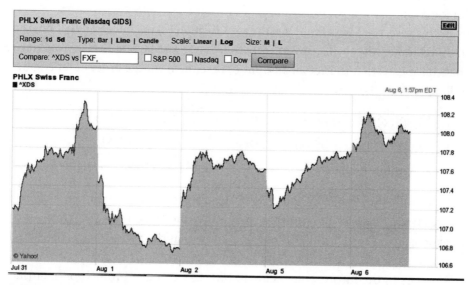

FIGURE 9-2 · PHLX Swiss Franc

In this example, an option would be entered into to buy 1,500,000 EUR six months in the future. The option works in the same manner as the future, except that with the option you are not obligated to take possession of the 1.5 million EUR at the expiration of the options contact. That is the nature of the option: The buyer has the "option" to exercise if it is financially advantageous.

So, you have a choice: You can enter into a futures contract that will lock in your EUR expense at a fixed rate. If you do this, you will lock in your EUR expenses in USD terms. At this point you are done, and you can do your financial planning for the job as far as expenses go.

On the other hand, you can enter into an options contract. If you go the options contract route, you can set up a contract that it is worth more at the same exact opposite rate that the EUR/USD spot rate makes a loss. The difference is that with the options contract, it is possible to structure the option in such a way that it will gain in value as you lose money in the spot market, but if the spot market gets better, the option will reach a floor and will become worthless. This is in stark contrast to the future, where the future can act in a mirror-like fashion (going up and down in value in opposite relation to the spot market). The options contract on the other hand, can be set up to go in one direction only: only gain in value when the spot market is less favorable, and not go below zero in value when the spot market is favorable.

Of course, all of these examples are very simplified and do not include interest costs, carrying costs, or transaction costs. Although this book is about Forex, this chapter attempts to give a brief introduction as to how derivatives are used in the Forex market to manage future expenses and receivables.

While simplified, the examples are not oversimplified and can serve to show you how an international business can have expenses in one currency and income in another currency. It also shows how the forward rate can be used to get a measure of what the 6- or 12-month expected exchange rate is being predicted to be by the market. The example also shows how, instead of going into the spot market to buy foreign currency in the future, derivatives such as futures and options can be bought to mirror the potential losses that might happen in the spot market. In this way gains can be made at the same rate as losses are incurred. Lastly, you have learned that you have the choice of using futures or options: futures lock in the FX rate, and options do just that—give you the option to use that FX rate.

QUIZ

1. You can use a Forex forward rate to determine what the markets are estimating the exchange rate will be in the future.
   A. True
   B. False

2. Forex futures can be bought or sold in such a way as to profit:
   A. When the exchange rate gets better
   B. When the exchange rate gets worse
   C. When the exchange rate stays the same
   D. A & B
   E. None of the above

3. It is possible to match the profits of a Forex derivative to _____the profits and losses of the FX spot rate.
   A. Equal
   B. Be the opposite of
   C. Mirror
   D. Lose
   E. B & C

4. A verbal contract to buy a certain product at a set time in the future at an agreed upon price is called a(n):
   A. Option
   B. Put
   C. Call
   D. Forward

5. Because futures trades settle daily, gains or losses are added to the margin balance at the end of the trading day.
   A. True
   B. False

6. A derivative has its value linked to a base financial product called a(n):
   A. FX grid
   B. Base trade
   C. Linked order
   D. Underlying

7. Finance managers at international companies have two choices: they can go into the_____market or the_____market to manage exchange-rate risk.
   A. Spot
   B. Futures
   C. Options
   D. Stock
   E. A, B, & C

8. Options contracts give the owners the _____ to buy or sell an underlying in the future.
   A. Right
   B. Obligation
   C. Chance
   D. Option
   E. A & D

9. Calls are options that give the right to buy an underlying and puts are options that give the right to sell an underlying.
   A. True
   B. False

10. It is possible to set up a Forex options contract that will gain in value when the underlying spot rate gets worse, yet doesn't go lower than a value of zero when the spot rate gets better.
    A. True
    B. False

Final Exam

1. A Forex trade will make money when the long currency gets stronger.
   A. True
   B. False

2. A Forex trade is two currencies and makes money when the value of one changes against the value of another.
   A. True
   B. False

3. Trading Forex involves... one currency and... another currency.
   A. Going long
   B. Going short
   C. Buying
   D. Selling
   E. All of the above

4. Going long one currency and shorting another is called a Forex pair.
   A. True
   B. False

5. Forex leverage is a form of...that is used to buy currency.
   A. Loan
   B. I.O.U.
   C. Credit card
   D. All of the above

6. **Leverage...the risk of trading.**
   A. Increases
   B. Decreases
   C. Leverage doesn't change the risk of Forex trading
   D. None of the above

7. **Leverage can be changed in a Forex account**
   A. True
   B. False

8. **Common leverage amounts are...**
   A. 1.5:1
   B. 20:1
   C. 50:1
   D. More than 50:1
   E. B, C, & D

9. **Forex traders are active all over the world as they can trade currency...**
   A. Anywhere with a computer
   B. 24 hours a day
   C. 6 days a week
   D. All of the above
   E. None of the above

10. **What is related to the "Gold Standard"?**
    A. Fixed rates of exchanges
    B. Gold's fixed price
    C. The Bretton Woods Agreement
    D. B & C
    E. All of the above

11. **"Going Short" a currency means that you have...**
    A. Sold that currency
    B. Will profit when that currency gets weaker
    C. Bought that currency
    D. Will profit when that currency gets stronger
    E. A & B

12. When you sell a currency and buy another you are trading…
   A. Forex pairs
   B. Money
   C. Equities
   D. Exchange rates
   E. A, B, & D

13. It is possible to put in a Short/Short trade and a Long/Long trade with the same currency pair.
   A. True
   B. False

14. The "Gold Window" refers to exchanging U.S. dollars for gold at a fixed rate.
   A. True
   B. False

15. Currently, foreign governments buy and sell gold for their treasury's vaults at a set price per ounce.
   A. True
   B. False

16. If the markets have mispriced a Forex trade and you think it is a good time to buy then you are a contrarian trader.
   A. True
   B. False

17. Currently, governments hold foreign currency and gold reserves in their treasuries as a safety measure.
   A. True
   B. False

18. It is common to want to experience ever-increasing risk levels when trading Forex.
   A. True
   B. False

19. Keeping up with…and…will make sure you are ready to trade FX.
    A. Market chatter
    B. FX internet news sites
    C. The economy of many countries
    D. Studying about Forex as much as you can
    E. All of the above

20. A good trade for a day that is "risk on" would be to go long a growth economy currency.
    A. True
    B. False

21. Your market skills can be learned, but your risk tolerance will probably remain the same.
    A. True
    B. False

22. One of the most difficult things to learn how to do is to not trade on emotions and greed.
    A. True
    B. False

23. When the world's financial markets are in full swing and doing well, it is often said that the market is…
    A. Risk off
    B. Risk adverse
    C. Risk on
    D. Risk hungry

24. One of the best ways to keep your trading perspective sharp is to change your time frames from long term to short term often when trading.
    A. True
    B. False

25. Forex mispricing is when the market has overreacted to economic or technical developments of a Forex pair.
    A. True
    B. False

26. "Risk Off" is a term that means world market investors and traders are seeking...investments.
    A. Better
    B. Worse
    C. Safer
    D. Growth
    E. Income

27. Market Chatter is a term that refers to the news, chat rooms, and public commentary about the economy, stock market, and currency market.
    A. True
    B. False

28. Forex trading is best done with many trades that have only the slightest chance of profit.
    A. True
    B. False

29. The time length for most Forex trades is...
    A. Longer term
    B. Shorter term
    C. It doesn't matter
    D. None of the above

30. Like investing, a long-term perspective in Forex might mean a trade lasts...
    A. Years
    B. Months
    C. Until retirement
    D. Buy and hold is the best strategy
    E. All of the above

31. Each Forex broker will have their version of trading software, called a trading platform.
    A. True
    B. False

32. Professional traders learn from good trades and bad trades. One of the best ways to do this is to…
    A. Learn from trades over the weeks and months
    B. Use a demo account
    C. Keep a trading log/trading journal
    D. All of the above

33. One of the best ways to learn how to actually place a Forex trade is to build up experience using a Forex demo account.
    A. True
    B. False

34. Each Forex broker will have its own software system which is called a trading platform.
    A. True
    B. False

35. It is best to practice trading Forex with a demo account before real money is traded.
    A. True
    B. False

36. Dollar cost averaging is a good risk-reduction method of…
    A. Buying
    B. Selling
    C. All of the above
    D. None of the above

37. Traders use a form of mini-dollar cost averaging to build up Forex positions. This is called…
    A. Spreading
    B. Averaging
    C. Long/shorting
    D. Position pyramiding

38. Position Pyramiding is best done by buying and selling off positions in 3, 5, or 7 equal parts.
    A. True
    B. False

39. **Capital Gains is another term for...**
    A. Money that is made from trading
    B. Money that is made from buying low and selling high
    C. Money that is made from collecting interest
    D. A & B

40. **Your risk tolerance is a measure of your ability to emotionally and financially tolerate a loss in your Forex account.**
    A. True
    B. False

41. **It is important to ask yourself what your risk tolerance is and match this with your Forex trading.**
    A. True
    B. False

42. **Forex should be enjoyable. Keeping it fun might mean...**
    A. Limiting your risk levels
    B. Limiting your margin
    C. Limiting the cash in your account to only what you are comfortable with
    D. All of the above

43. **One of the best things of Forex trading is the ability to hedge against...**
    A. Other Forex positions
    B. Stock portfolios
    C. Mutual fund portfolios
    D. B & C
    E. None of the above

44. **A Forex account will have higher levels of risk as the account is traded more and more often.**
    A. True
    B. False

45. **Moving the margin ratio from 500:1 to 50:1... the risk level of your Forex account.**
    A. Greatly lowers
    B. Greatly heightens
    C. Has no effect on
    D. Makes it easier to tolerate

46. AAA and AA rated bonds are considered to be one of the...
  A. Riskiest investments
  B. Best investments
  C. Least risky investments
  D. Safest investments
  E. C & D

47. A 90/10 portfolio of bonds and Forex trading can enhance returns while minimizing the risk of the entire investment portfolio.
  A. True
  B. False

48. If you trade daily or only weekly, it is best to keep your Forex portfolio within...
  A. High levels of risk
  B. Low levels of risk
  C. Your skill level
  D. Your risk-tolerance level
  E. C & D

49. Aggressive trading means a greater number of trades than carry trades and a higher level of risk.
  A. True
  B. False

50. The market's world traders are sensitive to good and bad economic news. Trading Forex according to these news developments is known as trading...
  A. The market's risk sentiment
  B. Risk on
  C. Risk off
  D. All of the above
  E. None of the above

51. One of the best times to trade the market's risk sentiment is to wait until...
  A. You can commit large amounts of capital
  B. The news says its "good to get into the market"
  C. There is a large percentage gain or loss in the markets world wide
  D. It doesn't matter, risk sentiment is too hard to predict

52. **Concentrated Forex positions are highly risky.**
    A. True
    B. False

53. **One of the best ways to minimize Forex risk is to...**
    A. Diversify between countries
    B. Diversify between interest rates
    C. Diversify across industries
    D. Diversify as many ways as possible

54. **One of the most difficult things to know is when to close out a profitable trade.**
    A. True
    B. False

55. **Forex trading is risky, but it is possible to...**
    A. Minimize risk by trading less
    B. Minimize risk by diversifying your FX portfolio
    C. Minimize risk by using less of your available margin
    D. A & B
    E. All of the above

56. **Short term traders must look for...**
    A. Getting into and out of trades quickly
    B. Carry trade opportunities
    C. Ways to amplify risk/reward ratios of trades
    D. A & C
    E. All of the above

57. **Even though you are in a long-term carry trade it is O.K. to close it out when there is a large gain.**
    A. True
    B. False

58. **Going long a high-yielding currency and shorting a low-yielding currency will usually gain when the stock markets are getting stronger.**
    A. True
    B. False

59. Playing the interest rate differentials is the same thing as…
    A. A long/short trade
    B. Going long a high-interest currency/shorting a low-interest currency
    C. A carry trade
    D. Scalping
    E. B & C

60. A good way to diversify a Forex portfolio is to trade across geography, economic zones, industrial outputs, and commodity production.
    A. True
    B. False

61. The study of economic indicators for Forex research is the same thing as…
    A. Government growth rates
    B. Technical analysis
    C. Central banking websites
    D. Fundamental research

62. There is usually at least one Central Banking website per
    A. Currency
    B. Economic zone
    C. Geographic region
    D. A & B
    E. All of the above

63. Because currency trading is done with…it is necessary to look at…to determine the quality of an FX trade.
    A. Money
    B. Hedging
    C. FX pairs
    D. Two separate currencies
    E. C & D

64. A well-executed carry trade will earn interest and also make capital gains.
    A. True
    B. False

65. Technical Research uses mathematics, statistics, and charting techniques.
    A. True
    B. False

66. Combining moving averages can show "crosses" which can indicate a "buy" or a "sell."
    A. True
    B. False

67. It is often required to have two computers to do Forex: one for trading the other for technical analysis.
    A. True
    B. False

68. Some Forex traders use…analysis, some traders use…analysis, but the best method to use is…
    A. High/low
    B. Fundamental
    C. Technical
    D. Both
    E. B, C, & D

69. Carry trades are also known as "playing the interest rate differential."
    A. True
    B. False

70. If you are searching a country's central banking website you are most likely looking at fundamental research.
    A. True
    B. False

71. A typical technical indicator is to look at the 200/50-day moving average.
    A. True
    B. False

72. A 200/50-day moving average can show the trader when to buy or sell a FX pair.
    A. True
    B. False

73. Support and resistance levels can show…and…levels.
    A. Upper
    B. Lower
    C. Support
    D. Resistance
    E. A & B
    F C & D

74. 200/50-day and 100/20-day moving averages work well because they are...
   A. Divided by 10
   B. Divided by 5
   C. They don't work well
   D. They are similar in values

75. High levels of Forex risk can be avoided by trading Currency ETFs.
   A. True
   B. False

76. Currency ETFs trade like a stock, but are invested in cash and cash equivalents that are in foreign currency. This makes them move up and down with the value of the FX exchange rate.
   A. True
   B. False

77. It is best to keep track of both your Forex gains and interest income when it comes time for income taxes.
   A. True
   B. False

78. Keeping up with your Forex skills might mean...
   A. Paying attention to world markets even when not trading
   B. Using a Forex demo account
   C. Using a Forex trading diary
   D. A & C
   E. All of the above

79. Keeping your Forex account within your risk limits will make you...
   A. A better trader
   B. A lazy trader
   C. A more relaxed trader
   D. None of the above, Forex is risky no matter what

80. It is best to keep your Forex trading money separate from your emergency money.
   A. True
   B. False

81. "Risk-On" and "Risk-Off" days are another way of describing the market's risk sentiment.
   A. True
   B. False

82. A good trade during a Risk-On day would be a long risky currency and a short low-risk currency.
   A. True
   B. False

83. Low-risk currencies are usually those that have a...
   A. High beta
   B. Low beta
   C. High interest rate
   D. Low interest rate

84. The Swiss franc, U.S. dollar, and the...have historically been low-risk currencies.
   A. Euro
   B. Great British pound
   C. Japanese yen
   D. All of the above
   E. None of the above, all currencies are risky

85. A growth-orientated country will most likely have a higher...
   A. Capital
   B. Interest rate
   C. Risk level
   D. Market beta
   E. B, C, & D

86. If a currency has a high market beta this means that it usually moves to a high degree in tandem with the ups and downs of the U.S. stock market.
   A. True
   B. False

87. You hear on CNBC that it is a "Risk-On day" and you note that the S&P 500 is up 1.5%. It would be safe to say that your...trades are up also.
    A. High beta
    B. Long high yield
    C. Too hard to tell, FX and the markets don't relate well.
    D. A & B
    E. None of the above

88. It is true that markets are trend following, but it is also true that they change direction every few days due to...
    A. Profit taking
    B. Bottom feeding
    C. When the market goes up it keeps going up
    D. A & B

89. Exotic currencies can add to the returns of a FX portfolio but can be high-risk trades.
    A. True
    B. False

90. It is best to take a break from trading after a series of successful trades as you may become too confident with your trading.
    A. True
    B. False

91. Keeping a "Financial Emergency Plan" won't help in your goal of financial independence.
    A. True
    B. False

92. In order to minimize risk in a long-term carry trade it is best to limit the amount of your available margin involved in the trade.
    A. True
    B. False

93. Scalping is a form of ultra-long term 6-12-month trades.
    A. True
    B. False

94. One of the best ways to forecast a FX exchange rate is to look at the…
    A. Spot rate
    B. Spot rate +3
    C. Dividend discount model
    D. Forward rate
    E. None of the above

95. Derivatives have their values based upon a financial product that is…
    A. Linked
    B. Related
    C. All of the above
    D. None of the above

96. Forex derivatives can be bought in such a way that they make a profit when the underlying FX spot rate goes up or down.
    A. True
    B. False

97. A Forex option has its value based upon the same FX spot rate. This FX spot rate is called the option's…
    A. Basic value
    B. Tied value
    C. Intrinsic value
    D. Underlying

98. Forex futures are settled up at the end of each trading day. This means that the trade's gains and losses are added and subtracted to the…at the end of the trading day.
    A. Bank account
    B. Score card
    C. Margin balance
    D. Tally sheet

99. Options work like futures except that the owner of an option has the right but not the obligation to buy the underlying.
    A. True
    B. False

100. Forex futures and Forex options work as a...by businesses that have accounts receivables and accounts payables that are in the future.
    A. Risk-management tool
    B. Hedge
    C. Expense planning tool
    D. Way to lock a FX exchange rate into U.S. dollars
    E. All of the above

Answers to Quizzes and Final Exam

Chapter 1	Chapter 3	Chapter 5	Chapter 7
1. D	1. T	1. D	1. A
2. A	2. B	2. E	2. B
3. D	3. D	3. E	3. A
4. A	4. D	4. A	4. E
5. D	5. D	5. A	5. A
6. D	6. A	6. B	6. D
7. D	7. A	7. A	7. E
8. D	8. D	8. D	8. A
9. A	9. A	9. A	9. E
10. C	10. A	10. A	10. E

Chapter 2	Chapter 4	Chapter 6	Chapter 8
1. A	1. D	1. D	1. E
2. D	2. D	2. D	2. A
3. D	3. C	3. E	3. E
4. A	4. E	4. D	4. A
5. E	5. A	5. A	5. D
6. C	6. D	6. D	6. B
7. D	7. D	7. A	7. E
8. D	8. F	8. D	8. D
9. A	9. E	9. A	9. D
10. D	10. E	10. A	10. A

Chapter 9	17. A	46. E	75. A
1. A	18. A	47. A	76. A
2. D	19. E	48. E	77. A
3. E	20. A	49. A	78. D
4. D	21. A	50. D	79. C
5. A	22. A	51. C	80. A
6. D	23. C	52. A	81. A
7. E	24. A	53. D	82. A
8. E	25. A	54. A	83. D
9. A	26. C	55. E	84. C
10. A	27. A	56. D	85. E
	28. B	57. A	86. A
Final Exam	29. B	58. A	87. D
1. A	30. B	59. E	88. D
2. A	31. A	60. A	89. A
3. E	32. D	61. D	90. A
4. A	33. A	62. D	91. B
5. D	34. C	63. E	92. A
6. A	35. A	64. A	93. B
7. A	36. A	65. A	94. D
8. E	37. D	66. A	95. C
9. D	38. A	67. B	96. A
10. E	39. D	68. E	97. D
11. E	40. A	69. A	98. C
12. E	41. A	70. A	99. A
13. B	42. D	71. A	100. E
14. A	43. D	72. A	
15. F	44. A	73. F	
16. A	45. A	74. D	

Glossary

200-day moving average
A technical analysis that uses the past 200 closing averages of an FX pair. The 200-day will show up on a bar chart as a smoothly flowing line indicating changes over time.

Automated take profit
The process of using the FX trading platform to automatically close out a trade at the exact moment a dollar or percentage gain is reached. It is used to allow traders to preprogram the profit points, thereby locking in gains even when they are not at their computers.

Bar chart
A graphic representation that shows the highs and lows of an FX pair. Each bar represents one time period, and that time period will change with the trader's adjustment of the time frame of the chart. In other words, when a trader is using technical analysis with a 15-minute chart, each bar represents the FX pair's price movement in that 15-minute time frame only.

Broker's reports
Technical and fundamental Forex research that is performed by a Forex broker's research department. Some full-service wealth management firms offer Forex broker's reports to their clients that can be used when trading Forex, other reports come from independent research houses and are then accessed by Forex brokers only.

Candlestick chart

A technical chart that shows the range of prices the FX pair made during that time frame, with the added information of the opening and closing prices of the pair during that time frame. The open price or "tail" will be on the left and the closing price will be on the right of the bar shown in the chart. *See* Bar chart.

Capital gains

The profits that are made from trading in a brokerage account, including a Forex account. Capital gains are earned in both long and short time frames. Short-term capital gains are earned from holding a security for less than a year, while long-term capital gains are earned from holding a security for a year or longer. The difference is important because oftentimes short- and long-term capital gains are taxed at different rates.

Capital preservation

The investing goal of putting the principal of the investment at minimal risk. Those who state that they have capital preservation as their investing goal will usually require that their invested capital be in solid, secure investments, even if this means limiting the potential for returns.

Carry trade

A long-term Forex trade that is designed to earn an amplified rate of interest income over a very long investment period. The trade is setup by shorting a low-yielding currency (called the funding currency) and using the proceeds to go long or buy a high-yielding currency. With this setup, the trade is borrowing at a very low rate and paying interest in one currency while earning at a high rate in another different currency. Carry trades often go on for months and years. They also can incur very large capital gains when closed out because the trade oftentimes becomes profitable during the carry.

Central bank

The economic manager of a country or an economic zone. Traders can visit a country's central bank website to learn about that country's interest rate, economic reports, inflation rate, and other important fundamental research information. A list of the world's central banks can be found on the Bank of International Settlements' website, http://www.bis.org/cbanks.htm.

Commodity currency

The currency from a country that produces commodities as its main source of export. Commodity currencies usually are high-yield currencies because of their high growth economies. They are also usually higher risk currencies and are often used in carry trades.

Market correction

When the equities, commodities, or Forex market go down in value sharply after a long slow rise in price. Market corrections are often event-driven, meaning they can be tied to specific news, but more often than not they are related to the herd effect and profit taking, where many people in the market are trying to lock in profits and there are more sellers than buyers. The market can be highly emotional during these times, which can lead to good contrarian or buying opportunities in the FX markets.

Exotic currencies

The group of currencies that are infrequently traded. They often move suddenly and in higher percentages than the more common currencies such as the EUR, GBP, JPY, and USD. They often are found in developing countries and are therefore considered a risk on trade that is dependent on good economic news. These currencies can become heavily traded in good times and then suddenly collapse in value as traders no longer favor them.

Fundamental analysis

When countries' exchange rates, growth rates, and economic situations are used to predict a currency pair's future movements.

Going long

Going long a trade refers to the end of the currency pair that is bought, as opposed to shorted, or sold.

Interest differential

The difference between the high-yielding currency and the low-yielding currency of a Forex pair. Interest differentials are the basis of carry trades, where the interest rate differential is upwards of 3%–5%.

Investment-grade bonds

IOUs that are issued by creditors with the highest credit rating. Typical companies are those that have credit ratings of AAA or AA. Many larger developed countries' government-issued debt is rated at investment grade.

Margin call

When a Forex broker automatically closes out a client's trades due to heavy losses. Most margin calls will allow the owner of the account until the end of the day to deposit more money in the account. If the client deposits more money in the account before the cut off period, the account will return to good standing and the losing trades will not be closed out.

Market risk appetite

A telling of the well-being or not-so-well-being of the traders and investors in the world's stock market. The market risk appetite will be either risky or safe. When the risk appetite is risky, most risky trades throughout the Forex market will do well, whereas safe appetite days will be days of risky trades doing relatively poorly.

Overnight trades

Forex trades that are placed during the evening hours (in the United States) and are held overnight, usually to be closed out in the early morning hours (Eastern Time). Overnight trades in the United States can be very successful because the heaviest trading periods of the FX day is during the times that the European and U.S. markets are overlapping. In this case, the European traders are at their desks at the same time the U.S. traders are, between 3 a.m. and 8 a.m. Eastern Time. The Forex market will usually see the heaviest volume during these hours, allowing FX pairs to move the greatest amount.

Pyramiding a position

Refers to knowing beforehand the amount of currency to be in a trade, and then making three, five, or seven equally measured purchases into the trade over time. The net effect is to minimize the risk of buying into a currency pair all at once, and possibly missing a better price. The same should be done when closing out a position, which allows the locking in of gains, while leaving some of the position in the trade to capture gains later at perhaps a higher level.

Risk/Return

Refers to how much risk is taken in a trade versus how much profit potential is in the trade.

Scalping

A form of Forex trading that is open and closed in a matter of minutes, usually no more than 15 minutes. Scalping uses a higher amount of available margin than a carry trade due to the short length and minimal Forex pair movement in the short time period.

Technical analysis

The use of charts, graphs, and statistics to estimate a Forex pair's future movement and determine the best time to enter and exit the market.

VIX Index

The VIX Index is a measure of the market's risk appetite. A high VIX indicates the market is volatile and nervous, and a lower VIX indicates the market is calm, steady, and otherwise overall positive in outlook. The VIX Index is calculated as a measure of the volatility of exchange-traded S&P 500 index options.

Index

Note: Page references followed by italic *f* refer to figures; a italic *t* indicates tables.

The simple way to ace your management accounting class!

Contents

All there is to know about financial statements— without the headache!

Contents

business math
DeMYSTiFieD

A SELF-TEACHING GUIDE

🔑 EASILY calculate MARKUP, sales tax, and DISCOUNTS

🔑 UNDERSTAND DEPRECIATION, inventory, and financial STATEMENTS for income tax purposes

🔑 MASTER a SCIENTIFIC CALCULATOR to do lengthy COMPUTATIONS

🔑 LEARN the MATHEMATICS of borrowing, SAVING, and INVESTING money

Allan G. Bluman

McGraw Hill

Learn the ins and outs of business math— the fast and easy way!

Contents

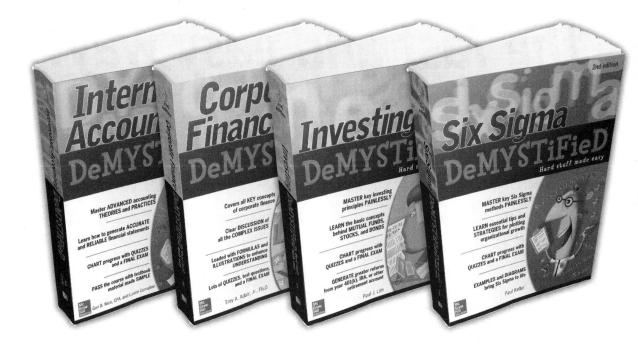